BOOK C

Macmillan McGraw-Hill **READING**

Skills Intervention

D1317087

wi... ers

Diagnostic Tests • Comprehension • Vocabulary Strategies
Study Skills • Leveled Books • Fluency

 Macmillan
McGraw-Hill

New York   Farmington

Macmillan/McGraw-Hill Skills Intervention

Macmillan/McGraw-Hill Skills Intervention program is designed to intervene when necessary and return students to the mainstream curriculum as quickly and effectively as possible.

Three highly motivating lessons for each skill offer corrective feedback and require minimal teacher preparation. Instruction is aligned with **Macmillan/McGraw-Hill Reading** so students can return to the mainstream as soon as they've completed the three lessons.

The **Macmillan/McGraw-Hill Skills Intervention Program** is so flexible, it can be used for In Class, Whole Class, Extended Day, Pullout, and Summer School Intervention Programs.

Macmillan/McGraw-Hill Skills Intervention ensures every child reads and every child succeeds.

Macmillan/McGraw-Hill Skills Intervention Components

Kit A (Grades 1–2) includes:
- Intervention Teacher's Guide (contains: Program Diagnostic Tests, Phonics and Decoding Skills, Comprehension Strategies, Vocabulary Strategies, and Fluency Lessons)
- Grade 1 Easy Leveled Books (24 titles)
- Grade 2 Easy Leveled Books (24 titles)
- Letter Cards

Kit B (Grades 3–4) and Kit C (Grades 5–6) include:
- Intervention Teacher's Guide (contains: Program Diagnostic Tests, Phonics and Decoding Skills, Comprehension Strategies, Vocabulary Strategies, Fluency Lessons)

Kit B includes the Grade 3 and Grade 4 Easy Leveled Books (24 titles each).

Kit C includes the Grade 5 and Grade 6 Easy Leveled Books (24 titles each).

The Phonics Intervention Guide (Grades 3–6) includes:
- Program Diagnostic Tests
- 50 carefully structured phonics and decoding lessons
- 10 decodable reading selections and unit reviews and assessments

Table of Contents

PART 1: INTERVENTION DIAGNOSTIC TESTS

PART 2: SKILLS SUPPORT LESSONS

COMPREHENSION STRATEGIES

VOCABULARY STRATEGIES

STUDY SKILLS

PART 3: LEVELED BOOKS
GRADE 5 LEVELED BOOKS

GRADE 6 LEVELED BOOKS

PART 4: FLUENCY

Macmillan/McGraw-Hill

READING

Skills Intervention
Content Analysis

Integrated, Systematic, and Explicit Instruction

Preventing Reading Difficulties in Young Children	Report of the National Reading Panel: Teaching Children to Read	Macmillan/McGraw-Hill Skills Intervention
Integrated: Reading instruction must "*integrate* attention to the alphabetic principle with attention to the construction of meaning and opportunities to develop fluency." (Addition to Preface, Third Printing) **Direct/Explicit Instruction is a teaching model that emphasizes:** • How print works and provides ample practice opportunities • Explicit instruction in letter-sound correspondences and spelling conventions • Opportunities to read using "graduated series of books" that review/practice sight words and phonics lessons • Development of reading strategies and phonics, spelling, and writing skills through reading of anthologies and trade books (p. 204)	"Systematic phonics instruction is only one component of a total reading program; systematic instruction should be integrated with reading instruction in phonemic awareness, fluency, and comprehension strategies to create a complete reading program." (p. 11)	Instruction in **phonics**, **comprehension** and **vocabulary** strategies, **study skills**, and **fluency** insures development of reading skills. Student's Graphic Organizer Skills Guide Book—A Teacher's Instruction Skills Guide—Book A A graduated series of books reviews and applies multiple readings skills.

Phonics Instruction

Preventing Reading Difficulties in Young Children	**Report of the National Reading Panel: Teaching Children to Read**	**Macmillan/McGraw-Hill Skills Intervention**
"There is evidence that explicit instruction that directs children's attention to the phonological structure of oral language and the connections between phonemes and spellings helps children who have not grasped the alphabetic principle or who do not apply it productively when they encounter unfamiliar printed word." (p. 321)	"The meta-analysis revealed that systematic phonics instruction produces significant benefits for students in kindergarten through 6th grade and for children having difficulty learning to read." (p. 9)	Systematic phonics instruction is provided for Grades 1and 2 in the **Skills Intervention Book A** and in an accelerated form for students in Grades 3-6 in the **Phonics Intervention Guide** to help children grasp the alphabetic principle.

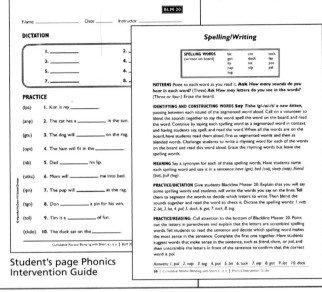

Student's page Phonics Intervention Guide

Teacher's Instruction Phonics Intervention Guide

Vocabulary Instruction

"Vocabulary instruction generally does result in measurable increase in students' specific word knowledge. Vocabulary instruction also appears to produce increases in children's reading comprehension… these gains are largest where passages contain explicitly taught words." (p. 217)

The largest gains in vocabulary and reading comprehension were registered when "children were given both information about the words' definitions and examples of the words' usages in a variety of contexts." (p. 217)

The findings on vocabulary yielded several specific implications for teaching reading. First, vocabulary should be taught directly and indirectly. Repetition and multiple exposures to vocabulary items are important." (p. 14)

Leveled Instruction in **vocabulary strategies**, as well as **high-frequency word** and **vocabulary** reviews in the **Leveled Books Lessons**, present words in multiple contexts to improve children's comprehension.

Comprehension Instruction

Preventing Reading Difficulties in Young Children	Report of the National Reading Panel: Teaching Children to Read	Macmillan/McGraw-Hill Skills Intervention
"Comprehension can be enhanced through instruction that is focused on concept and vocabulary growth…as well as by reading independently and interactively." (pp. 321-322) "Explicit instruction in comprehension strategies has been shown to lead to improved comprehension of texts." (p. 322)	The National Reading Panel identified 7 categories of text comprehension instruction that improve comprehension in non-impaired readers. They are: • Comprehension monitoring • Cooperative learning • Use of graphic and semantic organizers (including story maps) • Question answering • Question generation • Story structure • Summarization (p. 15)	Comprehension lessons include explicit instruction in **strategies,** use of **graphic organizers** and **oral summaries** to develop the students understanding of text. 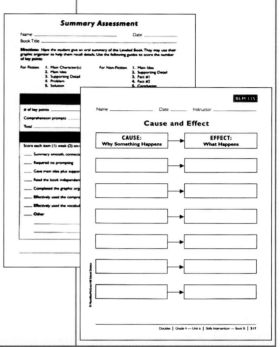

Fluency (Automaticity)

"When the goal is to help students conquer any particular text, one widely validated practice is that of asking students to read it several times over." (p. 214) "Gains in fluency (automaticity) come with increased experience, as does increased lexical knowledge [vocabulary] that supports word identification." (p. 79)	"…the Panel concluded that guided repeated oral reading procedures … had a significant and positive impact on word recognition, fluency, and comprehension." (p. 12) ### Macmillan/ McGraw-Hill Skills Intervention Motivational lessons in fluency include guided **repeated** readings, **choral** readings, **phrasing,** and **readers' theater** to improve students' word recognition and comprehension.	**Lesson 1** **Repeated Reading / Echo Reading** **MATERIALS** Fluency Passages Blackline Masters; Fluency Graphs; Timer **Lesson 2** **Repeated Reading / Choral Reading** **Lesson 3** **Phrasing** **MATERIALS** Fluency Passage Blackline Masters; Pencils **INTRODUCTION Phrase-Cued Text** Distribute copies of the level-appropriate Fluency Blackline Master. Explain to students that good readers learn to read groups of words together in phrases. They use these phrases along with punctuation to guide how they read a passage. **MODEL Choral Reading** Write the first few sentences of the passage on the board. Read them aloud with expression. **Ask When did I pause as I read the sentences?** As students respond, put a slash (/) after words on the board to indicate a pause, and two slashes (//) to denote a full stop at the end of a sentence. Tell students to follow along as you reread the passage aloud in an expressive voice, pausing at the slash marks. Point out how your pitch rises when reading a question and how you stress a word or phrase to indicate an exclamation. Repeat reading the passage chorally with students at least two more times. **PRACTICE Using Phrase-Cued Text** Have students work in pairs to read the remainder of the fluency passage. Invite them to discuss where the natural pauses occur between phrases and ask them to mark their text accordingly. Once they have penciled in the slashes, have them check their work by reading the passage aloud. Students should move or modify their markings until they agree that the phrasing is correct. Then invite partners to read their phrase-cued passage aloud to the whole group. Discuss why students marked their passages the way they did, and why some pairs may have marked theirs differently. **ASSESS/CLOSE** Provide students with an unmarked copy of the fluency passage. Have them test their skill by reading the passage aloud with the appropriate phrasing and expression. You may also invite students to read aloud a different, self-selected passage to the class. Invite them to discuss how working with phrase cues has improved their fluency.

Instructional Strategies

Preventing Reading Difficulties in Young Children	What Research Tells Us About Children with Diverse Learning Needs (Simmons and Kame'enui)	Macmillan/McGraw-Hill Skills Intervention
"The amount of improvement in word-reading skills appears to be associated with the degree of explicitness in the instructional method." (p. 206)	"The following appeared in interventions designed to increase reading comprehension: cognitive reading strategies, explicit instruction, modeling, interaction, guided practice, systematic feedback, increased student control."(Chapter 12)	Lessons are arranged in an easy to follow pattern: **explicit instruction, modeling, practice** and two opportunities for immediate **corrective feedback** to build students' independence.

Children with Exceptional Needs in Regular Classrooms (NEA, Cohen)	Teaching Reading to High-Risk Learners (Wood & Algozzine)	
The direct instruction lesson format includes; 1. Gain the learners' attention; 2. Communicate goals; 3. Model the skill; 4.Prompt for response; 5. Give corrective feedback; 6. Check skill mastery (p. 73)	Research has consistently shown that academic performance is improved when teachers provide instructional feedback. Feedback is most effective when it is explicit, systematic, and corrective. (p. 24)	

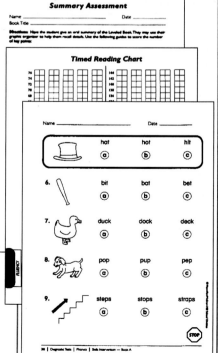

Draw Conclusions / C

TEACHING FRAME: BLM 18 Say Not all the information in a story is given directly. You need to use what you know and clues from the story to draw conclusions about story events. Have students repeat. **Ask** Who can explain what we do when we draw conclusions?

MODEL Read the first paragraph of the teaching frame together. **Say** This paragraph tells about someone in a particular place. The place is not named, but clues are given about the kind of place it is. Underline *worm as a bathtub, waves lapped at the island shore,* and *palm trees.* **Say** I know from these clues that Lonny is not dipping his toe in a freezing lake or in his own bathtub at home. As far as I know, very warm water and palm trees are only found in warm or tropical climates. By adding together the story clues and what I already know, I can conclude that Lonny is on a tropical island.

Say Now, as you read the next paragraph, think about what you are told and what you are not told. **Say** What does the last sentence mean? Is Lonny from a different planet that has a different sun? (No, it means that he is not used to the heat of the tropical sun.)

CORRECTIVE FEEDBACK

If students have difficulty drawing this conclusion, help them locate and underline clues. *Hopped quickly across the sand and moved his towel to the shade* imply that the sun is extremely hot.

PRACTICE Have students complete Blackline Master 18. **Say** Read the story. Then answer the questions. Circle the letter of the correct answer.

CORRECTIVE FEEDBACK

For each question students cannot answer, have them ask themselves: "What clues are given in the story about this?" Students should underline these clues. Then have them ask themselves: "What do I already know?" Remind students to use both the clues from the story and what they already know to draw conclusions.

Answers: 1. c 2. b 3. a

96 | Draw Conclusions / C | Skills Intervention · Book B

Assessment

Preventing Reading Difficulties in Young Children	Teaching Reading Sourcebook: From Kindergarten through Eighth Grade	
Successful intervention programs feature "carefully planned assessments that monitor the response of the child to the intervention." (p. 273)	"...reading assessment in the early grades needs to be frequent and specific. In the upper grades, assessment is necessary to monitor progress, but also to identify causes of reading weakness." (p. 21.2) On-going **assessment tools** include the **Summary Assessment, Fluency Charting** and **Diagnostic** tests to monitor progress, identify specific reading weaknesses, as well as motivate the student.	

Intervention Tips and Strategies

OVERVIEW

The Macmillan/McGraw-Hill INTERVENTION PROGRAM provides a flexible reading intervention program for struggling readers. These guides use explicit, systematic instruction in fast-paced lessons to help students accelerate their reading growth. The program is designed to be used for individual tutoring, small-group, or as a whole-class program.

This guide will help you design and deliver an effective instruction program that will fit the needs of your students.

WHAT IS A READING INTERVENTION PROGRAM?

Over the last decade, reading scores have dropped dramatically leaving teachers with students who are reading grossly below level (*Mullis, Campbell, & Farstrup, 1993*).

Students reading below grade level suffer in all classes, because they are unable to comprehend the subject material. Students reading below level need help to accelerate their reading as quickly as possible (*Allington & Walmsley, 1995*).

A reading intervention program is one that prevents or stops reading failure. The Macmillan/McGraw-Hill INTERVENTION PROGRAM provides explicit lessons in phonics and decoding, comprehension, vocabulary strategies, study skills, high-frequency and vocabulary word building, and reading fluency.

Teaching with the Skills Intervention Lessons

To assist the teacher, classroom aide, or parent volunteer tutor who may be new to reading intervention, each lesson is composed of a step-by-step teaching script. For the reading intervention specialist, the scripts will reduce preparation time and are easily adaptable to suit individual students' needs. The chart below presents the steps in a lesson.

Step	Description
Introduction	• Level A lessons - an interactive dialogue that engages the students by drawing on prior knowledge and gives a concrete example of the skill. • Level B and C lessons – define the skill and ask for a choral response to focus students' attention and define the task that will be explored in the lesson.
Teaching Frame/ Model/Demonstrate	The teacher uses the teaching frame at the top of the blackline master (BLM) and reads the script to model the skill.
Teaching Frame/ Apply & Practice	The student applies the skill to the second item in the frame.
First Corrective Feedback	For students who do not successfully apply the skill, the corrective feedback gives scaffolded dialogue to help spot and correct mistakes.
Practice	Activities for the students to complete while the teacher assesses the students' mastery of the skill.
Second Corrective Feedback	Suggestions to guide the student through the practice, reteach the skill, and how the student can self-correct.

Teacher Page   ### Student BLM

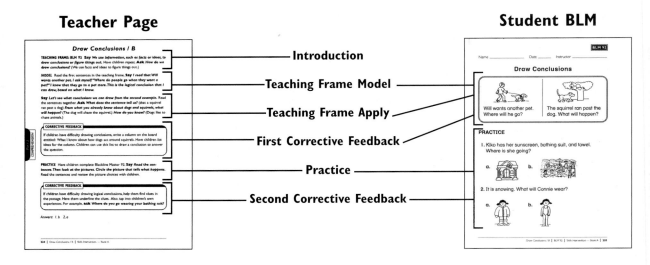

Inside Skills Intervention Guide — Book C

PART 1: PROGRAM DIAGNOSTIC TESTS

Each Skills Manual includes diagnostic tests to aid in placing students at the appropriate level within the Intervention Program as well as to retest for exiting the program.

The **SKILLS INTERVENTION GUIDES** include individual and group tests, administration instructions, student record charts, and guides for interpreting results of the tests.

PART 2: SKILLS SUPPORT LESSONS

This section of the Manual is divided into comprehension strategies, vocabulary strategies, and study skills. Each skill lesson is scaffolded into three levels, each increasing in difficulty.

- **Level A lesson plans** are designed for students reading two grade levels below expectation. The presentation of the concept is at its most introductory level and draws on students' prior knowledge while giving concrete examples. The focus is on how to apply the strategy. The practice exercises are written at an easy vocabulary reading level with all answers explicitly presented in the text.

- **Level B lesson plans** are designed to teach the full concept of the skill. The focus is on how and when to apply the strategy. The practice exercises are more complex than level A. They are written at a higher grade level of vocabulary and involve more multi-step tasks. All answers are explicitly presented in the text.

- **Level C lesson plans** are designed similarly to the level B lessons. However, answers in the practice exercises require inferential thinking and demand that the student combine information from the text with information outside the text. Lessons at this level provide an informal assessment of how completely the student has mastered the skill.

PART 3: LEVELED BOOK LESSONS

These lessons combine the above skills and require the student to apply them to an extended reading selection. Each lesson reviews high-frequency words, story vocabulary words, and introduces the book. The lesson contains a pupil blackline master (BLM) graphic organizer that is used with a guided reading as well as an independent reading. The lesson concludes with an assessment of skills through verbal summary and direct comprehension questions. The assessment and scoring chart are explained on page T15.

PART 4: FLUENCY

This section provides systematic instruction to help students improve fluency skills. The fluency section contains four lesson plans and multiple passages that increase in both vocabulary difficulty and sentence structure complexity

Identifying Students for Intervention and Exiting the Program

IDENTIFYING STUDENTS FOR INTERVENTION

- Observe students for two to three weeks.
- Compare the reading performance of potential candidates to the reading level of their classmates.
- Use the **Macmillan/McGraw-Hill Diagnostic Placement/Evaluation Tests** to see if the student's score is below instructional level.
- Use the **Skills Intervention Diagnostic** in the next section to place the student in the appropriate level of the intervention program.

TESTING

- The primary assessment tools for the intervention program are the **Summary Assessment** of the Leveled Books on page T15, an oral reading check with the fluency passages, and instructors' notes and observations from the **Student Progress Chart** on pages T16 and T17.
- Once the student is placed in the intervention program avoid adding more testing.
- For district purposes, use the **Macmillan/McGraw-Hill Reading Program Comprehensive Assessments** or a district standardized test for overall evaluation.

EXITING THE PROGRAM

1. Make the following observations:
   - Are the student's Leveled Book Summaries consistently scored acceptable?
   - Does the student need little or no corrective feedback?
   - Does the student complete the practice exercises independently?
   - Is the student reading the Leveled Books independently?
   - Is the student showing signs that the Leveled Books are too easy?
   - Is the student's fluency rate on grade level?

2. For tutors, aides, or intervention specialists, ask the student's classroom teacher:
   - Is the student improving in reading the grade-level material?
   - Has the student's comprehension improved?
   - Does the student's written response to reading show improved comprehension?

3. If the student has been in the intervention program for at least three months, retest with the **Skills Intervention Diagnostic Tests** and compare with original scores.

4. If the student has been in the intervention program for less than three months, retest using the **Macmillan/McGraw-Hill Diagnostic Placement/Evaluation Tests**.

Summary Assessment

Name _____   Date _____

Book Title _____

Directions: Have the student give an oral summary of the Leveled Book. They may use their graphic organizer to help them recall details. Use the following guides to score the number of key points:

For Fiction:
1. Main Character(s)
2. Main Idea
3. Supporting Detail
4. Problem
5. Solution

For Non-Fiction:
1. Main Idea
2. Supporting Detail
3. Fact #1
4. Fact #2
5. Conclusion

Summary Response	Scoring Chart	
# of key points _____ /5	(Circle one)	
Comprehension prompts _____ /5	Acceptable	7-10
Total _____ /10	Unacceptable	0-6

Observation Guide

Score each item (1) weak (2) on-target/developing appropriately (3) strong

_____ Summary smooth, connected, with events in order

_____ Required no prompting

_____ Gave main idea plus supporting details

_____ Read the book independently

_____ Completed the graphic organizer independently

_____ Effectively used the comprehension strategy

_____ Effectively used decoding skills

_____ Other

_____

_____

Student Progress Record

Name _____ Book _____

Start Date _____ Exit Date _____

Diagnostic Tests Score

Date	Score	Placement

Phonics Lessons

Lesson	Level	Performance/Comments

Comprehension Strategy Lessons

Lesson	Level	Performance/Comments

Vocabulary Strategy Lessons

Lesson	Level	Performance/Comments

Student Progress Record (Page 2)

Study Skill Lessons

Lesson	Level	Performance/Comments

Fluency Lessons

Passage #	WCPM	Performance/Comments

Leveled Book Lessons

Book Title	Grade Level	Performance/Comments

Summary Assessment

Book Title	Grade Level	Score	Performance/Comments

Guidelines for
Effective Intervention Instruction

Pace Lessons should be taught at a fast pace. Do not allow the students' attention to wander. Keep the students' focus on you or on the blackline master.

Modeling/Demonstration Read and rehearse the lesson script before teaching the lesson.

Corrective Feedback Be familiar with the following corrective feedback strategies:

1. Re-model: this technique shows how to "rethink" through the problem

2. Amplification and Rephrasing: rephrasing the concept as a question

3. Scaffolding: questions that lead the student to the correct answer

4. Checklists: provide self-checking procedures. The procedure must be taught in the modeling section. Teachers show "steps in the process" of figuring out the concept. These steps will be used as a checklist for students to use independently. Teachers must model this strategy in the feedback box as well.

5. Fix-up Strategies: rereading or restatement of the confusing text

6. Nonexample: giving the opposite of the example of the concept. This method should only be used in Level B and C lessons.

7. Repetition: return to the direct/explicit teaching process: a) provide the correct answer through a model/demonstration; b) practice the response again, with assistance as needed; c) have the student try the task again independently

Build Student Independence As the students progress through the program, choose parts of the corrective feedbacks that move from full modeling and support to moderate support to students working independently and self-correcting. Achieving the goal of student independence in the practice sections and Leveled Book reading is critical to success in the program.

Adapting the Lessons Consistency in presentation of each lesson is important to enable the students to be comfortable and focused on the task. It is important that each step in the lesson be followed as closely as possible.

- If students proceed through a lesson faster than you had anticipated, you may move on to the next level of lesson or skill on the same day.

- Avoid skipping parts.

- Complete each lesson. If the lesson is not finished in the allotted time, pick it up on the next day. Do not assign the remainder of the lesson as homework. It is important that the teacher be present to assess and give corrective feedback.

- If the student is a poor writer, to keep up the lesson pace have the student dictate the information as you record it on the blackline master. This is important in the Leveled Book lessons graphic organizers. Reading and comprehension should be the tasks that are the focus of the lesson.

Lesson Planner

Student/Class _____ Week of _____

	Day 1	Day 2	Day 3	Day 4	Day 5
Phonics					
Comprehension Strategy					
Vocabulary Strategy					
Study Skill					
Leveled Book					
Fluency					
Assessment					

Materials: _____

_____

Notes: _____

_____

Grade 5 Unit 1

Macmillan/McGraw-Hill Teacher's Edition Selections	Comprehension	Vocabulary Strategies
The Wise Old Woman pp 20-39	**Problem and Solution** Lesson A pp 60-61* Lesson B pp 62-63* Lesson C pp 64-65* **Make Inferences** Lesson A pp 84-85 Lesson B pp 86-87 Lesson C pp 88-89	**Antonyms and Synonyms** Lesson A pp 164-165 Lesson B pp 166-167 Lesson C pp 168-169
The Voyage of the Dawn Treader pp 46-60	**Story Elements** Lesson A pp 54-55 Lesson B pp 56-57 Lesson C pp 58-59 **Make Inferences** Lesson A pp 84-85 Lesson B pp 86-87 Lesson C pp 88-89	**Context Clues** Lesson A pp 146-147 Lesson B pp 148-149 Lesson C pp 150-151
Wilma Unlimited pp 69-88	**Cause and Effect** Lesson A pp 96-97 Lesson B pp 98-99 Lesson C pp 100-101 **Problem and Solution** Lesson A pp 60-61 Lesson B pp 62-63 Lesson C pp 64-65	**Context Clues** Lesson A pp 146-147 Lesson B pp 148-149 Lesson C pp 150-151
The Wreck of the Zephyr pp 96-117	**Story Elements** Lesson A pp 54-55 Lesson B pp 56-57 Lesson C pp 58-59 **Make Inferences** Lesson A pp 84-85 Lesson B pp 86-87 Lesson C pp 88-89	**Antonyms and Synonyms** Lesson A pp 164-165 Lesson B pp 166-167 Lesson C pp 168-169
TIME for Kids Tornadoes! pp 126-129	**Cause and Effect** Lesson A pp 96-97 Lesson B pp 98-99 Lesson C pp 100-101	**Antonyms and Synonyms** Lesson A pp 164-165 Lesson B pp 166-167 Lesson C pp 168-169 **Context Clues** Lesson A pp 146-147 Lesson B pp 148-149 Lesson C pp 150-151

* Lesson A - - -below level
Lesson B - - - - -on level
Lesson C - - - -transition

Unit Skills Plan

Study Skills	Leveled Book Lessons	Fluency/Assessment
Parts of a Book Lesson A pp 214-215 Lesson B pp 216-217 Lesson C pp 218-219	**Leveled Book Lesson** *Dan's Time* pp 246-247	**Fluency*** Lesson 1 p 347 **Leveled Book Summary Assessment** *Dan's Time* p W5
Parts of a Book Lesson A pp 214-215 Lesson B pp 216-217 Lesson C pp 218-219	**Leveled Book Lesson** *The Eye of the Hurricane* pp 248-249	**Fluency** Lesson 1 p 347 **Leveled Book Summary Assessment** *The Eye of the Hurricane* p W5
Parts of a Book Lesson A pp 214-215 Lesson B pp 216-217 Lesson C pp 218-219	**Leveled Book Lesson** *Franklin Delano Roosevelt* pp 250-251	**Fluency** Lesson 1 p 347 **Leveled Book Summary Assessment** *Franklin Delano Roosevelt* pW5
Parts of a Book Lesson A pp 214-215 Lesson B pp 216-217 Lesson C pp 218-219	**Leveled Book Lesson** *Diego's Sea Adventure* pp 252-253	**Fluency** Lesson 1 p 347 **Leveled Book Summary Assessment** *Diego's Sea Adventure* p W5
Parts of a Book Lesson A pp 214-215 Lesson B pp 216-217 Lesson C pp 218-219	**Leveled Book Lesson** *Teacher Selected Review Selection*	**Fluency** Lesson 1 p 347 **Leveled Book Summary Assessment** *Teacher Selected Review Selection* p W5

* To determine individual
student Fluency Passages
see page 40.

Grade 5 Unit 2

Macmillan/McGraw-Hill Teacher's Edition Selections	Comprehension	Vocabulary Strategies
The Gold Coin pp 140-161	**Make Predictions** Lesson A pp 48-49* Lesson B pp 50-51* Lesson C pp 52-53*	**Compound Words** Lesson A pp 158-159 Lesson B pp 160-161 Lesson C pp 162-163
John Henry pp 169-195	**Fact and Nonfact** Lesson A pp 114-115 Lesson B pp 116-117 Lesson C pp 118-119	**Inflectional Endings** Lesson A pp 152-153 Lesson B pp 154-155 Lesson C pp 156-157
It's our World Too pp 202-216	**Main Idea** Lesson A pp 66-67 Lesson B pp 68-69 Lesson C pp 70-71 **Fact and Nonfact** Lesson A pp 114-115 Lesson B pp 116-117 Lesson C pp 118-119	**Inflectional Endings** Lesson A pp 152-153 Lesson B pp 154-155 Lesson C pp 156-157
Dear Mr. Henshaw pp 224-236	**Make Predictions** Lesson A pp 48-49 Lesson B pp 50-51 Lesson C pp 52-53	**Compound Words** Lesson A pp 158-159 Lesson B pp 160-161 Lesson C pp 162-163
TIME for Kids Digging Up the Past pp 244-247	**Main Idea** Lesson A pp 66-67 Lesson B pp 68-69 Lesson C pp 70-71	**Inflectional Endings** Lesson A pp 152-153 Lesson B pp 154-155 Lesson C pp 156-157 **Compound Words** Lesson A pp 158-159 Lesson B pp 160-161 Lesson C pp 162-163

* Lesson A - - -below level
Lesson B - - - - -on level
Lesson C - - - -transition

Unit Skills Plan

Study Skills	Leveled Book Lessons	Fluency/Assessment
Reference Sources Lesson A pp 220-221 Lesson B pp 222-223 Lesson C pp 224-225	**Leveled Book Lesson** *From Dust to Hope* pp 254-255	**Fluency*** Lesson 1 p 347 **Leveled Book Summary Assessment** *From Dust to Hope* p W5
Reference Sources Lesson A pp 220-221 Lesson B pp 222-223 Lesson C pp 224-225	**Leveled Book Lesson** *Through a Mountain and Under a Sea* pp 256-257	**Fluency** Lesson 1 p 347 **Leveled Book Summary Assessment** *Through a Mountain and Under a Sea* p W5
Reference Sources Lesson A pp 220-221 Lesson B pp 222-223 Lesson C pp 224-225	**Leveled Book Lesson** *The Mills Green Team* pp 258-259	**Fluency** Lesson 2 p 348 **Leveled Book Summary Assessment** *The Mills Green Team* p W5
Reference Sources Lesson A pp 220-221 Lesson B pp 222-223 Lesson C pp 224-225	**Leveled Book Lesson** *Blue-Faced Blues* pp 260-261	**Fluency** Lesson 2 p 348 **Leveled Book Summary Assessment** *Blue-Faced Blues* p W5
Reference Sources Lesson A pp 220-221 Lesson B pp 222-223 Lesson C pp 224-225	**Leveled Book Lesson** *Teacher Selected Review Selection*	**Leveled Book Lesson** *Teacher Selected Review Selection* p w5

* To determine individual student Fluency Passages see page 40.

Grade 5 Unit 3

Macmillan/McGraw-Hill Teacher's Edition Selections	Comprehension	Vocabulary Strategies
The Marble Champ pp 258-268	**Steps in a Process** Lesson A pp 108-109* Lesson B pp 110-111* Lesson C pp 112-113* **Summarize** Lesson A pp 78-79 Lesson B pp 80-81 Lesson C pp 82-83	**Multi-Meaning Words** Lesson A pp 182-183 Lesson B pp 184-185 Lesson C pp 186-187
The Paper Dragon pp 276-303	**Sequence of Events** Lesson A pp 42-43 Lesson B pp 44-45 Lesson C pp 46-47 **Summarize** Lesson A pp 78-79 Lesson B pp 80-81 Lesson C pp 82-83	**Figurative Language** Lesson A pp 194-195 Lesson B pp 196-197 Lesson C pp 198-199
Grandma Essie's Covered Wagon pp 310-334	**Steps in a Process** Lesson A pp 108-109 Lesson B pp 110-111 Lesson C pp 112-113 **Sequence of Events** Lesson A pp 42-43 Lesson B pp 44-45 Lesson C pp 46-47	**Figurative Language** Lesson A pp 194-195 Lesson B pp 196-197 Lesson C pp 198-199
Going Back Home pp 342-367	**Author's Purpose, Point of View** Lesson A pp 102-103 Lesson B pp 104-105 Lesson C pp 106-107 **Summarize** Lesson A pp 78-79 Lesson B pp 80-81 Lesson C pp 82-83	**Multi-Meaning Words** Lesson A pp 182-183 Lesson B pp 184-185 Lesson C pp 186-187
TIME for Kids A Mountain of a Monument pp 374-377	**Sequence of Events** Lesson A pp 42-43 Lesson B pp 44-45 Lesson C pp 46-47	**Figurative Language** Lesson A pp 194-195 Lesson B pp 196-197 Lesson C pp 198-199 **Multi-Meaning Words** Lesson A pp 182-183 Lesson B pp 184-185 Lesson C pp 186-187

* Lesson A - - -below level
Lesson B - - - - -on level
Lesson C - - - -transition

Unit Skills Plan

Study Skills	Leveled Book Lessons	Fluency/Assessment
Graphic Aids Lesson A pp 226-227 Lesson B pp 228-229 Lesson C pp 230-231	**Leveled Book Lesson** *Dancer in the Spotlight* pp 262-263	**Fluency*** Lesson 1 p 347 **Leveled Book Summary Assessment** *Dancers in the Spotlight* p W5
Graphic Aids Lesson A pp 226-227 Lesson B pp 228-229 Lesson C pp 230-231	**Leveled Book Lesson** *Human Writes!* pp 264-265	**Fluency** Lesson 1 p 347 **Leveled Book Summary Assessment** *Human Writes!* p W5
Graphic Aids Lesson A pp 226-227 Lesson B pp 228-229 Lesson C pp 230-231	**Leveled Book Lesson** *Dear Diary* pp 266-267	**Fluency** Lesson 2 p 348 **Leveled Book Summary Assessment** *Dear Diary* p W5
Graphic Aids Lesson A pp 226-227 Lesson B pp 228-229 Lesson C pp 230-231	**Leveled Book Lesson** *Maya's Mural* pp 268-269	**Fluency** Lesson 2 p 348 **Leveled Book Summary Assessment** *Maya's Mural* p W5
Graphic Aids Lesson A pp 226-227 Lesson B pp 228-229 Lesson C pp 230-231	**Leveled Book Lesson** *Teacher Selected Review Selection*	**Fluency** Lessons 1 and 3 pp 347 and 349 **Leveled Book Summary Assessment** *Teacher Selected Review Selection* p W5

* To determine individual student Fluency Passages see page 40.

Grade 5 Unit 4

Macmillan/McGraw-Hill Teacher's Edition Selections	Comprehension	Vocabulary Strategies
Carlos and the Skunk pp 388-403	**Judgments and Decisions** Lesson A pp 120-121 Lesson B pp 122-123 Lesson C pp 124-125 **Draw Conclusions** Lesson A pp 72-73 Lesson B pp 74-75 Lesson C pp 76-77	**Suffixes** Lesson A pp 170-171 Lesson B pp 172-173 Lesson C pp 174-175
How to Think Like a Scientist pp 410-427	**Important and Unimportant Information** Lesson A pp 126-127 Lesson B pp 128-129 Lesson C pp 130-131 **Draw Conclusions** Lesson A pp 72-73 Lesson B pp 74-75 Lesson C pp 76-77	**Root Words** Lesson A pp 188-189 Lesson B pp 190-191 Lesson C pp 192-193
An Island Scrapbook pp 434-459	**Fact and Nonfact** Lesson A pp 114-115 Lesson B pp 116-117 Lesson C pp 118-119 **Important and Unimportant Information** Lesson A pp 126-127 Lesson B pp 128-129 Lesson C pp 130-131	**Suffixes** Lesson A pp 170-171 Lesson B pp 172-173 Lesson C pp 174-175
The Big Storm pp 466-487	**Judgments and Decisions** Lesson A pp 120-121 Lesson B pp 122-123 Lesson C pp 124-125 **Draw Conclusions** Lesson A pp 72-73 Lesson B pp 74-75 Lesson C pp 76-77	**Root Words** Lesson A pp 188-189 Lesson B pp 190-191 Lesson C pp 192-193
TIME for Kids Catching Up with Lewis and Clark pp 494-497	**Fact and Nonfact** Lesson A pp 114-115 Lesson B pp 116-117 Lesson C pp 118-119 **Important and Unimportant Information** Lesson A pp 126-127 Lesson B pp 128-129 Lesson C pp 130-131	**Root Words** Lesson A pp 188-189 Lesson B pp 190-191 Lesson C pp 192-193 **Suffixes** Lesson A pp 170-171 Lesson B pp 172-173 Lesson C pp 174-175

* Lesson A - - -below level
Lesson B - - - - -on level
Lesson C - - - -transition

Unit Skills Plan

Study Skills	Leveled Book Lessons	Fluency/Assessment
Graphic Aids Lesson A pp 226-227 Lesson B pp 228-229 Lesson C pp 230-231	**Leveled Book Lesson** *Kelley in Charge* pp 270-271	**Fluency*** Lesson 1 p 347 **Leveled Book Summary Assessment** *Kelley in Charge* p W5
Graphic Aids Lesson A pp 226-227 Lesson B pp 228-229 Lesson C pp 230-231	**Leveled Book Lesson** *On Track* pp 272-273	**Fluency** Lesson 1 p 347 **Leveled Book Summary Assessment** *On Track* p W5
Graphic Aids Lesson A pp 226-227 Lesson B pp 228-229 Lesson C pp 230-231	**Leveled Book Lesson** *Tourist Trap Island* pp 374-375	**Fluency** Lesson 2 p 348 **Leveled Book Summary Assessment** *Tourist Trap Island* p W5
Graphic Aids Lesson A pp 226-227 Lesson B pp 228-229 Lesson C pp 230-231	**Leveled Book Lesson** *Tornado!* pp 276-277	**Fluency** Lesson 2 p 348 **Leveled Book Summary Assessment** *Tornado!* p W5
Graphic Aids Lesson A pp 226-227 Lesson B pp 228-229 Lesson C pp 230-231	**Leveled Book Lesson** *Teacher Selected Review Selection*	**Fluency** Lessons 2 and 4 pp 348-350 **Leveled Book Summary Assessment** *Teacher Selected Review Selection* p W5

* To determine individua
student Fluency Passages
see page 40

Grade 5 Unit 5

Macmillan/McGraw-Hill Teacher's Edition Selections	Comprehension	Vocabulary Strategies
The Riddle pp 508-527	**Compare and Contrast** Lesson A pp 90-91* Lesson B pp 92-93* Lesson C pp 94-95* **Make Inferences** Lesson A pp 84-85 Lesson B pp 86-87 Lesson C pp 88-89	**Context Clues** Lesson A pp 146-147 Lesson B pp 148-149 Lesson C pp 150-151
Life in Flatland pp 534-549	**Author's Purpose, Point of View** Lesson A pp 102-103 Lesson B pp 104-105 Lesson C pp 106-107 **Make Inferences** Lesson A pp 84-85 Lesson B pp 86-87 Lesson C pp 88-89	**Prefixes** Lesson A pp 176-177 Lesson B pp 178-179 Lesson C pp 180-181
Tonweya and the Eagles pp 556-575	**Problem and Solution** Lesson A pp 60-61 Lesson B pp 62-63 Lesson C pp 64-65 **Author's Purpose, Point of View** Lesson A pp 102-103 Lesson B pp 104-105 Lesson C pp 106-107	**Context Clues** Lesson A pp 146-147 Lesson B pp 148-149 Lesson C pp 150-151
Breaker's Bridge pp 582-597	**Compare and Contrast** Lesson A pp 90-91 Lesson B pp 92-93 Lesson C pp 94-95 **Make Inferences** Lesson A pp 84-85 Lesson B pp 86-87 Lesson C pp 88-89	**Prefixes** Lesson A pp 176-177 Lesson B pp 178-179 Lesson C pp 180-181
TIME for Kids Cleaning Up America's Air pp 604-607	**Problem and Solution** Lesson A pp 60-61 Lesson B pp 62-63 Lesson C pp 64-65	**Prefixes** Lesson A pp 176-177 Lesson B pp 178-179 Lesson C pp 180-181 **Context Clues** Lesson A pp 146-147 Lesson B pp 148-149 Lesson C pp 150-151

* Lesson A - - -below level
Lesson B - - - - -on level
Lesson C - - - -transition

Unit Skills Plan

Study Skills	Leveled Book Lessons	Fluency/Assessment
Various Texts Lesson A pp 232-233 Lesson B pp 243-235 Lesson C pp 236-237	**Leveled Book Lesson** *The Riddle of the Sphinx* pp 278-279	**Fluency*** Lesson 1 p 347 **Leveled Book** **Summary Assessment** *The Riddle of the Sphinx* p W5
Various Texts Lesson A pp 232-233 Lesson B pp 243-235 Lesson C pp 236-237	**Leveled Book Lesson** *On the Ball* pp 280-281	**Fluency** Lesson 1 p 347 **Leveled Book** **Summary Assessment** *On the Ball* p W5
Various Texts Lesson A pp 232-233 Lesson B pp 243-235 Lesson C pp 236-237	**Leveled Book Lesson** *Teammates* pp 282-283	**Fluency** Lesson 2 p 348 **Leveled Book** **Summary Assessment** *Teammates* p W5
Various Texts Lesson A pp 232-233 Lesson B pp 243-235 Lesson C pp 236-237	**Leveled Book Lesson** *Unusual Bridges* pp 284-285	**Fluency** Lesson 2 p 348 **Leveled Book** **Summary Assessment** *Unusual Bridges* p W5
Various Texts Lesson A pp 232-233 Lesson B pp 243-235 Lesson C pp 236-237	**Leveled Book Lesson** *Teacher Selected Review Selection*	**Fluency** Lessons 1 and 3 pp 347 and 349 **Leveled Book Summary** **Assessment** *Teacher Selected Review Selection* p W5

* To determine individual
student Fluency Passages
see page 40.

Grade 5 Unit 6

Macmillan/McGraw-Hill Teacher's Edition Selections	Comprehension	Vocabulary Strategies
Amistad Rising: A Story of Freedom pp 618-643	**Judgments and Decisions** Lesson A pp 120-121* Lesson B pp 122-123* Lesson C pp 124-125* **Draw Conclusions** Lesson A pp 72-73 Lesson B pp 74-75 Lesson C pp 76-77	**Context Clues** Lesson A pp 146-147 Lesson B pp 148-149 Lesson C pp 150-151
Rip Van Winkle pp 650-669	**Cause and Effect** Lesson A pp 96-97 Lesson B pp 98-99 Lesson C pp 100-101 **Draw Conclusions** Lesson A pp 72-73 Lesson B pp 74-75 Lesson C pp 76-77	**Antonyms and Synonyms** Lesson A pp 164-165 Lesson B pp 166-167 Lesson C pp 168-169
Sea Maidens of Japan pp 676-691	**Sequence of Events** Lesson A pp 42-43 Lesson B pp 44-45 Lesson C pp 46-47 **Cause and Effect** Lesson A pp 96-97 Lesson B pp 98-99 Lesson C pp 100-101	**Context Clues** Lesson A pp 146-147 Lesson B pp 148-149 Lesson C pp 150-151
The Silent Lobby pp 700-712	**Judgments and Decisions** Lesson A pp 120-121 Lesson B pp 122-123 Lesson C pp 124-125 **Draw Conclusions** Lesson A pp 72-73 Lesson B pp 74-75 Lesson C pp 76-77	**Antonyms and Synonyms** Lesson A pp 164-165 Lesson B pp 166-167 Lesson C pp 168-169
TIME for Kids Amazon Alert pp 720-723	**Sequence of Events** Lesson A pp 42-43 Lesson B pp 44-45 Lesson C pp 46-47 **Cause and Effect** Lesson A pp 96-97 Lesson B pp 98-99 Lesson C pp 100-101	**Context Clues** Lesson A pp 146-147 Lesson B pp 148-149 Lesson C pp 150-151 **Antonyms and Synonyms** Lesson A pp 164-165 Lesson B pp 166-167 Lesson C pp 168-169

* Lesson A - - -below level
Lesson B - - - - -on level
Lesson C - - - -transition

Unit Skills Plan

Study Skills	Leveled Book Lessons	Fluency/Assessment
Reference Sources Lesson A pp 220-221 Lesson B pp 222-223 Lesson C pp 224-225	**Leveled Book Lesson** *Flight of the Trumpeters* pp 286-287	**Fluency*** Lesson 1 p 347 **Leveled Book Summary Assessment** *Flight of the Trumpeters* p W5
Reference Sources Lesson A pp 220-221 Lesson B pp 222-223 Lesson C pp 224-225	**Leveled Book Lesson** *A Matter of Time* pp 288-289	**Fluency** Lesson 1 p 347 **Leveled Book Summary Assessment** *A Matter of Time* pW5
Reference Sources Lesson A pp 220-221 Lesson B pp 222-223 Lesson C pp 224-225	**Leveled Book Lesson** *Making Pipes is His Bag* pp 290-291	**Fluency** Lesson 2 p 347 **Leveled Book Summary Assessment** *Making Pipes is His Bag* p W5
Reference Sources Lesson A pp 220-221 Lesson B pp 222-223 Lesson C pp 224-225	**Leveled Book Lesson** *The Day My Grandpa Voted* pp 292-293	**Fluency** Lesson 2 p 348 **Leveled Book Summary Assessment** *The Day My Grandpa Voted* p W5
Reference Sources Lesson A pp 220-221 Lesson B pp 222-223 Lesson C pp 224-225	**Leveled Book Lesson** *Teacher Selected Review Selection*	**Fluency** Lessons 2 and 4 pp 348-350 **Leveled Book Summary Assessment** *Teacher Selected Review Selection* p W5

*To determine individual student Fluency Passages see page 40.

Grade 6 Unit 1

Macmillan/McGraw-Hill Teacher's Edition Selections	Comprehension	Vocabulary Strategies
S.O.R. Losers pp 20-34	**Make Predictions** Lesson A pp 48-49 Lesson B pp 50-51 Lesson C pp 52-53 **Make Inferences** Lesson A pp 84-85 Lesson B pp 86-87 Lesson C pp 88-89	**Antonyms and Synonyms** Lesson A pp 164-165 Lesson B pp 166-167 Lesson C pp 168-169
The All-American Slurp pp 42-59	**Sequence of Events** Lesson A pp 42-43 Lesson B pp 44-45 Lesson C pp 46-47 **Make Inferences** Lesson A pp 84-85 Lesson B pp 86-87 Lesson C pp 88-89	**Context Clues** Lesson A pp 146-147 Lesson B pp 148-149 Lesson C pp 150-151
Viva New Jersey pp 66-79	**Story Elements** Lesson A pp 54-55 Lesson B pp 56-57 Lesson C pp 58-59 **Make Inferences** Lesson A pp 84-85 Lesson B pp 86-87 Lesson C pp 88-89	**Antonyms and Synonyms** Lesson A pp 164-165 Lesson B pp 166-167 Lesson C pp 168-169
Rain, Rain, Go Away pp 86-95	**Make Predictions** Lesson A pp 48-49 Lesson B pp 50-51 Lesson C pp 52-53 **Sequence of Events** Lesson A pp 42-43 Lesson B pp 44-45 Lesson C pp 46-47	**Context Clues** Lesson A pp 146-147 Lesson B pp 148-149 Lesson C pp 150-151
TIME for Kids A Viking Voyage pp 102-105	**Sequence of Events** Lesson A pp 42-43 Lesson B pp 44-45 Lesson C pp 46-47	**Antonyms and Synonyms** Lesson A pp 164-165 Lesson B pp 166-167 Lesson C pp 168-169 **Context Clues** Lesson A pp 146-147 Lesson B pp 148-149 Lesson C pp 150-151

* Lesson A - - -below level
Lesson B - - - - -on level
Lesson C - - - -transition

Unit Skills Plan

Study Skills	Leveled Book Lessons	Fluency/Assessment
Choose a Source Lesson A pp 238-239 Lesson B pp 240-241 Lesson C pp 242-245	**Leveled Book Lesson** *The Knitting Circle* pp 294-295	**Fluency*** Lesson 1 p 347 **Leveled Book** **Summary Assessment** *The Knitting Circle* p W5
Choose a Source Lesson A pp 238-239 Lesson B pp 240-241 Lesson C pp 242-245	**Leveled Book Lesson** *Letters from Lila* pp 296-297	**Fluency** Lesson 1 p 347 **Leveled Book** **Summary Assessment** *Letters from Lila* p W5
Choose a Source Lesson A pp 238-239 Lesson B pp 240-241 Lesson C pp 242-245	**Leveled Book Lesson** *Crossings* pp 298-299	**Fluency** Lesson 1 p 347 **Leveled Book** **Summary Assessment** *Crossings* p W5
Choose a Source Lesson A pp 238-239 Lesson B pp 240-241 Lesson C pp 242-245	**Leveled Book Lesson** *Tornado Alley* pp 300-301	**Fluency** Lesson 1 p 347 **Leveled Book** **Summary Assessment** *Tornado Alley* p W5
Choose a Source Lesson A pp 238-239 Lesson B pp 240-241 Lesson C pp 242-245	**Leveled Book Lesson** *Teacher Selected Review Selection*	**Fluency** Lesson 1 p 347 **Leveled Book** **Summary Assessment** *Teacher Selected Review Selection* p W5

*To determine individual student Fluency Passages see page 40.

Grade 6 Unit 2

Macmillan/McGraw-Hill Teacher's Edition Selections	Comprehension	Vocabulary Strategies
Last Summer With Maizon pp 116-132	**Compare and Contrast** Lesson A pp 90-91* Lesson B pp 92-93* Lesson C pp 94-95* **Draw Conclusions** Lesson A pp 72-73 Lesson B pp 74-75 Lesson C pp 76-77	**Multi-Meaning Words** Lesson A pp 182-183 Lesson B pp 184-185 Lesson C pp 186-187
Ta-Na-E-Ka pp 140-155	**Problem and Solution** Lesson A pp 60-61 Lesson B pp 62-63 Lesson C pp 64-65 **Draw Conclusions** Lesson A pp 72-73 Lesson B pp 74-75 Lesson C pp 76-77	**Compound Words** Lesson A pp 158-159 Lesson B pp 160-161 Lesson C pp 162-163
Number the Stars pp 162-182	**Compare and Contrast** Lesson A pp 90-91 Lesson B pp 92-93 Lesson C pp 94-95 **Problem and Solution** Lesson A pp 60-61 Lesson B pp 62-63 Lesson C pp 64-65	**Multi-Meaning Words** Lesson A pp 182-183 Lesson B pp 184-185 Lesson C pp 186-187
Opera, Karate and Bandits pp 192-203	**Main Idea** Lesson A pp 66-67 Lesson B pp 68-69 Lesson C pp 70-71 **Problem and Solution** Lesson A pp 60-61 Lesson B pp 62-63 Lesson C pp 64-65	**Compound Words** Lesson A pp 158-159 Lesson B pp 160-161 Lesson C pp 162-163
TIME for Kids Cleopatra's Lost Palace pp 210-213	**Draw Conclusions** Lesson A pp 72-73 Lesson B pp 74-75 Lesson C pp 76-77	**Multi-Meaning Words** Lesson A pp 182-183 Lesson B pp 184-185 Lesson C pp 186-187 **Compound Words** Lesson A pp 158-159 Lesson B pp 160-161 Lesson C pp 162-163

* Lesson A - - - -below level
Lesson B - - - - - -on level
Lesson C - - - - -transition

Unit Skills Plan

Study Skills	Leveled Book Lessons	Fluency/Assessment
Various Texts Lesson A pp 232-233 Lesson B pp 234-235 Lesson C pp 236-237	**Leveled Book Lesson** *A Summer Day* pp 302-303	**Fluency*** Lesson 1 p 347 **Leveled Book Summary Assessment** *A Summer Day* p W5
Various Texts Lesson A pp 232-233 Lesson B pp 234-235 Lesson C pp 236-237	**Leveled Book Lesson** *Laurie in Charge* pp 304-305	**Fluency** Lesson 1 p 347 **Leveled Book Summary Assessment** *Laurie in Charge* p W5
Various Texts Lesson A pp 232-233 Lesson B pp 234-235 Lesson C pp 236-237	**Leveled Book Lesson** *To the Rescue!* pp 306-307	**Fluency** Lesson 2 p 348 **Leveled Book Summary Assessment** *To the Rescue!* p W5
Various Texts Lesson A pp 232-233 Lesson B pp 234-235 Lesson C pp 236-237	**Leveled Book Lesson** *The History of Karate* pp 308-309	**Fluency** Lesson 2 p 348 **Leveled Book Summary Assessment** *The History of Karate* p W5
Various Texts Lesson A pp 232-233 Lesson B pp 234-235 Lesson C pp 236-237	**Leveled Book Lesson** *Teacher Selected Review Selection*	**Fluency** Lessons 2 and 4 pp 348-350 **Leveled Book Summary Assessment** *Teacher Selected Review Selection* p W5

* To determine individual student Fluency Passages see page 40.

Grade 6 Unit 3

Macmillan/McGraw-Hill Teacher's Edition Selections	Comprehension	Vocabulary Strategies
A Boy of Unusual Vision pp 224-235	**Author's Purpose, Point of View** Lesson A pp 102-103* Lesson B pp 104-105* Lesson C pp 106-107* **Summarize** Lesson A pp 78-79 Lesson B pp 80-81 Lesson C pp 82-83	**Context Clues** Lesson A pp 146-147 Lesson B pp 148-149 Lesson C pp 150-151
The School Play pp 242-255	**Steps in a Process** Lesson A pp 108-109 Lesson B pp 110-112 Lesson C pp 113-114 **Summarize** Lesson A pp 78-79 Lesson B pp 80-81 Lesson C pp 82-83	**Figurative Language** Lesson A pp 194-195 Lesson B pp 196-197 Lesson C pp 198-199
The Singing Man pp 262-282	**Cause and Effect** Lesson A pp 78-79 Lesson B pp 80-81 Lesson C pp 82-83 **Steps in a Process** Lesson A pp 108-109 Lesson B pp 110-112 Lesson C pp 113-114	**Figurative Language** Lesson A pp 194-195 Lesson B pp 196-197 Lesson C pp 198-199
Painters of the Cave pp 290-303	**Summarize** Lesson A pp 78-79 Lesson B pp 80-81 Lesson C pp 82-83 **Cause and Effect** Lesson A pp 78-79 Lesson B pp 80-81 Lesson C pp 82-83	**Context Clues** Lesson A pp 146-147 Lesson B pp 148-149 Lesson C pp 150-151
TIME for Kids Is this Ancient Bone the World's First Flute? pp 310-313	**Steps in a Process** Lesson A pp 108-109 Lesson B pp 110-112 Lesson C pp 113-114 **Context Clues** Lesson A pp 146-147 Lesson B pp 148-149 Lesson C pp 150-151	**Figurative Language** Lesson A pp 194-195 Lesson B pp 196-197 Lesson C pp 198-199

* Lesson A - - -below level
Lesson B - - - - -on level
Lesson C - - - -transition

Unit Skills Plan

Study Skills	Leveled Book Lessons	Fluency/Assessment
Graphic Aids Lesson A pp 226-227 Lesson B pp 228-229 Lesson C pp 230-231	**Leveled Book Lesson** *Ron's Story: Talking Baseball* pp 310-311	**Fluency*** Lesson 1 p 347 **Leveled Book Summary Assessment** *Ron's Story: Talking Baseball* p W5
Graphic Aids Lesson A pp 226-227 Lesson B pp 228-229 Lesson C pp 230-231	**Leveled Book Lesson** *George Blanchine, A Life of Dance* pp 312-313	**Fluency** Lesson 1 p 347 **Leveled Book Summary Assessment** *George Blanchine, A Life of Dance* p W5
Graphic Aids Lesson A pp 226-227 Lesson B pp 228-229 Lesson C pp 230-231	**Leveled Book Lesson** *Meet the Band* pp 314-315	**Fluency** Lesson 2 p 348 **Leveled Book Summary Assessment** *Meet the Band* p W5
Graphic Aids Lesson A pp 226-227 Lesson B pp 228-229 Lesson C pp 230-231	**Leveled Book Lesson** *Through Alexandra's Eyes* pp 316-317	**Fluency** Lesson 2 p 348 **Leveled Book Summary Assessment** *Through Alexandra's Eyes* p W5
Graphic Aids Lesson A pp 226-227 Lesson B pp 228-229 Lesson C pp 230-231	**Leveled Book Lesson** *Teacher Selected Review Selection*	**Fluency** Lessons 1 and 3 **Leveled Book Summary Assessment** *Teacher Selected Review Selection* p W5

*To determine individual student Fluency Passages see page 40.

Grade 6 Unit 4

Macmillan/McGraw-Hill Teacher's Edition Selections	Comprehension	Vocabulary Strategies
Mummies, Tombs, and Treasure pp 324-337	**Fact and Nonfact** Lesson A pp 114-115* Lesson B pp 116-117* Lesson C pp 118-119*	**Suffixes** Lesson A pp 170-171 Lesson B pp 172-173 Lesson C pp 174-175
Over the Top of the World pp 344-363	**Important and Unimportant Information** Lesson A pp 126-127 Lesson B pp 128-129 Lesson C pp 130-131 **Fact and Nonfact** Lesson A pp 114-115 Lesson B pp 116-117 Lesson C pp 118-119	**Root Words** Lesson A pp 188-189 Lesson B pp 190-191 Lesson C pp 192-193
The Phantom Tollbooth 370-401	**Story Elements** Lesson A pp 52-53 Lesson B pp 54-55 Lesson C pp 56-57	**Root Words** Lesson A pp 188-189 Lesson B pp 190-191 Lesson C pp 192-193
Exploring the Titanic 408-427	**Important and Unimportant Information** Lesson A pp 126-127 Lesson B pp 128-129 Lesson C pp 130-131 **Sequence of Events** Lesson A pp 42-43 Lesson B pp 44-45 Lesson C pp 46-47	**Suffixes** Lesson A pp 170-171 Lesson B pp 172-173 Lesson C pp 174-175
TIME for Kids Back to the Moon pp 434-437	**Fact and Nonfact** Lesson A pp 114-115 Lesson B pp 116-117 Lesson C pp 118-119	**Suffixes** Lesson A pp 170-171 Lesson B pp 172-173 Lesson C pp 174-175 **Root Words** Lesson A pp 188-189 Lesson B pp 190-191 Lesson C pp 192-193

* Lesson A - - -below level
Lesson B - - - - -on level
Lesson C - - - -transition

Unit Skills Plan

Study Skills	Leveled Book Lessons	Fluency/Assessment
Graphic Aids Lesson A pp 226-227 Lesson B pp 228-229 Lesson C pp 230-231	**Leveled Book Lesson** *Nate, Steffi, and the Great Pyramid* pp 318-319	**Fluency*** Lesson 1 p 347 **Leveled Book Summary Assessment** *Nate, Steffi, and the Great Pyramid* p W5
Graphic Aids Lesson A pp 226-227 Lesson B pp 228-229 Lesson C pp 230-231	**Leveled Book Lesson** *Mining the Moon* pp 320-321	**Fluency** Lesson 1 p 347 **Leveled Book Summary Assessment** *Mining the Moon* p W5
Graphic Aids Lesson A pp 226-227 Lesson B pp 228-229 Lesson C pp 230-231	**Leveled Book Lesson** *Across the Country* pp 322-323	**Fluency** Lesson 2 p 348 **Leveled Book Summary Assessment** *Across the Country* p W5
Graphic Aids Lesson A pp 226-227 Lesson B pp 228-229 Lesson C pp 230-231	**Leveled Book Lesson** *Sea of Treasures* pp 324-325	**Fluency** Lesson 2 p 348 **Leveled Book Summary Assessment** *Sea of Treasures* p W5
Graphic Aids Lesson A pp 226-227 Lesson B pp 228-229 Lesson C pp 230-231	**Leveled Book Lesson** *Teacher Selected Review Selection*	**Fluency** Lessons 2 and 4 pp 348 and 350 **Leveled Book Summary Assessment** *Teacher Selected Review Selection* p W5

* To determine individual student Fluency Passages see page 40.

Grade 6 Unit 5

Macmillan/McGraw-Hill Teacher's Edition Selections	Comprehension	Vocabulary Strategies
Child of the Owl pp 448-462	**Story Elements** Lesson A pp 54-55* Lesson B pp 56-57* Lesson C pp 58-59* **Make Inferences** Lesson A pp 84-85 Lesson B pp 86-87 Lesson C pp 88-89	**Denotation and Connotation** Lesson A pp 200-201 Lesson B pp 202-203 Lesson C pp 204-205
Bellerophon and the Flying Horse pp 470-477	**Sequence of Events** Lesson A pp 42-43 Lesson B pp 44-45 Lesson C pp 46-47 **Make Inferences** Lesson A pp 84-85 Lesson B pp 86-87 Lesson C pp 88-89	**Context Clues** Lesson A pp 146-147 Lesson B pp 148-149 Lesson C pp 150-151
Adventure in Space pp 484-497	**Judgments and Decisions** Lesson A pp 120-121 Lesson B pp 122-123 Lesson C pp 124-125 **Sequence of Events** Lesson A pp 42-43 Lesson B pp 44-45 Lesson C pp 46-47	**Context Clues** Lesson A pp 146-147 Lesson B pp 148-149 Lesson C pp 150-151
Rumpelstiltskin's Daughter pp 504-526	**Story Elements** Lesson A pp 54-55 Lesson B pp 56-57 Lesson C pp 58-59 **Make Inferences** Lesson A pp 84-85 Lesson B pp 86-87 Lesson C pp 88-89	**Denotation and Connotation** Lesson A pp 200-201 Lesson B pp 202-203 Lesson C pp 204-205
TIME for Kids The History of Money pp 534-536	**Sequence of Events** Lesson A pp 42-43 Lesson B pp 44-45 Lesson C pp 46-47	**Denotation and Connotation** Lesson A pp 200-201 Lesson B pp 202-203 Lesson C pp 204-205 **Context Clues** Lesson A pp 146-147 Lesson B pp 148-149 Lesson C pp 150-151

* Lesson A - - -below level
Lesson B - - - - -on level
Lesson C - - - -transition

Unit Skills Plan

Study Skills	Leveled Book Lessons	Fluency/Assessment
Graphic Aids Lesson A pp 226-227 Lesson B pp 228-229 Lesson C pp 230-231	**Leveled Book Lesson** *A Tune for Lucy* pp 326-327	**Fluency** Lesson 1 p 347 **Leveled Book Summary Assessment** *A Tune for Lucy* p W5
Graphic Aids Lesson A pp 226-227 Lesson B pp 228-229 Lesson C pp 230-231	**Leveled Book Lesson** *Hercules* pp 328-329	**Fluency** Lesson 1 p 347 **Leveled Book Summary Assessment** *Hercules* p W5
Graphic Aids Lesson A pp 226-227 Lesson B pp 228-229 Lesson C pp 230-231	**Leveled Book Lesson** *John Glenn: Space Pioneer* pp 330-331	**Fluency** Lesson 2 p 348 **Leveled Book Summary Assessment** *John Glenn: Space Pioneer* p W5
Graphic Aids Lesson A pp 226-227 Lesson B pp 228-229 Lesson C pp 230-231	**Leveled Book Lesson** *Rosa Parks* pp 332-333	**Fluency** Lesson 2 p 348 **Leveled Book Summary Assessment** *Rosa Parks* p W5
Graphic Aids Lesson A pp 226-227 Lesson B pp 228-229 Lesson C pp 230-231	**Leveled Book Lesson** *Teacher Selected Review Selection*	**Fluency** Lessons 1 and 3 Pages 347 and 350 **Leveled Book Summary Assessment** *Teacher's Selected Review Selection* p W5

* To determine individual student Fluency Passages see page 40.

Grade 6 Unit 6

Macmillan/McGraw-Hill Teacher's Edition Selections	Comprehension	Vocabulary Strategies
Mandela pp 548-568	**Recognize Techniques of Persuasion** Lesson A pp 132-133* Lesson B pp 134-135* Lesson C pp 136-137* **Draw Conclusions** Lesson A pp 72-73 Lesson B pp 74-75 Lesson C pp 76-77	**Prefixes** Lesson A pp 176-177 Lesson B pp 178-179 Lesson C pp 180-181
My Friend Flicka pp 576-595	**Problem and Solution** Lesson A pp 60-61 Lesson B pp 62-63 Lesson C pp 64-65 **Recognize Techniques of Persuasion** Lesson A pp 132-133 Lesson B pp 134-135 Lesson C pp 136-137	**Prefixes** Lesson A pp 176-177 Lesson B pp 178-179 Lesson C pp 180-181
Alexander the Great pp 602-615	**Evaluate Evidence and Sources** Lesson A pp 138-139 Lesson B pp 140-141 Lesson C pp 142-143 **Draw Conclusions** Lesson A pp 72-73 Lesson B pp 74-75 Lesson C pp 76-77	**Analogies** Lesson A pp 206-207 Lesson B pp 208-209 Lesson C pp 210-211
The Circuit pp 622-631	**Problem and Solution** Lesson A pp 60-61 Lesson B pp 62-63 Lesson C pp 64-65 **Draw Conclusions** Lesson A pp 72-73 Lesson B pp 74-75 Lesson C pp 76-77	**Analogies** Lesson A pp 206-207 Lesson B pp 208-209 Lesson C pp 210-211
TIME for Kids A Great Wall? pp 638-641	**Recognize Techniques of Persuasion** Lesson A pp 132-133 Lesson B pp 134-135 Lesson C pp 136-137	**Prefixes** Lesson A pp 176-177 Lesson B pp 178-179 Lesson C pp 180-181

* Lesson A - - -below level
Lesson B - - - - -on level
Lesson C - - - -transition

Unit Skills Plan

Study Skills	Leveled Book Lessons	Fluency/Assessment
Reference Sources Lesson A pp 220-221 Lesson B pp 222-223 Lesson C pp 224-225	**Leveled Book Lesson** *Last Summer at Camp Woodside* pp 334-335	**Fluency*** Lesson 1 p 347 **Leveled Book Summary Assessment** *Last Summer at Camp Woodside* p W5
Reference Sources Lesson A pp 220-221 Lesson B pp 222-223 Lesson C pp 224-225	**Leveled Book Lesson** *Symphony Weekend* pp 336-337	**Fluency** Lesson 1 p 347 **Leveled Book Summary Assessment** *Symphony Weekend* p W5
Reference Sources Lesson A pp 220-221 Lesson B pp 222-223 Lesson C pp 224-225	**Leveled Book Lesson** *The Reluctant Princess* pp 338-339	**Fluency** Lesson 2 p 348 **Leveled Book Summary Assessment** *The Reluctant Princess* p W5
Reference Sources Lesson A pp 220-221 Lesson B pp 222-223 Lesson C pp 224-225	**Leveled Book Lesson** *Lake Joy, at Last* pp 340-341	**Fluency** Lesson 2 p 348 **Leveled Book Summary Assessment** *Lake Joy, at Last* p W5
Reference Sources Lesson A pp 220-221 Lesson B pp 222-223 Lesson C pp 224-225	**Leveled Book Lesson** *Teacher Selected Review Selection*	**Fluency** Lessons 2 and 4 pp 348 and 350 **Leveled Book Summary Assessment** *Teacher Selected Review Selection* p W5

*To determine individual student Fluency Passages see page 40.

Intervention Diagnostic Tests

PART 1 INDIVIDUAL ASSESSMENTS

PART 2 GROUP ASSESSMENTS

Introduction to Intervention Diagnostic Tests

Part One of the Intervention Guide provides tools for assessing student competency in key skill areas. The Diagnostic Tests are divided into two sections:

Section 1 **Individually** Administered Assessments

- Word Recognition Test
- Running Record (RR)
- Informal Reading Inventory (IRI)

Section 2 **Group** Administered multiple-choice tests that measure student competency in

- phonics
- vocabulary
- reading comprehension.

The information provided by the individual and group assessments can be used to help you make decisions about where to place a child within the intervention program. Assessment results can also be used to help you determine if and when a child should exit the intervention program.

Guidelines for Administering the Individual Assessments

Word Recognition Test

The first test to be administered to students is the Word Recognition Test found on pages 6-7. The lists on page 7 feature basic reading vocabulary words at three levels.

You may administer the test in one of two ways:

- have the student read each word aloud from the list, OR
- have the student identify each word from the list as you read them aloud.

The Word Recognition Test is not timed. You should, however, set aside 10-15 minutes for testing each student.

PROCEDURE:

1. Begin with the first word on list one.
2. If the student makes less than two errors in a list, move on to the next list.
3. If the student makes more than two errors in a list, DO NOT GO ON TO THE NEXT LIST.
4. Stop the student when a total of five errors have been made ON ANY LIST.

The Running Record

The Running Record (RR) provides valuable information about a student's reading patterns. It is the primary tool used to determine the student's starting point in the fluency section of the intervention program. The RR is designed to measure two facets of the student's oral reading ability:

- accuracy (correctly reading the actual words on the page)
- fluency (phrasing, intonation, and reading rate)

The student is given a passage to read aloud. As the student begins reading, the starting time is noted. Any mistakes made by the student are noted on the teacher's copy of the passage. Other behaviors are observed and described as well. When the student finishes reading, the ending time is recorded.

The RR should be administered **after** the student has taken the Word Recognition Test, since the results of the Word Recognition Test are used to determine the difficulty level of the passage the student is asked to read. **Students unable to identify more than half of the words in list one in the Word Recognition test should not be assessed with the RR.**

There is no time limit for administering the RR. For planning purposes, you should expect to spend 5-10 minutes administering the RR to each student.

Please note: Before administering the RR, you should familiarize yourself with examples of the types of errors likely to be noted, and the notations used to record each type. This information is provided on page 4.

As you administer the RR it is important to remember the following:

- If the student hesitates while reading, you should wait at least five seconds before reading that word for the student and marking it as an error.
- If the student repeats the same error several times (such as mispronouncing the same word again and again), you should treat these repetitions as single error.
- If the student makes an error but self-corrects before proceeding, you should not record the initial error.
- If you observe student behaviors other than errors, you should note those behaviors in the space provided on the reading chart.

PROCEDURE:

1. Use the chart below to select the passage the student will read for the RR.

Word Recognition Test	Running Record
If the student read most or all of list one only,	then have the student read passage one on page 13.
If the student read only list one and part or all of list two,	then have the student read passage two on page 15.
If the student read lists one and two, and part or all of list three,	then have the student read passage three on page 17.

2. Give the student a copy of the appropriate passage. Write the time the student begins reading at the top of your copy of the passage.
3. As the student reads, record errors on your copy of the passage. Follow the notation system shown on page 4 of this guide.
4. Observe any behaviors not categorized as errors. As time allows, record these behaviors in the space provided on your page.
5. When the student has finished reading the passage, note the time and record it in the appropriate space.

CALCULATING THE STUDENT'S READING ACCURACY SCORE:

1. Tally the number of errors recorded for that passage.
2. Calculate the percentage score using this formula:

$$\frac{\text{Total \# of Words} - \text{\# of Errors}}{\text{Total \# of Words}} \times 100 = \underline{\hspace{1cm}} \%$$

CALCULATING THE STUDENT'S WORDS CORRECT PER MINUTE:

1. Subtract the student's start time from the finish time. This will give you the amount of time the student spent reading. Express this figure in seconds.
2. Tally the number of errors recorded for the passage and subtract that amount from the total number of words in the passage. This will give you the number of words correct.
3. Divide the student's words correct by the number of seconds spent reading.
4. Multiply that figure by 60 to determine the student's words correct per minute.

Example

A student reads a passage in 1 minute and 24 seconds, or 84 seconds.
   (1 minute x 60 seconds) + 24 seconds = 84 seconds
The passage is 180 words in length, and the student missed 20 words.
   180 – 20 = 160 words correct read
The student's reading rate is 1.9 words correct per second.
   160 words correct ÷ 84 seconds = 1.9 words correct per second
The student's reading rate is 114 words correct per minute.
   1.9 words correct per second x 60 seconds = 114 words correct per minute

READING ERRORS

A student's oral reading accuracy score is based on the number of reading errors noted. In the chart below, the left column shows the types of errors which should be noted as the student reads aloud. The right column shows examples of how to record each error.

Reading Errors	Examples and Notations
1. Omission (words or parts of words omitted)	The girl reads a̧ book.
2. Insertion (words or parts of words inserted)	The girl reads a good book.
3. Mispronunciation/Misreading	The girl reds a book.
4. Substitution (words or parts of words substituted for those in the text)	The girl sees a book.
5. Hesitation (teacher provides word)	The (girl) reads a book.

• If the student hesitates, wait at least five seconds before providing the word.

• If the student repeats the same error, it is scored as one error.

• If the student self-corrects an error before proceeding, it is not counted as an error.

READING BEHAVIORS

During oral reading, the student may exhibit any number of specific reading behaviors. These behaviors should not be considered errors and should not be included in the score.

Reading Behaviors (not scored)	Examples and Notations
1. Repetition (the student repeats words or parts of words.)	The girl <u>reads</u> a book.
2. Self-Correction (the student repeats a word or words to correct an error.)	The girl c/reds a book.
3. Mispronunciation or Substitution/ Dialect (words are pronounced in a nonstandard way	The girl writes with a pen. (pin)
4. Phrasing (the student reads with phrasing that does not some coincide with punctuation or emphasis in the text.)	The girl/has/a/pen, paper, and some/crayons.

The Informal Reading Inventory

The Informal Reading Inventory (IRI) is an assessment tool that provides information about a student's ability to read and understand continuous text of increasing difficulty. The IRI is used to assess both silent reading and oral reading. The student reads a short passage, either silently or out loud, and responds orally to several questions about that passage.

Like the Running Record (RR), the IRI should be administered **after** the student has taken the Word Recognition Test, since the results of the Word Recognition Test are used to determine the difficulty level of the first passage the student is asked to read. **Students unable to identify more than half of the words in list one in the Word Recognition test <u>should not</u> be assessed with the IRI.**

The three types of questions in the IRI are:

- Vocabulary (V): require students use context clues from the passage to determine word meaning.

- Comprehension (C): measure student understanding of text at the literal, inferential, and evaluative levels.

- Metacognitive (M): provide information about the student's self-monitoring strategies, literary appreciation, and motivation.

There is no time limit for administering the IRI. Students should be allowed as much time as needed to read the passages and answer the questions. For planning purposes, you should expect to spend 15-20 minutes administering the IRI to each student.

PROCEDURE:

1. Use the chart below to select the first passage the student will read for the IRI.

Word Recognition Test	Informal Reading Inventory
If the student read most or all of list one,	then begin with passage one on page 13.
If the student read only list one and part or all of list two,	then begin the IRI with passage two. on page 15.
If the student read lists one and two, and part or all of list three,	then begin with passage three on page 17.

2. Have the student silently read the passage. Let the student take as much time as necessary.
3. When the student finishes reading the passage, read the first question from the Teacher Page to the student. Let the student take as much time as necessary to respond orally to the question.
4. Score the student's answer in the scoring box on the Teacher Page.
5. Continue with the rest of the questions.
6. After the student has answered all the questions, calculate what percentage of the questions the student answered correctly.

Use the chart below to determine if testing needs to be continued.

	WCPM(RR)	COMPREHENSION
Independent Level	96%-99%	7/8 answers correct
Instructional Level	90%-95%	5/8 answers correct
Frustration Level	below 90%	below 7/8 answers correct

The student's placement should be based on the difficulty level of the passage for which he/she answered between 70-90% of the questions correctly. Testing should continue until the student achieves a score within that range.

Word Recognition Test

Word Recognition Test

The targeted vocabulary in the Word Recognition test is drawn from the reading selections and is based on high-frequency and basic reading vocabulary word lists. You may administer the test in one of two ways:

- have the student read each word aloud from the list, OR

- have the student identify each word from the list as you read them aloud.

The Word Recognition Test is not timed. You should, however, set aside 10-15 minutes for testing each student.

PROCEDURE:

1. Begin with the first word on list one.
2. If the student makes less than two errors in a list, move on to the next list.
3. If the student makes more than two errors in a list, DO NOT GO ON TO THE NEXT LIST.
4. Stop the student when a total of five errors have been made ON ANY LIST.

Name _____ Date _____ Instructor _____

LIST 1	LIST 2	LIST 3
fan	helmet	willow
creek	partner	hamster
dawn	treasure	thunderstorm
match	mystery	solution
juice	fireworks	permanent
alive	searches	beginnings
season	bicycling	reappear
planet	invisible	science
disbelief	thoughtful	comfortably
weight	dangerous	mournful

Informal Reading Inventory (/RI/)

IRI Passage I

DIRECTIONS

You are going to read a story about two boys who are best friends and must race against each other. How do you suppose the boys will feel about having to race against each other? Read the story to find out.

QUESTIONS

C.1 **What sports do John and Mike both like to play?** (running and baseball)

C.2 **What did classes in the same grade do at the spring field day?** (Classes in the same grade played against each other in sporting events.)

C.3 **Why were John and Mike selected to be the last runners for their teams?** (The boys enjoyed running, and they probably ran very fast.)

C.4 **What thought did John and Mike both have before the race?** (Both boys thought, "May the fastest runner win.")

C.5 **Do you think their positive approach to the race will strengthen their friendship? Explain your answer.** (Their friendship will be stronger because they both realize that their friendship is more important than winning the race.)

V.6 **John and Mike competed against each other. What does *competed* mean?** (raced against each other to win)

M.7 **What are some reasons why John and Mike might be best friends?** (They like the same sports, they go to the same school, they are the same age, and they probably live near each other.)

M.8 **Where could you find out more about relay races?** (The student could ask a teacher or coach, look at running books in the library, or search the Internet.)

M.9 **Do you think the boys will still be friends when the race is over? Explain your answer.** (They probably will still be friends because they both realized that only one — the fastest runner — could win.)

Reading Comprehension	
# Correct	**% Score**
/8	%

IRI Passage I

John and Mike were best friends. Both boys were in the fourth grade at the same school, but they were in different classes. The two friends enjoyed sports, especially running and baseball.

At spring field day, classes in the same grade competed against each other. Five students from each class were chosen to run in a relay race. John was selected to be on the last runner for his class, and Mike was chosen to run last for his class.

The two friends looked at each other. Each boy realized that only one would win. Neither boy wanted to hurt his friend, but neither wanted his team to lose. They both had the same thought, "May the best runner win."

When they heard the starting whistle, the first runners took off in a flash. They quickly passed the stick to the second runners, and the second passed it to the third, and third to the fourth. Finally, it was up to John and Mike to decide which team would win.

IRI Passage II

DIRECTIONS

You are going to read about ants in nature. They often work together to help each other survive. Read the passage to find out how.

QUESTIONS

C.1 **What kind of living things are ants?** (Ants are insects.)

C.2 **What are two ways ants communicate with each other?** (Ants communicate by rubbing the antennae of another ant and by leaving a special liquid for other ants to follow.)

C.3 **Why is it important for the queen ant to lay eggs?** (The eggs will hatch into baby ants, and the colony will have new members.)

C.4 **Why might an ant find meat on the ground?** (The meat might be left over from a meal or it may be from the body of a small dead animal such as a bird.)

V.5 **Each ant colony lives in its own nest. What does *nest* mean?** (A nest is a place in or near dirt where a colony of ants live.)

M.6 **How would you describe an ant colony?** (An ant colony is a busy place where many ants live together and where each type of ant has a special job.)

M.7 **Why is it important for the queen ant to lay eggs?** (The eggs will hatch into baby ants, and the colony will have new members.)

M.8 **Which special job in an ant colony do you think is most interesting? Explain your answer.** (The student should evaluate the function of the job selected and explain its relevance to the survival of the colony.)

Reading Comprehension	
# Correct	% Score
/8	%

IRI Passage II

Ants are insects that live in large *colonies*. Ants work together for the good of the whole colony. Each ant has a special job. The queen's job is to lay eggs. Worker ants gather food and care for the young. Soldier ants protect their colony.

Each ant colony lives in its own nest. Some ants build their nests under an old log or large stone, and others make a nest in the ground or in a *mound* of dirt.

Some ants eat meat, such as *leftover* food or dead animals. *Harvester* ants collect the grass seeds and store them in their nest for food. Some ants cut pieces of leaves off plants and transport them back to the nest.

Ants have fascinating ways of *communicating*. Sometimes they "talk" by touching the *antennae* of other ants. Other times, they mark a spot with a special liquid. When an ant finds food, it will leave a message for other ants to follow the trail of this special liquid.

IRI Passage III

DIRECTIONS

You are going to read about a girl who has an excellent imagination. She has an interesting way of using her creativity and sense of humor. Read the story to find out how.

QUESTIONS

C.1 **Why did the other children think Gina's shoes were special?** (Her shoes had lightning bolts painted on them.)

C.2 **What did Kate and the other children think the shoes would help Gina do?** (They thought that the shoes would make Gina run fast.)

C.3 **Why were the other children surprised when they saw Gina the next day?** (They were surprised because Gina was wearing a different pair of shoes, ones with pictures of jumping kangaroos and not lightning bolts .)

C.4 **Why did all the children paint lightning bolts on their shoes?** (They like Gina's shoes and wanted to be fast runners.

V.5 **These shoes had illustrations of jumping kangaroos painted on them. What does _illustrations_ mean?** (pictures; drawings)

M.6 **Why does Gina say she plans to paint a picture of a brain on the shoes she will wear tomorrow?** (She is joking that the picture of the brain will make her smart so she will do well on her spelling test.)

M.7 **Where might you learn more about how to do good experiments?** (The student might look in a science book, in library reference books, and on the Internet.)

M.8 **How would you describe Gina?** (She is creative, and she has a good sense of humor.)

Reading Comprehension	
# Correct	**% Score**
/8	%

IRI Passage III

Gina was wearing a new pair of shoes.

"The shoes you're wearing are amazing," Nate exclaimed.

"They are really incredible shoes!" Jim said.

"I bet you can run faster than anybody," said Tim.

"They're only regular shoes," Gina said. "I just painted lightning bolts on them, that's all."

"They look awesome!" cried Fred.

"Let's try an experiment," Kate said. "Run to the tree and we'll see time you to see how fast you go."

Gina ran to the tree and it seemed that her feet never touched the ground.

"Wow!" the kids said. The next day everybody except Gina had shoes with lightning bolts painted on them.

Gina was wearing different shoes. These shoes had illustrations of jumping kangaroos painted on them.

"Watch me jump," she said. With one bounce she reached as high as the treetop.

"Wow!" the kids said. "That's fantastic!"

"What are you going to paint on your shoes tomorrow?" Matt asked.

"A brain," said Gina. "I have a spelling test."

Student Record Chart
Score Summary

Name _____ Grade _____

Administrator _____ Date _____

Comprehension Analysis Chart

Skill	Passage 1	Passage 2	Passage 3
Comprehension	/4	/4	/4
Vocabulary	/1	/1	/1
Metacognitive	/3	/3	/3
Total	/8	/8	/8

Running Record

Skill	Passage 1	Passage 2	Passage 3
Fluency Rate (WCPM)			
Reading accuracy rate			

Oral Reading Miscue Analysis Chart

Skill	Passage 1	Passage 2	Passage 3
Omission			
Insertion			
Mispronunciation/ Misreading			
Substitution			
Hesitation			

Word Recognition Test

	Number of errors
List 1	
List 2	
List 3	

Group Assessments

Phonics Test

SHORT VOWELS

Have students turn to page 23.

Find the row marked S. Look at the picture. Name the picture to yourself. Notice the vowel sound. Then fill in the circle beside the word that names the picture. What is the letter of the circle you filled in? Yes, the answer is b, pot.

Continue with the other items on this page. Go on to page 24 and complete that page. Then stop and look up at me.

CONSONANT BLENDS WITH SHORT VOWELS

Have students turn to page 25.

Find the row marked S. Look at the picture. Name the picture to yourself. Notice the sounds in the word. Then fill in the circle beside the word that names the picture. Which circle did you fill in? Yes, the answer is a, chop.

Continue with the other items on this page. Then stop and look up at me.

LONG VOWELS

Have students turn to page 26.

Find the row marked S. Look at the picture. Name the picture to yourself. Notice the vowel sound. Then fill in the circle beside the word that names the picture. Which circle did you fill in? Yes, the answer is c, pole.

Continue with the other items on this page. Go on to page 27 and complete that page. Then stop and look up at me.

VARIANT VOWELS

Have students turn to page 28.

Find the row marked S. Look at the first word in the row. Say the word to yourself. Notice the sound the underlined letters make. Then fill in the circle beside the word that has the same vowel sound as those underlined letters. Which circle did you fill in? Yes, b, stew, has the same vowel sound as clue.

Continue with the other items on this page. Go on to page 29 and complete that page. Then stop and look up at me.

R-CONTROLLED VOWELS

Have students turn to page 30.

Find the row marked S. Look at the first word in the row. Say the word to yourself. Notice the sound the underlined letters make. Then fill in the circle beside the word that has the same sound as those underlined letters. Which circle did you fill in? Yes, c, stair, has the same vowel sound as bear.

Continue with the other items on this page. Then STOP.

Tally results using the answer key and scorebox below.

ANSWERS

1. a 2. c 3. a 4. b 5. c

6. b 7. a 8. b 9. c 10. b

11. a 12. b 13. c 14. a 15. a

16. c 17. a 18. b 19. c 20. a

Phonics	
# Correct	**% Score**
/20	%

Vocabulary Strategies Test

COMPOUND WORDS

Have students turn to page 31.

Read the directions to yourself as I read them aloud.

Read the directions aloud.

Find the example marked S. Read the sentence. Look for the compound word. Fill in the circle under the compound word. Did you mark a, wildflowers? Wildflowers is a compound word. It is made up of two smaller words, wild and flowers.

Continue with the other items on this page. Then stop and look up at me.

SYNONYMS AND ANTONYMS

Have students turn to page 32.

Read the directions to yourself as I read them aloud.

Read the directions aloud.

Notice that the correct answer will mean the same thing as the underlined word.

Find the example marked S. Read the sentence. Then fill in the circle beside the word that means the same as the underlined word. Which word was underlined? That's right, voyage was underlined. Which word means the same as voyage? You should have marked c. journey means the same thing as voyage. Complete number 4.

Now you need to find the opposite of the underlined words.

Continue with the other items on this page. Then stop and look up at me.

CONTEXT CLUES

Have students turn to page 33.

Read the directions to yourself as I read them aloud.

Read the directions aloud.

Find the example marked S. Read the sentence. Think about the clues these words give about the meaning of the missing word. Fill in the circle next to the best choice for the missing word. You should have marked b, terrible. The clues tell you that the movie was bad so only terrible fits.

Continue with the other items on this page. Then stop and look up at me.

MULTI-MEANING WORDS

Have students turn to page 34.

Read the directions to yourself as I read them aloud.

Read the directions aloud.

Find the example marked S. Read the sentence. Think about which meaning of rows is meant. Fill in the circle next to that meaning. You should have marked a, straight lines. Only that meaning fits the sentence.

Continue with the other items on this page. Then STOP.

Tally results using the answer key and scorebox below.

ANSWERS

1. c   2. b   3. a   4. b   5. a

6. c   7. c   8. a   9. b   10. c

11. b   12. a

Vocabulary Strategies	
# Correct	**% Score**
/12	%

Comprehension Skills Test

Have students turn to page 35.

Read the story in the box silently as I read it aloud.

Read the story aloud.

Now read the sentence marked S. Read the answer choices. Which choice best completes the sentence? That's right. This story is mostly about c, Jeb's first time fishing with his grandfather. That is the main idea of the story.

Do you have any questions? If not, turn to page 36. Read the story silently. Then answer the questions by filling in the correct circle. Continue through page 38. You will read three more stories. When you see the word STOP, look up at me.

Tally results using the answer key and scorebox below.

ANSWERS

1. b 2. a 3. c 4. c 5. a

6. b 7. b 8. c 9. a

Comprehension Skills	
# Correct	**% Score**
/9	%

S.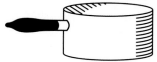

    a pet   **b** pot   **c** put

1.

    a cap   **b** cup   **c** cape

2.

    a bad   **b** bud   **c** bed

GO ON

Name _____ Date _____

3.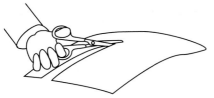

   a cut   **b** cute   **c** cat

4.

   a droops   **b** drops   **c** drapes

5.

   a stuck   **b** stock   **c** stack

STOP

S.

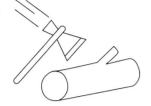

(**a**) chop   (**b**) chap   (**c**) chip

6.

(**a**) stir   (**b**) star   (**c**) steer

7.

(**a**) truck   (**b**) trick   (**c**) track

STOP

Name _____   Date _____

S.

➡

a pale   **b** pile   **c** pole

8.

a can   **b** cane   **c** come

9.

a sled   **b** slid   **c** slide

GO ON ➡

Name _____   Date _____

10.

   (**a**) got   (**b**) goat   (**c**) gate

11.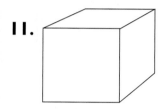

   (**a**) cube   (**b**) cub   (**c**) cup

12.

   (**a**) strip   (**b**) stripe   (**c**) strap

STOP

S. cl<u>ue</u>   (**a**) squeak   (**b**) stew   (**c**) cow

13. d<u>aw</u>n   (**a**) grown   (**b**) coin   (**c**) thought

14. g<u>oo</u>d   (**a**) could   (**b**) smooth   (**c**) globe

GO ON →

15. ch<u>ew</u>   (**a**) true   (**b**) lawn   (**c**) trout

16. b<u>oy</u>   (**a**) hoe   (**b**) mop   (**c**) soil

17. s<u>au</u>cer   (**a**) song   (**b**) spoon   (**c**) hook

STOP

Name _____   Date _____

S. b<u>ea</u>r   (**a**) born   (**b**) germ   (**c**) stair

18. t<u>or</u>n   (**a**) crown   (**b**) hoarse   (**c**) cart

19. th<u>ir</u>d   (**a**) rear   (**b**) hire   (**c**) germ

20. f<u>er</u>n   (**a**) curb   (**b**) chart   (**c**) rear

Directions Read each sentence. Mark the circle below the word that is a compound word.

S. The wildflowers have bloomed beautifully.
  (a)   (b)   (c)

1. Summer days are long and filled with sunlight.
  (a)   (b)   (c)

2. Mother's homemade soup was delicious.
  (a)   (b)   (c)

3. A thunderstorm frightened the children playing on the beach.
      (a)   (b)   (c)

STOP

Name _____   Date _____

Directions   Read each sentence. Pick the word that means **the same** as the underlined word. Mark your answer.

> **S.** The <u>voyage</u> across the ocean took two weeks.
>
> **a** visit   **b** story   **c** journey

4. The road was <u>slippery</u> from all the icy rain.

a wet   **b** slick   **c** clean

Directions   Pick the word that means **the opposite** of each underlined word.

5. Did you <u>remember</u> the way to the lake?

a forget   **b** lose   **c** find

6. He <u>inserted</u> two new batteries in the toy.

a found   **b** looked for   **c** removed

Name _____   Date _____

Directions   Read each sentence. Which word correctly completes the sentence? Mark your answer.

S. The movie was a failure because the acting was really _____.

    (a) terrific   **(b)** terrible   **(c)** special

7. The audience laughed because they found the jokes to be _____.

    (a) interesting   **(b)** unforgettable   **(c)** amusing

8. The waiting room of the dentist's office was packed with new
_____.

    (a) patients   **(b)** workers   **(c)** friends

9. Everyone did a poor job, and the home owner thought the work was
_____.

    (a) miraculous   **(b)** disastrous   **(c)** acceptable

STOP

Name _____   Date _____

Directions   Read each sentence. Which word or group of words defines the underlined word as it is used in the sentence? Mark your answer.

> **S.** The vegetable seeds were planted in <u>rows</u> in the garden.
>   **a** straight lines   **b** flowers   **c** paddles

10. The player <u>ducks</u> his head just before the baseball hits it.

  a birds   **b** lowers   **c** cloth

11. He carefully read each name on the <u>roll</u>.

  a piece of bread   **b** list   **c** move

12. Tommy's house is only three <u>blocks</u> from my house.

  a streets   **b** wooden cubes   **c** obstacles

STOP

The first time Jeb went fishing with his grandfather he asked, "What will I do if I catch a big fish and it pulls me in the water?"

Grandpa laughed, "Well, let's cross that bridge when we come to it."

"I didn't know we had to cross a bridge," said Jeb nervously. "What happens if it falls down and we're thrown into the river? What will we do?"

Grandpa laughed again. "Jeb, that was just an old saying."

Later that morning, Jeb felt a big tug on his fishing line.

"Oh, no!" he cried. "Grandpa help the fish is pulling me into the river." Grandpa got behind Jeb and helped him reel in a big trout.

"That's a beautiful fish you caught, Jeb," said grandpa. "Let's put him in the basket and your mom and grandma can prepare him for dinner."

When they got home that afternoon, Jeb showed his mother and his grandmother the fish he had caught. He told them about being afraid of ending up in the river and how grandfather helped.

Mom laughed, "That's some fish story, but I'm still proud of you."

S. This story is mostly about —

(a) Jeb's fears of being thrown into the water

(b) Jeb's mother being proud of the fish he caught

(c) Jeb's first time fishing with his grandfather

GO ON ⇒

Dad got a new job and Rachel's family would be moving at the end of the summer.

"It will be fine," said Rachel's mom. "You'll make lots of new friends."

"Yes, and you can invite them to play in your big, new back yard," added her father.

"But I love this house and the friends I already have!" cried Rachel. "How can I keep my old friends if we are living miles away," asked Rachel.

"That's easy," said Rachel's dad. "You can stay in touch everyday with the new computer." mom and I bought for you this afternoon," he answered. Rachel smiled for the first time since she heard the news about moving.

1. What will Rachel do after her family moves?
- **a** She will talk to her old friends on the telephone everyday.
- **b** She will use her computer to write to her old friends every day.
- **c** She will forget about her old friends quickly.

2. Why does Rachel smile when her father tells her about the computer?
- **a** She realizes that she will be able to stay in touch with her friends.
- **b** She has wanted a computer for a long time.
- **c** Her mom and dad want her to forget about her problems.

3. To summarize, this story tells about —
- **a** a girl who is angry because her parents don't understand her
- **b** a girl who is upset because she wants a computer
- **c** a girl who wants to stay in touch with her friends after she moves

GO ON ➡

Name _____   Date _____

As soon as they saw the old house in the moonlight, Randy became frightened. The paint was peeling. The porch sagged like the back of an old horse. The stairs made creaking sounds when they climbed them.

"I'm sure I saw Mrs. Fuller's cat go inside just before dinner," said Sandy. "Don't you want the five dollar reward she is offering?"

"Did you hear that noise? That's it! I'm leaving!" Randy turned. "Wait a minute. Here, kitty, kitty. Meow. Meow," Sandy said. Within a moment, Mrs. Fuller's cat jumped through a broken window.

"See, I told you the cat was here," said Sandy as she picked it up.

"The sooner we are out of here the better!" said Randy as he turned and began running down the stairs.

"Well, the sooner I collect the reward the better," Sandy laughed.

4. This story is mostly about —
- (a) two children scaring each other
- (b) two children talking to each other
- (c) two children looking for a missing cat

5. Why does Sandy want to find Mrs. Fuller's cat?
- (a) She wants the five dollar reward.
- (b) She wants to prove she is brave.
- (c) She saw the cat near the old house before dinner.

6. Where does this story take place?
- (a) in front of Mrs. Fuller's house
- (b) on the porch of an old rundown house
- (c) inside an old rundown house

GO ON ⟹

Thousands of years ago, people lived outdoors. They learned to use fire to cook and keep warm. Once people began building real houses, they took the fire inside. At first, people just built a fire in a nook in the wall. The smoke was let out through a hole in the ceiling.

On a windy day, however, the wind might blow the smoke back inside the house. Sometimes the wind fanned the flames, and the house caught fire. About 500 years ago, solutions to these problems were found.

Indoor fireplaces made of brick became common. Bricks did not catch fire easily. Soon, a tall shaft of brick was placed outside the house. It reached several feet beyond the roof of the house. This was called the chimney. In time, the chimney was lined with metal. It carried the smoke outside the house. It stopped smoke from blowing back inside. It also prevented the wind from fanning the flames and causing a fire.

7. Before chimneys, how did the smoke from indoor fires get out of a house?

(a) The smoke got out through a nearby window.

(b) The smoke got out through a hole in the ceiling.

(c) The smoke got out through the front door.

8. Why were chimneys built several feet beyond the roof?

(a) to help the people cook

(b) to keep the people inside warm

(c) to carry smoke away from the house

9. How did having an indoor fire help people?

(a) It kept them warm and helped them cook.

(b) It stopped the wind from fanning the flames.

(c) It stopped the house from burning down.

Name _____   Date _____

Score Summary Chart

Assessment	Correct Number	Notes
1. Phonics	/20	_____ _____ _____ _____ _____
2. Vocabulary Strategies	/12	_____ _____ _____ _____ _____
3. Comprehension Skills	/9	_____ _____ _____ _____ _____

Interpreting the Results

As with most assessment devices, interpretation relies on a wide range of individual factors. Student results may vary dramatically from one part of the test to the next, though in most instances this will not be the case. For that reason, the tables below suggest representative ranges of achievement on the assessments. Teachers should use their own discretion in placement based on observation, prior student records, and results from the Diagnostic Tests.

INDIVIDUAL ASSESSMENTS Refer to the Student Record Chart on p. 18.

Word Recognition	Reading Accuracy	Comprehension	Placement Recommendation
Student could read most or all of list 1.	below 90% on Passage 1	less than 6/8 on Passage 1	• Have student take the Individual Assessment Tests for Skills InterventionGuide Book B. • If needed, have student take the Diagnostic Assessment in the Phonics Intervention Guide. • Use only Level A lessons. • Have the students begin with Fluency Passage F1.
Student could read most or all of list 2.	at least 90% on passage 2	at least 6/8 on passage 2	• Use Level B lessons. • Have the student begin with Fluency Passage F14. • Begin with Grade 5 Level Book "Dan's Time" on p. 246.
Student could read most or all of list 3.	at least 90% on passage 3	at least 6/8 on passage 3	• Use Level C lessons. • Have the student begin with Fluency Passage F26. • Begin with Grade 6 Level Book "The Knitting Circle" on p. 294.

GROUP ASSESSMENTS Refer to the Score Summary Chart on p. 39.

Phonics	Vocabulary	Comprehension	Placement Recommendation
10/20 or less	4/12 or less	3/9 or less	• Have students take the Diagnostic Tests for Skills Intervention Guide Book B. • If needed, have students take the Diagnostic Assessment in the Phonics Intervention Guide. • Use only Level A lessons. • Have students start with Fluency Passage F1.
11/20 to 15/20	5/12 to 8/12	4/9 to 6/9	• Use Level B lessons. • Have students start with Fluency Passage F14. • Begin with Grade 5 Level Book "Dan's Time" on p. 246.
16/20 or cmore	9/12 or more	7/9 or more	• Use Level C lessons. • Have students start with Fluency Passage F26. • Begin with Grade 6 Level Book "The Knitting Circle" on p. 294.

Comprehension Strategies

Sequence of Events / A

TEACHING FRAME: BLM 1 Ask students to think about the order of movements as they draw a capital A in the air. **Ask** *What do you do first? What do you do next? What do you do last? Would it be a good idea to start with the cross-bar of the A?* (probably not; the letter would be more difficult to make) **Say** *The order, or sequence, of events is important in stories, too.*

Ask students to read along with you as you read the first paragraph. **Ask** *What did Darcy do first?* (put a tablecloth on the table) *I'll circle the word* **first.** *It's a good clue as to the order of events. What did Darcy do next?* (set out paper plates and cups) *I'll circle the word* **next.** *What did Darcy do last?* (brought out the food) *I'll circle the word* **last.** *So Darcy did three actions in order. Does the sequence make sense? Would it be better to bring out the food before putting on the tablecloth?* **Say** *Read the second paragraph and number the order in which things happen.* **Ask** *Which three words give you clues about when things happened?* (first, next, last) *What happened first? What happened next? What happened last?*

CORRECTIVE FEEDBACK

If students have trouble naming the order of events, have them circle the clue words and write the numbers 1, 2, and 3 over those words. Then ask them to tell what happened first, next, and last.

PRACTICE Have students complete Blackline Master 1. **Say** *Read each paragraph. Decide what happened first, next, and last. Write 1, 2, or 3 before each sentence to show the order of events.*

CORRECTIVE FEEDBACK

If students cannot number events in sequence, have them circle the clue words *First, Next,* and *Last* in each paragraph and write the numbers 1, 2, and 3 over those words. Then have them use those numbers to number the events below.

Answers: 1. 1, 3, 2   2. 3, 2, 1

Name _____ Date _____ Instructor _____

Sequence of Events

Darcy prepared carefully for the picnic. First, she put a checked table-cloth over the table. Next, she set out paper plates and cups. Last, Darcy brought out the food. She put the cold chicken and salad in the center of the table.

Olivia and Kate set up a treasure hunt for their friends. First, they tied the ends of balls of yarn around little stuffed dogs. Next, they unrolled the yarn in twisted paths all through the garden. Last, they hid the little dogs in bushes and under logs. They called this game the "Hound Hunt."

PRACTICE

1. The party began at two in the afternoon. First, all of the children watched Skippy the Clown. Next, they sat around the big table for ice cream and cake. Last, Kirby opened the presents his friends had brought.

_____ The children watched a clown.

_____ Kirby opened his presents.

_____ The children had ice cream and cake.

2. Dan went for a run this morning. First, he did some stretches to warm up his muscles. Next, he started at a slow jogging pace down the quiet lane. Last, he finished with a sprint up the hill to his home.

_____ Dan sprinted up the hill.

_____ Dan jogged slowly down the lane.

_____ Dan stretched his muscles.

Sequence of Events / B

TEACHING FRAME: BLM 2 Say *The sequence of events in a story is the order in which things happen.* Have students repeat. **Ask** *What is the sequence of events in a story?* **Say** *Writers often use clue words such as* first, next, then, *and* last, *to tell us the sequence of events.*

MODEL Read the first paragraph on the teaching frame. **Say** *The paragraph is about going to the State Fair. What happened first, second, third, and so on? There are clue words that help me keep the events straight.* Circle the words *First, Once we got there,* and *Finally.* **Say** *These words and phrases tell me that the narrator crossed the footbridge first, bought tickets second, and entered through the gates third. I need to keep the sequence of events clear in my mind if I want to understand the story.* **Say** *Think about the sequence of events in the next paragraph.* Read the paragraph. **Ask** *Are there any clue words that help you identify the sequence of events? What are they?* (first, Then, After that) Circle these as they are mentioned. *Where did the family go first at the fair?* (They went to the dairy barn.) *Where did they go second?* (They went to see the pigs.) *Where did they go third?* (They went to the midway to ride the Ferris wheel.)

CORRECTIVE FEEDBACK

If students have trouble identifying the sequence of events, ask them to tell which events happened *before* and *after* the visit to the pigs.

PRACTICE Have students complete Blackline Master 2. **Say** *Read each paragraph. Decide what happened first, second, and third. Write 1, 2, or 3 before each sentence to show the sequence of events.*

CORRECTIVE FEEDBACK

If students cannot identify the sequence of events, have them circle the clue words in each paragraph and write the numbers 1, 2, and 3 over those words. Then have them use those numbers to number the events below.

Answers: 1. 2, 1, 3, 2. 3, 2, 1

Name _____ Date _____ Instructor _____

Sequence of Events

We had a wonderful time at the State Fair. We drove up on Saturday morning. First, we crossed the long footbridge to get to the entrance. Once we got there, we bought four tickets. Finally, we slipped inside the gates into the hustle and bustle of the fair.

There were so many things to see! I dragged everyone to the dairy barn first. They always have great ice cream. Then Jasmine wanted to see the pigs. She thinks all pigs are like the one in *Babe*. She was a bit surprised to see those porkers! After that, of course, we went to the midway to ride the enormous Ferris wheel.

PRACTICE

1. Kara started her routine with a run of cartwheels. Then she turned and did forward rolls to the end of the mat. Her routine ended with a straddle jump that ended in a split. All of the parents were very impressed.

   _____ Kara did a series of forward rolls.
   _____ Kara did a run of cartwheels.
   _____ Kara did a straddle jump and split.

2. The guest speaker was very interesting. He began by showing us slides of his travels. Then he explained what he was studying and why it was important. Last, he allowed us to handle some of the unusual fossils he had brought.

   _____ The speaker let us handle some fossils.
   _____ The speaker explained his studies.
   _____ The speaker showed slides of his travels.

Sequence of Events / C

TEACHING FRAME: BLM 3 Say *The sequence of events in a story is the order in which things happen.* Have students repeat. **Say** *Sometimes writers use time-order words to give us clues about the sequence of events. Words such as* first, next, then, *and* last *tell us when things happen. Phrases such as* before that, after five minutes, *or* during that time *also give clues about sequence.*

MODEL Read the first part of the teaching frame together. **Say** *The story tells about taking a singing lesson. As I read, I want to keep the order of events clear in my mind. Time-order words can help.* Circle the words *began, Next,* and *Nearly half an hour had gone by before.* **Say** *The teacher is giving his pupil things to do in a specific sequence. Before he can sing, he has to stretch his muscles and warm up his voice. So the sequence is I, yawn and stretch; II, say the vowels; III, sing.* Write I, II, III over the sentences in question. **Say** *This sequence is important. The teacher would not want his pupil to sing before warming up properly.* **Say** *Think about the sequence of events in the next paragraph.* Read the paragraph. **Say** *Think about the sequence of events in the next paragraph.* Read the paragraph. **Say** *There are clue words in this paragraph, too. What are they?* (First, After I heard that, then) Circle these as they are mentioned. *What happened first? What happened next? What happened last? Why doesn't the narrator sing first?*

> ## CORRECTIVE FEEDBACK
>
> If students have trouble identifying the sequence of events, show them how to pull out the events and write them in an outline form.

PRACTICE Have students complete Blackline Master 3. **Say** *Read each paragraph. Decide what happened first, second, and third. Write the events in order in the outline.*

> ## CORRECTIVE FEEDBACK
>
> If students cannot outline the events, have them circle the clue words in each paragraph and write Roman numerals I, II, and III over those words. Then have them use those numbers to outline the events.

Answers: 1. I Mary found the bakery section. II Mary picked out food in the fish section. III Mary found the produce section. 2. I The car turned over properly. II The car died. III The car roared into life.

Name _____ Date _____ Instructor _____

Sequence of Events

Today I took a beginning singing lesson. It was very interesting. We began simply by yawning and stretching. This opens the throat and makes singing easier. Next, the teacher had me say the vowels over and over in a normal speaking voice. Nearly half an hour had gone by before I sang a note.

"All right," said Mr. Munson. "It's time to do some scales." First, he hit middle C on the piano. After I heard that, I sang "OHHHHHHH." We then continued up the scale, with me singing "OHHHHHHH" for each note. It felt a little strange.

PRACTICE

1. Mary wandered down the aisles of the supermarket. She started in the bakery section, since it smelled so good. There she found some bread and a lovely pie. Next, she visited the fish section, where she picked out two pounds of mussels. She finished up in the produce section for broccoli and mushrooms.

   I. _____

   II. _____

   III. _____

2. The car was always hard to start on cold, winter mornings. It usually began by starting up properly, but then it would sputter and die. After a few minutes, it would suddenly roar into life. Dad said he wasted most mornings in January waiting for the car to start.

   I. _____

   II. _____

   III. _____

Make Predictions / A

TEACHING FRAME: BLM 4 Ask students to watch you carefully. Take a set of keys that are sitting on a desk and put them in your hand. **Ask** *What might happen next? What made you think this would happen?* **Say** *When you look ahead to what might happen in the future, you are making a prediction. You make predictions when you read, as well. Based on clues in the story, you make guesses about what might happen.*

Ask students to read along with you as you read the first paragraph aloud. **Ask** *What did Lynn put in her pocket? Now, let's circle the word* **sandwich**. *What did Lynn feel in her pocket later on? Let's circle* **something strange, too**. *What do you think might happen next?* (Lynn will find a squashed sandwich in her pocket.) **Say** *Each clue we circled helped us to predict what might happen next. Now let's read the second paragraph together.* Read the paragraph. **Ask** *What do you predict will happen next?* (Rain might cancel the picnic so Frank won't miss it.) *Which details gave you clues about what might happen?* (Frank really wanted to go to the picnic but was too sick to go as the rain clouds appeared.)

CORRECTIVE FEEDBACK

If students have trouble predicting, **ask** *What does Frank want to do?* (go to the picnic) *Why can't he do it?* (He's feeling sick.) *What happens that might change things?* (black clouds appear.)

PRACTICE Have students complete Blackline Master 4. **Say** *Read the paragraph and predict what might happen next. Read each possible answer and select the best choice. Circle a, b, or c.*

CORRECTIVE FEEDBACK

If students are not able to choose the best prediction, have them read each sentence carefully and identify the clue. Ask them to circle each clue then make a prediction in their own words. Have them compare the predictions they made to the choices given.

Answers: 1. b 2. a

Name _____ Date _____ Instructor _____

Make Predictions

At lunch time, Lynn played kickball. She crammed her sandwich in her back pocket. Sliding into a base, Lynn felt something strange in her pocket. "Oh no," Lynn said.

Today was the picnic. Suddenly, Frank began to feel queasy. "You can't go with a fever," his mom told him. Frank looked out the window and saw black clouds.

PRACTICE

1. Bonnie had not worn her winter coat for 9 months. She put it on and put her hands in the pockets. Inside the right pocket she felt a piece of paper folded up. Then she remembered that five-dollar bill she had lost last March.

a. Bonnie pulled out the paper and saw that it was torn.

b. Bonnie pulled a five-dollar bill out of her pocket.

c. Bonnie pulled a hundred-dollar bill out of her pocket.

2. Lucky the dog didn't like the new mailman. He started barking as soon as he came near. The mailman smiled. He felt in his pocket for a plastic bag. Inside the bag was a small bone.

a. The mailman gave Lucky the bone.

b. Lucky bit the mailman.

c. The mailman threw the bone across the street.

Make Predictions / B

TEACHING FRAME: BLM 5 Say *A prediction is a guess, based on clues and knowledge, of what might happen next in a story.* Ask students to repeat the definition, then ask, *How do you make a good prediction?*

MODEL: Read the first paragraph of the teaching frame together. **Say** *This first paragraph is about cherry picking. I'm looking for clues as to what might happen as I read. The paragraph says that the birds are likely to eat all of the cherries if Alba doesn't take action.* Circle *eat them.* **Say** *Alba notices a scarecrow.* Circle *scarecrow.* **Say** *I predict that Alba will use the scarecrow to protect the cherries. Making a prediction helps me be an active reader and gets me really involved in what happens in the story. See if you can make your own predictions as you read the next paragraph.* Read the paragraph. **Ask** *What did Alba do before she went to the tree?* Circle the words *pie tin.* **Say** *How did the scarecrow affect the birds?* Circle the words *warded off.* **Ask** *What was Alba able to do with the help of the scarecrow? What do you think Alba will do with the cherries?*

> **CORRECTIVE FEEDBACK**
>
> If the students have difficulty making predictions, tell them to read the paragraph again, then ask *What kind of pie might Alba make?*

PRACTICE Have students complete Blackline Master 5. **Say** *After reading the paragraph, make a prediction about what might happen next. Write your prediction on the line, then go on to make another prediction for the second paragraph.*

> **CORRECTIVE FEEDBACK**
>
> If students are not successful at making predictions, guide them in asking questions about the text: *What was Cass doing? What seemed to happen? What do you think Cass will do next? What happened during the storm? How might it affect the ice cream? What do you predict Mike will do next?*

Answers: 1. Cass will look down to see that her tire is flat. 2. Mike will eat the ice cream before it melts.

---

50 | Make Predictions / B | Skills Intervention — Book C

Name _____ Date _____ Instructor _____

Make Predictions

> The cherries Alba picked were sweet, ripe, and ready. The birds would eat them all up if Alba didn't do something. Just then, Alba glanced at an old scarecrow nearby.
>
> The next day Alba took out a pie tin. She went to the tree and saw that the scarecrow had warded off the birds. Alba then picked a huge bowl of cherries.

PRACTICE

1. Cass was riding her bike through the empty lot when she heard a noise. It sounded like a pop. After the pop, Cass heard a hissing noise. After that she began having trouble keeping up her speed. She then looked down at her tire.

   Cass _____

2. During the storm, a big bolt of lightning knocked out all the electricity in the house. Mike brought out candles. "This is fun," he said. Then he remembered that they had just bought a big carton of ice cream for tomorrow.

   Mike _____

Make Predictions / C

TEACHING FRAME: BLM 6 Say *Making predictions uses your own knowledge and clues from the text to guess what might happen next.* Have students repeat the definition. **Say** *A prediction is useful if it makes sense and is supported by evidence from the story.*

MODEL Go over the teaching frame together. Begin by saying **This first paragraph describes what happened in the soup shop. Ned bought soup and left his keys.** Circle the words *purchasing soup* and *left his keys.* **Say What does Ms. Cox want to do? She wants to return the keys, but she doesn't know where Ned lives. But then she sees a clue, a trail of soup on the floor. This tells Ms. Cox that there may be a way to follow Ned.** Circle the words *trail of soup* **Ask What do you think will happen next? Say I can use clues from this paragraph to guess that Ms. Cox might try to follow the trail of soup to Ned's home. To find out if my prediction is correct, I need to read on. Now use what you know to make predictions for the second paragraph.** Read the paragraph aloud. **Ask Was my prediction correct?** Point out that even if it hadn't been correct, it still helped you understand the story. You can now use new information to change your prediction. What is this second paragraph about? **Ask What clues do I see that indicate what might happen next? Using these clues, what do you think will happen?**

CORRECTIVE FEEDBACK

If students have trouble making predictions, tell them to outline any clues they come across. Upon completing each paragraph, they can use the outline as reference to make predictions.

PRACTICE Have students complete Blackline Master 6. **Say Read the paragraphs. Predict what will happen next. Write your predictions.**

CORRECTIVE FEEDBACK

If students have trouble making predictions, tell them to reread the paragraph and circle clues. Instruct them to use the clues to change their predictions or make new predictions about what will happen next.

Answers: 1. Jake will walk to the store in snow shoes 2. Juanita will give Sparky a bath.

Part 2
COMPREHENSION

Name _____   Date _____   Instructor _____

Make Predictions

After purchasing soup, Ned forgot his keys. "Wait!" cried Ms. Cox, but he was gone. If only she could discover where he lived. Then she saw a trail of soup leading outside. Ned's container must have had a leak! Ms. Cox had an idea.

The drips led to a house with a big herb garden. When Ms. Cox returned the keys to Ned, he asked, "How can I thank you?" Ms. Cox peered at the garden. At her soup shop, she used large quantities of natural herbs.

PRACTICE

1. The snow was coming down hard. Jake needed food, but could he risk driving in this weather? He looked at the street. There were no cars in any direction. Then Jake noticed a pair of snow shoes in the closet.

What will happen next? _____

_____

2. Juanita smelled something terrible outside. Then she saw Sparky barking at a black and white animal in the bushes. A few minutes later, Sparky came running in. "You're coming with me," Juanita said, heading for the backyard hose.

What will happen next? _____

_____

Story Elements / A

TEACHING FRAME BLM 7 Bring up a familiar story, such as Cinderella. **Ask** *Who are the characters in the story?* (Cinderella, the prince, her step-family) *Where does the story take place?* (in a kingdom) *What happens in the story?* **Say** *All stories are like Cinderella in some ways. They have special features or elements that tell the reader whom the story is about, where the story takes place, and what happens in the story.*

Read the first paragraph aloud. **Ask** *Who is in this story? Where does the story take place? What is the story about?* Circle the elements: *lake, canoe, Jill, Megan, paddles.* **Say** *Seeing story elements helps you understand the meaning of a story.*

Say *Let's read the second paragraph together.* **Ask** *Who is the story about?* (Ty and Rick) *Where does the story take place?* (on a desert road) *What happens in the story?* (The riders stop to look at the starry sky.) Circle the following story elements: *Ty, Rick, desert, stars.*

CORRECTIVE FEEDBACK

If students have trouble identifying story elements, **Say** *To find out who the story is about, look for names. Do you see any names in the story? To find out where the story takes place, look for places? Can you find names of places? Finally, To find out what happens, look for action words. Can you find any action words in the story?*

PRACTICE Have students complete Blackline Master 7. **Say** *Read each paragraph. Find out who each story is about, where each story takes place, and what happens in each story. Write your answers in the spaces of the chart.*

CORRECTIVE FEEDBACK

If students have trouble identifying story elements, ask them to reread the stories and circle clues about characters, setting, and events. Have them use the clues that they circled to fill in a Who/Where and When/What Happened chart.

Answers: 1. Who: Oscar; Where and When: on a race course, during a race; What Happens: Oscar decides to keep going 2. Who: Lucia, Uncle Wilfredo; Where and When: in a hospital; What Happens: Lucia finds Uncle Wilfredo's room.

Name _____ Date _____ Instructor _____

Story Elements

> The water in the lake was still and clear. Jill sat in the back of the canoe while Megan was in the front. They were both holding paddles. "Now what?" Jill said.
>
> They had been driving in the desert for hours. Finally, Ty and Rick stopped. They looked up at the dark sky. There were more stars than anyone could ever imagine!

PRACTICE

1. All Oscar could think was, "There are 2 miles to go." His legs hurt. He was tired. But when he saw all the other runners, he didn't want to give up. Soon, it would all be over.

Who
Where and When
What Happens

2. The halls of the hospital were quiet. Lucia got lost trying to find Room 305. Finally, a nurse took her to see Uncle Wilfredo. He was sitting up in bed. He had a smile on his face.

Who
Where and When
What Happens

Story Elements / B

TEACHING FRAME BLM 8 Say *All stories have three elements in common: characters, setting, and plot. Characters are the people or animals that the story is about. The setting is where and when the story takes place. The plot is how the events in the story unfold.* Ask students to repeat these definitions.

MODEL Go over the teaching frame. **Say** *To find a story's characters I ask "Who is the story about? Who is carrying out the actions in the story?"* Circle *prince* and *frog*. **Say** *To identify the setting, I ask, "Where and when do the events take place?"* Circle *pond*. **Say** *To identify elements of the plot, I look for a problem. In this case, the frog claims that she is really a princess.* Circle *princess.* Point out that the rest of this story will probably describe the frog's actions.

Say *Try to identify story elements in the second paragraph.* Read the paragraph together. **Ask** *Who are the characters in the story?* Circle the two names. *Where does the story take place?* Circle the words *theater* and *stage*. **Ask** *What problem does the main character face?* Circle the words *better dancer.*

CORRECTIVE FEEDBACK

If students experience difficulty in identifying story elements, have them ask questions such as, "What things are happening in the story?" "Who is doing these things?" and "Where are these things taking place?"

PRACTICE Have students complete Blackline Master 8. **Say** *After reading the paragraph, find the characters, setting, and problem that each character faces. Write your answers in the spaces given.*

CORRECTIVE FEEDBACK

If students have trouble completing the chart, have them change the chart headings to questions: "Who is in the story?" "Where and when does the story take place?" "What problem does the main character have?"

Answers: 1. Characters: Rosa, George; Setting: Cave, sunset; Problem: no flashlight. 2. Characters: Jay, Rachel; Setting: Old house, day; Problem: Spending the night in the house.

Name _____ Date _____ Instructor _____

Story Elements

A voice from the edge of the pond addressed the prince on his horse. It was a hideous green frog. "I need your help," the frog said. "I'm really a beautiful princess."

The theater stage was empty except for Nikki. When Mr. Fox asked her what she was doing, Nikki replied, "I'm practicing. I want to become a better dancer."

PRACTICE

1. When they got to the mouth of the cave at sunset, Rosa told George that he would need his flash light. "Oh no," George said. "I must have left it back on the bus."

Characters	
Setting	
Problem	

2. To Jay, the house seemed very old but not so spooky. But this was during the day time. "How would you feel about spending the night in this old place?" Rachel asked Jay.

Characters	
Setting	
Problem	

Story Elements / C

TEACHING FRAME: BLM 9 Say *The main elements of a story are character, setting, and plot. The animals or people who do things in the story are its characters. Setting is the time and place in which the story takes place. Plot is the action that takes place in the story.* **Ask** *What are the three important elements of a story? Who are characters? What is setting? What is plot?*

MODEL Go over the teaching frame with students. **Say** *The first paragraph sets up the story by identifying its character, setting, and part of its plot. The paragraph describes the actions of Dr. Pitt, the story's main character.* Circle Dr. Pitt. **The setting of the story is late at night in Dr. Pitt's lab.** Circle the words *late at night* and *lab*. **Ask** *What problem does Dr. Pitt have?* **Say** *I think she might use the spilled formula to solve the problem as the story continues.*

Say *While you read the second paragraph, think about the story elements you already know about. You know the main character, the setting and the problem that the character faces. But now you see how the character's problem changes. She may not be able to invent a new soft drink, but she can invent something else useful.* **Ask** *What does she invent?*

CORRECTIVE FEEDBACK

If students have difficulty identifying story elements, have them ask, *Who is carrying out the actions in the story? That person is the main character. Where is the main character? That location and time is the story's setting. And finally, what problem is the main character struggling with? That problem will determine the plot.*

PRACTICE: Have students complete Blackline Master 9. **Say** *Read the story and circle the letter of each correct answer.*

CORRECTIVE FEEDBACK

If students are not able to answer the story element questions, have them reread the story and circle the following items: all people or animals; all places and times; all actions that the main character takes. Then have them make a second attempt at answering the questions.

Answers: 1. c 2. b 3. a 4. b

Name _____ Date _____ Instructor _____

Story Elements

> It was late at night and Dr. Pitt was still working in the lab. She was trying to find a new formula for a soft drink. The mixture she tried looked promising. Then she accidentally spilled some of the mixture on a hair brush.
>
> When she tried to pick up the brush, it wouldn't budge. "Oh my!" Dr. Pitt cried. "I've discovered a formula for a fast-drying glue!" And that is how Dr. Pitt's Super Secret Quick Drying Glue got its start.

PRACTICE

Both Dee and Jeff claimed they had the slowest bike on the playground. So they decided to race. But how could they make the race fair? Neither rider would try to win. Both riders would go as slowly as they could. It was a tough problem until Dee finally thought of a solution.

"You ride my bike and I'll ride yours," she said. "That way we'll both try to win. And we'll see whose bike is really slower."

1. Who is the main character or characters of the story?

    a. Dee   **b.** Jeff   **c.** Dee and Jeff

2. Where does the story take place?

    a. in the gym   **b.** on the playground   **c.** on a race course

3. When does the story take place?

    a. now   **b.** in ancient times   **c.** in the future

4. What problem do the main characters face?

    a. slow bikes   **b.** how to race fairly   **c.** how to go fast

Problem and Solution / A

TEACHING FRAME: BLM 10 Say *Have you ever tried to solve a difficult problem? How did you solve the problem? Have you noticed that usually the main character of the story faces a problem? The key to many stories is also a problem. The story's plot shows how the character solves his or her problem.*

Read the first paragraph out loud. **Ask** *Who is the main character in the story?* (Sam) *Where is the main character?* (probably at home) *What problem does the main character face?* (She can't read the directions to her game.) Underline the phrase *the directions were in German.* **Say** *The problem that a character faces is usually described at the beginning of the story. The rest of the story is used to explain how the character solves the problem.*

Say *Follow along with me as I read the second paragraph. As I read, try to identify the problem that the character in the story faces. What problem does this character need to solve?* (She needs to get to soccer practice.) Underline sentences 1 and 2.

CORRECTIVE FEEDBACK

If students still have trouble identifying the story problem, suggest that they use questions such as: *Who is the story's main character? What does he or she want to do? What is stopping this character from doing what he or she wants?*

PRACTICE Have students complete Blackline Master 10. **Say Read each paragraph and identify the problem. Circle the letter of the correct answer.**

CORRECTIVE FEEDBACK

If students have trouble identifying problems, have them reread the stories and circle the actions of the main character. Have them use these actions to state the main character's problem in their own words. Then have them return to the questions and try answering them a second time.

Answers: 1. c   2. a

Part 2 COMPREHENSION

Name _____ Date _____ Instructor _____

Problem and Solution

The directions for Sam's new video game were in German! What could Sam do? Then she remembered that Ian spoke German. He could show Sam how to play.

Soccer practice was starting and Lia's mom was late. Her brother Bo could not be left alone. So Lia decided to take Bo with her to practice. He'd have a splendid time!

PRACTICE

1. Gino loved to read at night. But sometimes, reading made him stay up too late. Then he had a hard time getting out of bed in the morning. "Why don't you try reading earlier in the evening?" Gino's aunt suggested.

What is the problem?

a. Gino's aunt does not like reading

b. Gino can't sleep in the morning.

c. Gino can't wake up in the morning.

2. Something was wrong with Dava's computer. The screen was frozen. The mouse wouldn't move. Nothing would work. Dava tried everything. Then she simply turned the computer off and then on again. Would this work? She would soon find out!

What is the problem?

a. Dava's computer wouldn't work.

b. Dava knew nothing about computers.

c. Dava's computer was too old.

Problem and Solution / B

TEACHING FRAME: BLM 11 Say *The heart of a story is based on a problem and its solution. The problem may be something that the main character wants or needs, a situation that calls for change, or a goal that the main character has.* Have students repeat this definition.

MODEL Go over the teaching frame together. **Say** *I can identify the problem by recognizing the main character and determining what is important to this character.* Circle *alarm clock* and *broken.* **Say** *The problem here is that Amy needs to wake up. Now, I identify the solution by noticing what the main character does. Here, Amy calls Fred and asks him to wake her up.* Circle *call Fred.* **Say** *Calling Fred to wake Amy up solved the story's problem.*

Say *Read the second paragraph.* **Ask** *Can you identify the problem?* Circle *Jim* and *shower.* **Ask** *Why can't Jim take this shower?* Circle *hot water* and *out.* *How does the main character solve the problem?* Circle *heated, pots, poured,* and *tub.*

> **CORRECTIVE FEEDBACK**
>
> If students have trouble recognizing this problem and solution, have them ask questions such as: "Who is the main character?" "What goal does he have?" "What does he do to accomplish this goal?"

PRACTICE Have students complete Blackline Master 11. **Say** *Read each paragraph. Find the problem and solution and write each in the chart.*

> **CORRECTIVE FEEDBACK**
>
> Have students who cannot complete the chart reread the story and retell the plot in their own words. Then instruct them to use the summaries they made to complete the chart.

Answers: 1. Problem: Walt is having trouble with Math; Solution: He treats Math like basketball and practices. 2. Problem: Carmen is afraid of spiders; Solution: She reads about a spider and learns to like spiders.

Name _____ Date _____ Instructor _____

Problem and Solution

> Amy's alarm clock was broken. How could she wake up at six tomorrow? She decided to call Fred. "Call me tomorrow at six, will you?" Amy politely requested.
>
> Jim wanted to take a shower, but the hot water was out for the day! Jim heated water in pots on the stove. Then he poured the heated water in the tub for a nice hot bath!

PRACTICE

1. "I just don't get Math," Walt said. Then Coach Beal told Walt that Math was like basketball. To get good, you needed to practice. So Walt practiced and his Math scores went way up!

Problem	
Solution	

2. Carmen was afraid of spiders. Then she read a book about spiders called *Charlotte's Web*. Carmen liked the spider in the book so much that she was never afraid of spiders again.

Problem	
Solution	

Problem and Solution / C

TEACHING FRAME: BLM 12 Say *A story's problem is something the main character wants or needs or a situation that calls for change.* Ask students to repeat. **Say** *Solutions are the steps or actions that the main character takes to solve a problem. These steps make up the plot.*

MODEL Read the teaching frame together. **Ask** *Who is the main character of this paragraph?* Circle the words *American Toad.* **Say** *The problem the American Toad has is stated in the second sentence.* Underline the second sentence. **Say** *I can restate the toad's problem: It wants to avoid being eaten.* **Ask** *What is the solution to this?* **Say** *It has ways to protect itself. It has a color that blends in with its surroundings.* Underline the third sentence. **Say** *The toad has poison in its skin. These two features protect the toad from enemies.* Circle the words *color blends* in the story. Then circle the word *poison.* **Say** *These are the steps that the toad takes to protect itself.*

Say *As you read the second paragraph, focus on the problem and its solution.* **Ask** *Who is the main character?* Circle the frog's name. **Ask** *What problem does this frog face?* Circle the words *protect itself.* **Ask** *What solution does the frog have?* Circle the word *attack.* **Say** *Find some actions that the frog takes to solve its problem.* Circle *bite down hard* and *never lets go.*

> **CORRECTIVE FEEDBACK**
>
> If students have trouble identifying the actions that the frog takes to protect itself, have them reread the paragraph and make a list of the frog's defense features.

PRACTICE Have students complete Blackline Master 12. **Say** *Read the story and complete the chart. List the steps to solve each problem.*

> **CORRECTIVE FEEDBACK**
>
> If students have trouble completing the chart, have them ask: "Who has a problem?" "What is the problem?" "How will they solve it?"

Answers: 1. Problem: Mice were hunted. Step 1: Have a meeting. Step 2: They want to put a bell around cat's neck. Step 3: Put the bell on the cat.

Part 2 COMPREHENSION

Name _____ Date _____ Instructor _____

Problem and Solution

American Toads are slow-moving creatures. Without sharp teeth, how do they keep from being eaten? First, their color blends in with their surroundings. They also have poison in their skin. Holding a toad can make you sick!

The Argentine Horned Frog has a different way to protect itself. Unlike most frogs, this creature will attack anything. Its jaws bite down hard on an enemy. And once it gets a hold, the Horned Frog never lets go!

PRACTICE

1. The mice were tired of being hunted by the cat. They had a big meeting. At the meeting, they decided to put a bell around the cat's neck. This would warn them whenever the cat came near. Now there was only one problem: who would do it?

Problem	
Solution	
Step 1	
Step 2	
Step 3	

Main Idea / A

TEACHING FRAME: BLM 13 Sit on a chair. **Ask** *What am I sitting on? What holds the chair up? What things are supporting the chair, and keeping it off the floor?* **Say** *A story is like this chair. The main idea of a story is like the seat of this chair. The supporting details of a story are the things that hold it up, like the chair's legs.* **Ask** *Have you noticed that all books and movies have titles?* **Say** *The title tells what a book or movie is about. The title gives a good clue to the main idea.*

Ask students to listen carefully as you read the first paragraph. **Ask** *What's a good title for that? What supporting details or sentences helped you think of the title?* (made friends, played, went to movies, etc.) **Say** *Let's underline those sentences. They're the legs that support the main idea of "My Summer Vacation."*

Say *Let's try giving a title to the next paragraph.* Read the paragraph aloud. **Ask** *What's a good title for that? What sentences or supporting details helped you think of that title?* Underline the sentences as students mention them.

CORRECTIVE FEEDBACK

If students can't find a title, or come up with an inappropriate one, ask them to point out the supporting details. Guide them to underlining details. **Ask** *Do you have another title you might like even better?*

PRACTICE Have students complete Blackline Master 13. **Say** *Read the paragraphs. Underline the best titles for each paragraph.*

CORRECTIVE FEEDBACK

If students select incorrectly, ask them *What happens in the paragraph? Let's look at the supporting details.* Lead them in finding and underlining the details, and then help them think of new title.

Answers: 1. b 2. c

Name _____ Date _____ Instructor _____

Main Idea

I loved my summer vacation. My family rented a beach house. I made lots of friends and played in the water. On rainy days, we went to the movies or played games. I learned how to cook out. I hope we rent a house next summer, too.

My best friend, Juan, is very funny. He knows a lot of great jokes. He also knows how to make all kinds of silly sounds. Even Mom and Dad smile a lot when he comes over. It's hard to be around Juan and not laugh every minute.

PRACTICE

1. Everyone calls my sister "Champ." That's because she is good at sports. She runs very fast. She can throw a ball really well, too, and her aim is perfect. Once, she even hit a home run in baseball. Mom and Dad were proud of her, and so was I!

    a. Perfect Aim   **b.** My Sister, Champ   **c.** I Am Proud

2. Yesterday I read a great book. It wasn't for homework, but just for fun. The book was about a boy who reminded me of myself. All kinds of exciting things happened to him. He got the other boys to do his chores. He was trapped in a cave, and he helped catch some bad people.

    a. Trapped in a Cave   **b.** Not For Homework   **c.** A Great Book

Main Idea / B

TEACHING FRAME: BLM 14 Say *The main idea is the most important thing the writer wants you to know.* **Ask** *What's the main idea?* Repeat the concept together. **Say** *Supporting details are the sentences that give more information about the main idea.* **Ask** *What are supporting details?* Repeat as above.

MODEL Read the teaching frame together. **Say** *The first paragraph is about going to the movies. We can prove it, by looking at the other sentences, such as "I love to go the movies?" "It's fun to sit in the dark," "I enjoy laughing," "when we all cheer." Those are all examples of why "I love to go the movies." Those are supporting details of the main idea.* **Say** *Let's circle the main idea and underline the supporting details.*

Say *Let's try the same thing with the second paragraph.* Read the paragraph together. *The first sentence is about getting popcorn. Could that be the main idea? Why not? Can the second sentence be the main idea? Why not?* **Say** *The first three sentences are about different foods. The last sentence says "No matter what I eat, I have a great time." If that's the main idea, some of the other sentences should give examples of different foods? Do they?* **Say** *The main idea is "No matter what I eat, I have a great time."* Circle the main idea and underline the supporting details, as above.

> ### CORRECTIVE FEEDBACK
>
> If students have difficulty selecting supporting details, have them ask themselves, "What happens in the story?" Then have them underline the details and use them as reference.

PRACTICE Have students complete Blackline Master 14. **Say** *Read the main idea and the sentences after it. Decide which sentences are supporting details that support the main idea. Mark only those supporting details with an x.*

> ### CORRECTIVE FEEDBACK
>
> If students select incorrect supporting details, rephrase the main idea as a question: *Why is drawing a wonderful way to express yourself?*

Answers: 1. b, c, 2. a, c

Main Idea

I love to go the movies. It's fun to sit in the dark and watch a story as it happens. I enjoy laughing at the jokes with everyone else. When we all cheer for the star, I smile.

Sometimes, I get popcorn at the movies. At other times, I bring a piece of fruit with me from home. Once in a while, I munch on some nuts. No matter what I eat, I have a great time.

PRACTICE

1. MAIN IDEA: Drawing is a wonderful way to express yourself.
SUPPORTING DETAILS:

A. _____ Colored pencils are better than plain ones.

B. _____ You can put your ideas into pictures.

C. _____ A drawing can show your feelings.

D. _____ My mother bought me new crayons.

2. MAIN IDEA: My father loves music.
SUPPORTING DETAILS:

A. _____ He always sings along with the radio.

B. _____ He reads every night after supper.

C. _____ He tries to see a concert at least once a month.

D. _____ He works in the post office.

Main Idea / C

TEACHING FRAME: BLM 15 Say *The main idea is the most important thing the writer wants you to know.* **Ask** *What's the main idea?* Have students repeat the concept. **Say** *Supporting details are the sentences that give more information about the main idea.* **Ask** *What are supporting details?* Repeat as above.

MODEL Read the teaching frame together with the class. **Say** *The first paragraph is all about the author at the museum. The first sentence says that the museum was a treat for the author's senses. That may be the main idea, but how can I know for sure? If it is, other sentences should back it up by giving examples of how it was a treat. The colors tickled my eyes, the guide's voice was happy, I could feel the paintings in my mind. Those are definitely supporting details of the main idea that "The museum was a treat for my senses." Let's circle the main idea and underline the supporting details.*

Say *Let's look for the main idea of the second paragraph. Can it be the first sentence? Why not? So which sentence is it? Who can find the main idea?* (It's the last sentence. The other sentences are examples of different things artists like to paint.) **Say** *In this paragraph the main idea comes last. It's "I'm glad artists like to paint so many different things.* Circle the main idea and underline the supporting details, as above.

> **CORRECTIVE FEEDBACK**
>
> If students select incorrect details, have them write down the main idea in their own words. Then have them explain what led them to understand that fact. Have them write down the details.

PRACTICE Have students complete Blackline Master 15. **Say** *Read the main idea. Six sentences are below it, but only three are supporting details for that main idea. Decide which three they are. Then write their numbers on the lines below the main idea.*

> **CORRECTIVE FEEDBACK**
>
> If students select incorrect details, rephrase the main idea as a question. **Ask** *What makes the circus "The Greatest Show on Earth?"*

Answers: 1 ,3,6

Name _____ Date _____ Instructor _____

Main Idea

The museum was a treat for my senses. The paintings had colors that tickled my eyes. I enjoyed listening to the guide's happy voice when she talked about the artists. And even though we weren't allowed to touch anything, I could feel the pictures in my mind.

The guide told us that some artists mainly like to paint nature. Other artists would much rather paint people. There are even artists who just want to make interesting designs. I'm glad artists like to paint so many different things.

PRACTICE

MAIN IDEA

The circus really is "The Greatest Show on Earth."

_____   _____   _____

1. Nothing in the world is funnier than a clown.

2. TV and movies are both great, too.

3. The animals do the most amazing things.

4. I think the circus is wonderful.

5. Most people who go to the circus buy something to help them remember it later.

6. It's hard to imagine anything as exciting as the tightrope walker.

Draw Conclusions / A

TEACHING FRAME: BLM 16 Have students observe as you try to staple a stack of papers together using an empty stapler. **Ask** *What do you know about this stapler?* **Say** *Authors often show you a situation by using details. They give you clues about what is happening. But you must put these clues together, along with what you already know, to draw a conclusion about what is happening.*

Have the students listen as you read the first paragraph. **Ask** *Who is in the story? What does she do?* (She throws her glove and shakes her head sadly.) Underline these actions. **Say** *This paragraph doesn't directly tell you who won the game. But it does tell you that Brianna threw her glove and shook her head sadly. Those clues allow you to draw the conclusion that Brianna lost the game.*

Read the second paragraph aloud. **Say** *In this second paragraph, try to picture what is happening. What characters appear in the story? What does Marta say to Jon?* (She makes comments about how he looks.) *What happened to Jon?* (He got a haircut.)

CORRECTIVE FEEDBACK

If students are unable to draw conclusions, have them circle these clues from the paragraph and try again: *short, Turn around, the back, stylish.* **Ask** *What do all of these clues have in common?*

PRACTICE Have students complete Blackline Master 16. **Say** *Read each paragraph. Answer each question by circling the letter of the correct answer.*

CORRECTIVE FEEDBACK

If students have trouble drawing conclusions, suggest that they go over the answers one by one and ask, "Is this conclusion possible? What clues lead to this conclusion?"

Answers: 1. a   2. c

Name _____ Date _____ Instructor _____

Draw Conclusions

Brianna still had her uniform on when she came in. She threw her baseball glove on the floor. "Well?" her sister asked. Brianna shook her head sadly.

"I like it," Marta said, when she saw Jon. "It's short, but not extremely short. Turn around." As Jon turned, Marta said, "I like the back, too — it's very stylish."

PRACTICE

1. Roscoe filled his pockets with change from the piggy bank. As he walked along, he felt something fall down his leg into his shoe.
What does Roscoe have?

    a. a hole in his pocket

    b. no more money

    c. a hole in his shoe

2. Che watched Derek unwrap his first gift. It looked familiar. In fact, it was a book about frogs! "Oh no," Che thought. She put the wrapped gift she had brought into her pocket. Maybe she could exchange it for a different book.
What was wrong with Che's gift?

    a. It was broken.

    b. It was not wrapped.

    c. It was the same book that Derek just got.

Draw Conclusions / B

TEACHING FRAME: BLM 17 Say *Authors can't explain everything in a story. You need to draw some conclusions by using clues from the story and your own knowledge.* Have students repeat this definition. **Ask** *Who can tell me what it means to draw conclusions?* **Say** *Drawing conclusions helps you figure out how a character feels, what happened, or why a character does something.*

MODEL Read the teaching frame together. **Say** *To find out how someone feels, I look at what they do. I also use my own knowledge to make sure my conclusions are reasonable. Here, I imagine myself in Suvi's position. I am nervous. The facts that Logan had more votes and Suvi ended up smiling let me draw the conclusion that Suvi must have supported Logan in the election. Suvi's words tell that she is relieved to have won by such a small amount.*

Say *Try to draw a conclusion about what has happened in the second paragraph.* Read the paragraph aloud. **Say** *What clues indicate what has happened?* Circle each clue. **Say** *Is the car likely to be broken? Why or why not? Did something else happen to the car? What do you think it was? What clues tell you this?* Finally, **say** *Draw a conclusion about the the end of this story. Where is Jim headed?*

CORRECTIVE FEEDBACK

If students are unable to draw conclusions, have them circle the clues. They should then ask themselves, "What do all these clues have in common?"

PRACTICE Have students complete Blackline Master 17. **Say** *Read each paragraph. Use clues and your own knowledge to draw conclusions. Write your conclusions.*

CORRECTIVE FEEDBACK

If students are unable to draw conclusions, have them make a chart with two headings: "Clue" and "Meaning of Clue." Help them list clues on the chart and draw conclusions from their meanings.

Answers: 1. perform in front of an audience. 2. very hot

74 | Draw Conclusions / B | Skills Intervention — Book C

Part 2 COMPREHENSION

Draw Conclusions

Suvi waited as Mr. Evans wrote the election results on the board. Arthur got 112 votes. Logan had 114. Suvi smiled. "That was too close!" Suvi said.

The engine stopped running and the car came to a halt. "I knew this would happen," Jim said. He opened the trunk and took out a gasoline can. Then he started to walk.

PRACTICE

1. Karen stood back stage waiting for the show to start. Her heart was beating fast. Her stomach felt funny. She hoped her family was out there.

   Karen is about to _____

2. Alex put the pepper in his mouth. How hot could it be? Nothing happened for a few seconds. Then Alex's face turned color. He started to sweat. "I need water!" he cried.

   The pepper is _____

Draw Conclusions / C

TEACHING FRAME: BLM 18 **Say** *Information in a story is not always given to the reader directly. Sometimes you need to draw conclusions about events from details in the story and what you already know.* Have students repeat the statements you have just made. **Ask** *Who can tell me what it means to draw conclusions?* Point out *To understand a story completely, you may need to draw several conclusions about the events that happen and why they happen.*

MODEL Read the first paragraph of the teaching frame out loud. Model how to draw conclusions using the first paragraph. **Say** *This paragraph shows a person in an unnamed place. To understand what I am reading I want to know what the setting is. Clues that help identify the place include the character's words, the microphone, the money, and the request to drive up to the window.* Circle these clues. **Say** *I can tell from the way that the customer orders and is told to "drive to the window" that Hal is working in a fast food restaurant. Do you see other clues that go along with this conclusion?*

Say *As you read the second paragraph, look for clues that tell you how long Hal has worked in the restaurant. Do you think he is new to the job or has been working there for a long time? What clues helped you answer this question?*

CORRECTIVE FEEDBACK

If students have trouble drawing this conclusion, have them go to the text and mark off clues. Then have them put their clues together to draw a conclusion.

PRACTICE Have students complete Blackline Master 18. **Say** *Read the story. Answer each question by circling the letter of the correct answer.*

CORRECTIVE FEEDBACK

Go over the questions that the students have trouble with. Review each answer choice and ask *What clues in the story support this answer?* Tell students to choose only those answers that are supported by story clues or their own personal knowledge.

Answers: 1. b, 2. a, 3. b, 4. c

Draw Conclusions

"May I help you?" Hal said into the microphone. The customer took a while to place her order. Hal repeated the order aloud. Then Hal told the customer, "That will be five dollars and six cents. Please drive up to the window."

At five o'clock it got crowded. Hal worked steadily until the manager came and told him he could go. "How did I do?" Hal asked. She held her thumb up and promised Hal that everything would seem a lot easier tomorrow.

Diane and Dana both played the cello. Normally, Diane saw Mr. Stern on Thursdays, and Dana saw him on Fridays. But this week Diane had swimming practice on Thursday. She didn't know what to do. Finally, Dana said, "I'll go to Mr. Stern's on Thursday for you."

So Dana went to see Mr. Stern on Thursday. "There's something different about you today," Mr. Stern said. "You seem to be playing like your sister."

On Friday, Diane went to Dana's lesson. Mr. Stern thought she seemed different too, but he wasn't sure. Finally, Dana told him, "Diane and I switched places. I'm sorry. We'll never do it again."

1. Dana and Diane are probably ___

    a. friends

    b. twin sisters

    c. cousins

2. Mr. Stern is probably ___

    a. a music teacher

    b. the mayor

    c. their father

3. Mr. Stern was confused because___

    a. the two played badly

    b. he thought Diane was Dana

    c. he thought Diane played well

4. Dana was sorry because ___

    a. she had played badly

    b. Diane had played badly

    c. they had played a trick on Mr. Stern

Summarize / A

TEACHING FRAME: BLM 19 Ask *How was your day yesterday? What did you do?* **Say** *That is how you summarize your day when someone asks about it. You share the main events and leave out the little details. When you summarize a story or article, you tell what its main events are. You do not mention most of the details.*

Ask students to listen as you read the first paragraph. **Ask** *What is the story's main idea? What title would fit this story? Give a summary of the story in a single sentence.* Underline the words *cleaned, cooked,* and *scrubbed.* **Say** *These words help summarize what Dave did.*

Say *Now we can summarize the second paragraph of the story. Who is this second paragraph about?* (Molly) Circle *Molly.* **Ask** *What is Molly doing in this paragraph?* (entering a typing contest) **Ask** *What are the major events and final outcome in the story?* (Molly entered a contest; Molly won a prize) **Say** *Now you should be ready to write a summary. Make sure your summary is brief and contains the most important ideas and events in the story.* (Molly entered a typing contest and won a third place prize.)

> **CORRECTIVE FEEDBACK**
>
> If students have trouble summarizing, have them circle each detail in the story once, then circle the most important details twice. Tell them to make sure they include the double-circled details in their summaries.

PRACTICE Have students complete Blackline Master 19. **Say** *Read each paragraph. Then circle the letter that contains the best summary.*

> **CORRECTIVE FEEDBACK**
>
> If students are unable to select the best summary, have them read each answer. Then **Ask** *Which sentence tells all the important details?*

Answers: I. c 2. b

Part 2
COMPREHENSION

Name _____ Date _____ Instructor _____

Summarize

For his mom's birthday, Dave cleaned the house. He tidied, dusted, and vacuumed. Then he cooked pasta with cheese sauce for dinner. He even scrubbed the dishes after dinner. It wasn't as bad as he thought it would be. "What a terrific present!" his mom cried.

Molly practiced her typing all year. Her teacher entered her in a speed-typing contest. In the finals, Molly typed 76 words a minute. This was good enough to earn her a third place prize.

PRACTICE

1. Sally searched everywhere for her twenty dollar bill. She hunted through every part of the house, including the garage. Finally, she gave up and sat down to read. When she opened her book, she found the money. She'd used it as a book mark!

   a. The money wasn't in the garage.

   b. Sally searched through every book in the house.

   c. Sally searched everywhere and finally found her money in a book.

2. In January, the stock market was at 2000. It went down in the spring, then up in the summer. In the fall, it went way up, then it dropped. By the end of the year it was back at 2000.

   a. The market went up more than down.

   b. The market went up and down but ended up at the same place.

   c. The market went up in the summer and way up in the fall.

Summarize / B

TEACHING FRAME: BLM 20 Say *To summarize a story, give a brief account of what happened in your own words.* Ask students to repeat this definition. **Ask** *Who can tell me the definition of a summary?* **Say** *To make a good summary you need to have a solid understanding of the main idea of the story, its major events, and what they mean.*

MODEL Read the first paragraph of the teaching frame together. **Say** *To summarize, I first try to get an understanding of what the story is about and what its key events are. In this story, Molly is learning to type.* Circle *Molly* and *type.* *Then I look at the most important events in the story. I want to include the idea that Molly learned to touch-type.* Circle this phrase. **Here is my summary:** *Last year, after much practice, Molly taught herself to touch-type.*

Read the second paragraph aloud. **Say** *Try to tell what happened in a single sentence. Think, what is the main idea of the paragraph?* Underline the final sentence. **Say** *The way Martha played in each individual set is not as important as the final outcome of the match.*

> ## CORRECTIVE FEEDBACK
>
> If students have trouble summarizing, suggest that they mark each story detail with a number, ranking them from least to most important. Then suggest that they include only their most highly ranked details in their summaries.

PRACTICE Have students complete Blackline Master 20. **Say** *Read the paragraph. Write a title for the paragraph on the top line. Then write a summary of the paragraph below.*

> ## CORRECTIVE FEEDBACK
>
> If students are unable to summarize or write titles, have them make a chart that lists details from the story. Next to each detail they should write "important," "very important," and "not so important." Then they should use their chart to make a new summary.

Answers: Title: Max Steps Out; Summary: Max gives up being a movie star and goes home.

Name _____   Date _____   Instructor _____

Summarize

Last year, Molly was in sixth grade. She took word-processing as an elective. First, she learned to position her fingers on the keyboard. Then she practiced. She practiced a lot. Before long, she could "touch-type" without looking at the keyboard.

If Martha won this last match she could enter the city-wide championships. In the first game she did not score one point, and she thought it was over. In the second game, her opponent seemed tired. Martha won easily. The third game was a battle, but Martha couldn't be stopped. She won the match 2 games to 1, and went on the the city-wide championships.

PRACTICE

_____

The movie is about a talking dog named Max. In the movie, Max gets discovered by a big "howlywood" agent. The agent is a poodle that drives a car. Max goes to Howlywood and becomes a star. He lives the high life: parties, late nights, and has fun times. But through it all he misses his family. He calls them his co-dogs. There are two little girls named Lizzie and Kate that he misses most of all. In the end, Max goes back home and becomes an ordinary dog again. Lizzie and Kate never even know about his secret life as a star.

Summary of the Story: _____

_____

_____

_____

Summarize / C

TEACHING FRAME: BLM 21 Say *To summarize a story or article, you state its main points or events in a few brief sentences.* Have students repeat. **Ask Who can tell me how to summarize a story or article?**

MODEL Read the first paragraph of the teaching frame together. **Say** *This paragraph lists the steps that take place when you hit a baseball. Underline Image enters eyes; signal to brain; brain signal: Swing!* **Ask** *How can I put all of these details together? What happens in just a few words?* **Say** *Here's my summary: The image of the ball enters my eyes, goes to my brain as a nerve signal, and causes my brain to send out a signal to swing. This summary accurately reflects the path of information in the paragraph and includes only the important details.*

Say *Try summarizing the second paragraph of the article.* **Ask** *What steps are described?* Circle *nerves to spine; spine to muscles; twitch; swing.* Make a diagram on the board of this pathway showing the nerve signal traveling from the brain to the spine, then from the spine to the arm muscles. **Say** *Using a diagram will help you to summarize.* (The signal goes from the brain to the spine to the muscles, causing them to swing.)

CORRECTIVE FEEDBACK

If students have trouble summarizing, have them make their own diagrams and label what happens. Have them ask themselves: "Is this summary too brief or too long?" "Does it only give key information?" "Does it leave out any important information?"

PRACTICE Have students complete Blackline Master 21. **Say** *Read the article. Then write a title and a brief summary of two or three sentences.*

CORRECTIVE FEEDBACK

If students have trouble summarizing, have them make a list of the major points in the article and rate each point from A to D according to importance. Then have them write their summaries, making sure to include only highly ranked details.

Answer: The experiment showed that a plant does not gain weight from soil. Instead, it uses three things to grow: water, sunlight, and air. Without these, a plant will not grow.

Name _____ Date _____ Instructor _____

Summarize

What happens when you hit a ball? The image of the moving ball enters your eyes as light. Your eyes send a nerve signal to your brain. Brain cells interpret the signal as: Ball coming! Your brain then sends out a new signal: Swing!

From your brain, the signal travels to your spine. Nerves coming out of the spine then carry the signal to muscle cells in your arms. These cells twitch, causing your arms to move. Your arms then swing the bat and you hit a home run!

A 17th century doctor named Jean van Helmont put a tiny plant in a pot of soil. The plant weighed only a few ounces. Five years later the plant grew to a weight of over 150 pounds. How did the plant gain so much weight? van Helmont thought that the plant had gained its weight from the soil. But no soil had been lost from the pot.

In fact, van Helmont showed that the plant used three things to make itself larger: water, sunlight, and air. If a plant doesn't have these three things, it won't grow.

Summary: _____

_____

_____

_____

_____

_____

Make Inferences / A

TEACHING FRAME: BLM 22 **Say** *Imagine that you saw me watching TV. You couldn't see the TV or hear what was on. I was clapping and yelling "Go team!" What would you think I was watching?* **Say** *You figured that out from clues. What were they? You also used your life experience. You know enough about what might be on TV to figure it out. Sometimes writers show rather than tell. Then, you use clues and your personal experience to make a good guess.*

Have students listen as you read the first paragraph. **Ask** *What characters are mentioned in this story? What does the author tell us Tommy does?* Underline these as they are mentioned. **Ask** *What do you think he was doing?* **Say** *The author doesn't ever say that, but you used clues and your own experience with school and homework to figure it out. Who do you think Mrs. Amati is?*

Say *Now let's read the second paragraph.* Read it aloud. **Say** *I am going to draw a chart to help me make inferences. One column is for clues, and one column is for personal experience.* Draw the chart. **Ask** *What are the first clues in the paragraph?* Write these on the chart. **Say** *Based on your experience, what do you know about putting on a new dress and styling one's hair?* Write this on the chart.

CORRECTIVE FEEDBACK

If students have difficulty with finding clues, help them underline the clues in the text. If they have difficulty with personal experience ask related questions such as *Have you ever styled your hair? What reason did you have?*

PRACTICE Have students complete Blackline Master 22. **Say** *Read each paragraph. Then answer the question. Circle the letter of the answer.*

CORRECTIVE FEEDBACK

If students are unable to answer correctly, help them make a chart of clues and experiences. Then help them draw inferences by relating clues and experiences.

Answers: 1. c   2. b

Name _____ Date _____ Instructor _____

Make Inferences

Tommy put down his pencil and closed his book. "Finished!" he said, happily. "I thought I'd never get those questions answered. But I did them all." He smiled. He could imagine how proud he would make Mrs. Amati tomorrow in school.

Lisa put on her new dress. She styled her hair. Her mother even let her borrow a pearl necklace. Lisa stared at herself in the mirror. She could hardly wait! Today her cousin Jim was getting married.

PRACTICE

1. Jim held the book in his hands. He cleared his throat. One of his friends put on a voice like an old woman. She said, "Well, hello dear." It was Jim's turn to speak.

   What is Jim doing?

   a. walking with an old woman

   b. writing a poem for homework

   c. reading a play aloud

2. Kim felt something soft rub against her foot. She looked down and saw Happy. Happy had finished drinking his milk. He looked like he was going to go to sleep there on the rug. Kim could hear him purring.

   Who is Happy?

   a. Kim's favorite toy

   b. Kim's pet cat

   c. Kim's little brother

Make Inferences / B

TEACHING FRAME: BLM 23 **Say** *Authors don't always tell you everything. They often show rather than tell.* **Say** *Then, you use the author's clues and combine them with what you already know to make inferences.* **Ask** *What two things do we use when we make inferences? You might make inferences about characters: How does he feel? Where is she going? What are they doing? You might even make inferences about the setting of a story. Where does this take place?*

MODEL Read the first paragraph on the teaching frame together. **Say** *The author doesn't tell me specifically how Mickey feels, but I think I can infer it.* **Ask** *What does the author show?* **Say** *There are lots of clues.* Circle each clue as you mention it. *Mickey is waiting for a ride at the theme park. His hands are shaking, his forehead is getting wet, his heart is beating fast.* **Say** *If I think about these clues, I can imagine just how Mickey feels. These things happen when I get scared or nervous. I can infer that Mickey is nervous about going on the ride. Even though the author doesn't say he's nervous, the story gives me enough clues to infer that he is.* **Say** *Now read the next paragraph. Try to guess what Mickey is doing.* Read the paragraph aloud. **Say** *It sounds like a lot of things are happening. What are some clues about what's going on?* Circle each clue as it's mentioned. **Ask** *Is he still standing in line? Why not? Does he decide not to go on the ride? What do you think Mickey's doing?*

CORRECTIVE FEEDBACK

If students have trouble making inferences, ask them to reread the paragraph and write the clues in a chart with personal experiences in another column.

PRACTICE Have students complete Blackline Master 23. **Say** *Read each paragraph. Use clues and what you know to answer the questions.*

CORRECTIVE FEEDBACK

If students cannot make inferences, help them make a chart with clues and personal experiences. Work with them to connect clues and what they know from experience to make inferences.

Answers: 1. at the grocery 2. painting her room

Make Inferences

Mickey is nearing the front of the line for the ride. He feels his hands starting to shake. Suddenly, his forehead is dripping wet. As he gets closer and closer, he can hear his heart beating faster and faster.

It's as if Mickey is in a dream. He hears someone say, "Next car." He feels his father take his hand and pull him into a seat. He clicks a seat belt closed. He hears the sound of a motor starting, and senses something moving — with him in it!

PRACTICE

1. Robert looked at his handwritten list. It said "milk, bread, cereal, apples." He had already put both the bread and the cereal in his cart. "Now where are the apples?" he asked himself.

   Where is Robert?

   _____

2. Melanie was covered from head to toe in yellow. So were her Mom and Dad. It was a good thing everybody had old clothes to work in. She looked at the brushes, and into the open cans. More yellow! Pretty soon her room would look brand new.

   What is Melanie's family doing?

   _____

Make Inferences / C

Part 2
COMPREHENSION

TEACHING FRAME: BLM 24 Say *Authors don't always tell everything. So you need to make inferences if you want to completely follow the story. To make inferences, you use clues in the story, your own knowledge, and personal experience.* Have students repeat. **Ask** *How do you make inferences?* **Say** *As you read, look for important details, and use what you already know.*

MODEL Read the first paragraph on the teaching frame together. **Say** *This paragraph introduces a group of people waiting for someone. We aren't told much, but we have some definite clues about what's going on.* Underline each phrase as you mention it. *Everybody seems to be related. There's an aunt, and an uncle, and a mom.* **Say** *Two of them mention birthdays. I can infer from these clues that they're waiting for someone whose birthday it is. When I read what Mom says, I see she's talking about their father. She says he loves parties. By applying what I know, I can infer that Mom's father must be the author's grandfather. Everybody's waiting for him at his birthday party.* **Say** *Now, as you read the next paragraph, use clues and what you already know to make inferences about where the party takes place.* Read the paragraph. **Ask** *Where would you find tables and a server?* **Ask** *Does the author give us a clue about what kind of restaurant it is?*

CORRECTIVE FEEDBACK

If students have trouble making inferences, help them make a chart of clues and personal experiences, and relate them to make inferences.

PRACTICE Have students complete Blackline Master 24. **Say** *Read the story. Then answer the questions. Circle the letter of the correct answer.*

CORRECTIVE FEEDBACK

If students can't answer a question, have them ask themselves: "What clues are given in the story about this? How can my own knowledge and experience help me figure this out?" Help them put the information in a chart.

Answers: 1. b 2. a

Name _____ Date _____ Instructor _____

Make Inferences

All of us were waiting. Aunt Emily asked, "Where's the birthday boy?" Uncle Simon said, "When you've already had that many birthdays, maybe you don't care about another one." Mom said, "I know our father, and he loves parties. He'll be here!"

The server came over to our table. "Would you like to order now?" he asked. Aunt Emily thought we should still wait for Grandpa. She reminded us that he couldn't stand it when his spaghetti and meatballs got cold. He also hated cold pizza.

PRACTICE

Sarah could feel the gentle squishing under her toes. It reminded her of last July. Today, though, her feet were chilly, and the sound of the water made her shiver. She took off a mitten, and picked up a shell. Smiling at Jody, she slipped the shell into Jody's coat pocket.

"Let's try to enjoy the rest of our holiday here," Sarah said. "Don't worry. Tomorrow we'll need a different calendar. Lots of things will change at midnight tonight." Jody snorted, rolled her eyes, and pulled her hood over her head.

1. Where are Sarah and Jody?

   a. in a park

   b. at the beach

   c. on a farm

2. Why will Sarah and Jody need a different calendar tomorrow?

   a. It will be a new year.

   b. The calendar they already have must have gotten wet.

   c. They are getting tired of the old one.

Compare and Contrast / A

TEACHING FRAME: BLM 25 Say *Can you name some ways in which a cat and a dog are similar?* Say *Writers often compare one thing to another in articles and stories. They point out how two things are alike.*

Read the first paragraph aloud. **Ask** *What things are being compared?* (pine and oak trees). Underline *pine* and *oak*. **Ask** *In what ways are these two things alike?* (They're both strong and tall; they both have leaves) Underline the words *strong*, *tall*, and *leaves*. **Say** *The writer does not claim that the two trees are alike in every way, just that they are alike in some ways.*

Read the second paragraph aloud. **Say** *What things are being compared in this paragraph?* Underline *Jake's* and *Ann's* in the text. **Say** *In what ways does the writer claim that the two types of pizza are alike?*

> ### CORRECTIVE FEEDBACK
>
> If students have trouble comparing, have them circle each pizza feature that they can find in the text. Then tell them to match up features to make comparisons.

PRACTICE Have students complete Blackline Master 25. **Say** *Read each paragraph, then list three things that are alike about the two things being compared.*

> ### CORRECTIVE FEEDBACK
>
> If students are unable to identify comparisons and contrasts, have them circle phrases such as *in common, both, also, alike, to tell them apart, but*. Then have them list the comparisons and contrasts related to each phrase.

Answers: 1. a. Both speak English, b. Laws are based on English system, c. Both have 2 government houses   2. a. Both are meat-eaters, b. Both are reptiles, c. Both live in swamps, rivers, and lakes

Compare and Contrast

Pine and oak trees are both strong and tall. Pine trees have tiny leaves that stay green all year. Oaks have larger leaves. They turn color and drop off in the fall.

Jake's pizza costs less than Ann's and it also has free delivery. Jake's pizza tastes great, but Ann's is even better. Ann's has more cheese, too. If you ask me, get Ann's.

PRACTICE

1. The United States and England have much in common. English is the main language of both countries. The laws of the U.S. are based on English laws. England's government has two houses: the House of Commons and the House of Lords. The U.S. also has two houses, the House of Representatives and the Senate.

   a. _____

   b. _____

   c. _____

2. Crocodiles and alligators are very much alike. Both are meat-eating reptiles that live in swamps, rivers, and lakes. To tell them apart, look at the fourth tooth. This fourth tooth sticks out of a crocodile's mouth, but not an alligator's.

   a. _____

   b. _____

   c. _____

Compare and Contrast / B

Part 2

COMPREHENSION

TEACHING FRAME: BLM 26 Say *When you compare, you tell how things are alike. When you contrast you tell how things are different.* Have students repeat each definition. **Say** *Writers compare and contrast things in their writing to paint or describe a more accurate picture of what these things are really like.*

MODEL Read the first paragraph of the teaching frame together. **Say** *I want to get an idea of what's being related. This paragraph focuses on apes and monkeys.* Circle the words *apes* and *monkeys*. *In some cases, it says how they are alike; in others it says how they are different. Special clue words are* share, same, both, *and* unlike. *I pay special attention to whether the two things are being shown to be the same or different. For example, apes and monkeys are shown to have the same body shape.* (they are alike) *It also says that apes have longer arms than monkeys.*

Say *Now compare and contrast the items in the second paragraph. What things are being compared or contrasted?* Circle the two monkey types. **Say** *I notice the clue words:* both, also, *and* only. Circle each word. *In what ways does this paragraph tell how the two types of monkey are the same? In what ways are they different?* Underline all of these examples.

CORRECTIVE FEEDBACK

If students have trouble comparing and contrasting, have them ask themselves, "Which examples mention a feature that both monkey types have?" "Which examples mention a feature that only one monkey type has?"

PRACTICE Have students complete Blackline Master 26. **Say** *Read each paragraph. Answer the questions that follow.*

CORRECTIVE FEEDBACK

Tell students who have difficulty comparing and contrasting to make a chart that lists and matches up features of each related item. Then have them use their chart to compare and contrast.

Answers: 1. Alike: a. quick, b. great shooters; Different: Beagles are better rebounders 2. Alike: class party; Different: a. shorter hours, b. date of party

Name _____ Date _____ Instructor _____

Compare and Contrast

Apes and monkeys share the same body shape, diet, and life style. Apes are larger than monkeys, have longer arms, and bigger brains. Unlike monkeys, apes do not have tails.

Both New and Old World monkeys dwell in trees. Some Old World monkeys can also live on the ground. Both monkeys have tails. Only New World monkeys can grasp things with their tails.

PRACTICE

1. The Beagles and Blue Socks are both good basketball teams. The Beagles are better rebounders. Both teams are quick, but the Blue Socks are better at defense. Both teams have great shooters.

   How are the teams alike?

   a. _____

   b. _____

   How are the teams different?

   a. _____

2. The candidates for school president are both excellent. Laura Chin supports a shorter school day. Lance Rose is not for a shorter day. Both candidates want to organize a class party. Laura wants the party to be held in May. Lance wants to have it in October.

   How are the candidates alike?

   a. _____

   How are the candidates different?

   a. _____

   b. _____

Compare and Contrast / C

TEACHING FRAME: BLM 27 Say *When you compare you find how two related things are alike. When you contrast you find how two related things are different.* Have students repeat each definition.

MODEL Read the first paragraph of the teaching frame together aloud. **Say** *To compare or contrast, I first need to identify two related things. Here, I can see that the paragraph focuses on different types of ice skates.* Circle *speed skates, figure skates,* and *hockey skates.* *I'm going to look for examples that show the skates to be the same or different. For example, I see that all three have sharp blades. This feature is the same. On the other hand, I see how speed skates are unlike the other two because they have long blades. This is a difference.* Underline these comparisons and contrasts as you mention them. **Say** *Let's read the second paragraph together.* Read the second paragraph. **Say** *What related things does this paragraph focus on?* Underline these items as they are mentioned. **Say** *What are speed skates good for? What are they not good for?* Underline each item. *Now look at hockey skates: what are they good for?* Underline each item. *How are speed skates and hockey skates the same? How are they different?*

> ### CORRECTIVE FEEDBACK
>
> If students have trouble comparing and contrasting, have them ask themselves: "Which features does only one type of skate have?" "Which features are common to all of the skates?"

PRACTICE Have students complete Blackline Master 27. **Say** *Read the article. Then complete the chart.*

> ### CORRECTIVE FEEDBACK
>
> If students have trouble comparing and contrasting, have them reread the article and circle the items that show similarities between Mars and Earth and underline items that show differences.

Answers: Likenesses: both planets, 24 hour day, have had water in the past, have atmosphere, may have life. Differences: size, distance from sun, length of year, amount of water and atmosphere, temperature, oxygen, ease of finding life

Part 2 COMPREHENSION

Name _____ Date _____ Instructor _____

Compare and Contrast

There are three kinds of ice skates: speed skates, figure skates, and hockey skates. All three have sharp blades and strong boots. Speed skates have the longest blades. Hockey and figure skates have much shorter blades.

Speed skates are superb for speed but clumsy on turns and stops. Hockey blades are also fast. They're best for making quick turns and stops. The toes of figure skates have jagged "teeth." This makes them perfect for jumps and twirls.

Mars and Earth have many differences. Earth is almost twice as big across as Mars, and almost 50 million miles closer to the sun. Both planets have a day that lasts about 24 hours. However, the year on Mars lasts 687 days compared to the 365-day year we have on Earth.

Does Mars have life? Living things need water and there is good evidence that Mars once had water. However, scientists know that Mars has very little atmosphere, no oxygen, and very cold temperatures. If life exists on Mars, it will probably not be easy to find.

Mars and Earth	
Likenesses	Differences

Cause and Effect / A

TEACHING FRAME: BLM 28 Ask *When your alarm clock goes off, what do you do?* **Say** *The alarm clock makes noise. That causes you to wake up. Imagine that you're about to go outside and you notice that it's raining.* **Ask** *What might you want to take with you? Rain causes you to take an umbrella. Many times in a story, events are connected. One event causes another to happen.*

Have students listen as you read the first paragraph. **Ask** *What caused Katrina to wake up?* Draw an arrow connecting sentence 1 to sentence 2. **Ask** *What caused Katrina to decide to take an umbrella?* Draw an arrow connecting sentence 4 to sentence 5. **Say** *You can figure out the cause of an event by asking yourself, "Why did this happen?"*

Say *Now let's look at the second paragraph. This story has a lot of connections.* Read the paragraph. **Ask** *What caused Skippy to bark and jump?* Draw an arrow connecting sentence 1 to sentence 2. **Ask** *What caused Bob to grab Skippy's leash?* Draw an arrow connecting sentence 2 to sentence 3. **Ask** *What caused Skippy to come racing over to Bob?* Draw an arrow connecting sentence 3 to sentence 4.

CORRECTIVE FEEDBACK

If students have trouble identifying causes, have them ask: "Why did this happen?" Have them identify the cause by circling that sentence.

PRACTICE Have students complete Blackline Master 28. **Say** *Read each paragraph. Then answer the question. Circle the letter of the best answer.*

CORRECTIVE FEEDBACK

If students have trouble identifying causes, ask them to read each answer choice to find the one that is mentioned in the paragraph.

Answers: 1. a   2. b

Name _____ Date _____ Instructor _____

Cause and Effect

Katrina's alarm clock went off. She woke up and got out of bed. The first thing she did every morning was look out the window. When she did, she saw that it was raining. "I'll take an umbrella with me to school today," she decided.

Bob's dog Skippy wanted to go out. The dog began barking and jumping up and down near the door. Bob walked to the closet, and grabbed Skippy's leash. A happy Skippy came racing over to Bob.

PRACTICE

1. Teresa loved playing in the snow. She built a man with it. She rolled around in it. She even rubbed some on her face and laughed. But then she started shivering, and went inside. Her mother made her hot cocoa.

What caused Teresa's mother to make her hot cocoa?

    a. Teresa was shivering.

    b. Teresa asked for some.

    c. Teresa loved the snow.

2. It was a cloudy night, and the sky was dark. They could hardly see each other as they sat outside the tent. Then there was a break in the clouds. Suddenly, The moon came out. Jerry saw his father smiling.

What caused Jerry to see his father smiling?

    a. His father was glad they were outside together.

    b. There was a break in the clouds, and the moon came out.

    c. Jerry suddenly noticed that his father was smiling.

Cause and Effect / B

TEACHING FRAME: BLM 29 Say *As you read, you need to understand the connections between events. Knowing why things happen helps you follow a story better.* **Say** *A* cause *is an event that makes another event happen. An* effect *is an event that results from a cause.* Have students repeat these definitions. Explain *When you notice causes and effects, you see the connections between events.*

MODEL Read the first paragraph on the teaching frame together. **Say** *This paragraph begins with a sentence about Mark and his father. Mark wants to learn about birds. His father buys him a guidebook. There's a clue word* since. Since *tells me that two things are connected.* Circle *since.* **Say** *The fact that Mark wants to learn* causes *his father to buy the book.* Draw an arrow connecting cause and effect. *That Mark wants to learn is the cause. His father buying the book is the effect. In the next sentence, I see another clue word:* so. Circle *so.* *This tells me that two events are connected.* **Say** Mark wasn't sure how to use it, *is the cause.* His father showed him *is the effect.* Draw an arrow connecting cause and effect.

Say *Now try another paragraph.* Read the next paragraph aloud. **Ask** *What clue words do you see?* Circle *them.* **Ask** *Why did John get angry?* Draw an arrow connecting cause to effect. **Ask** *What is the effect of Brenda's leaving John alone?* Draw an arrow connecting cause to effect.

CORRECTIVE FEEDBACK

If students have trouble identifying cause and effect, have them ask themselves: "Why did John get angry?" "What happened because Brenda left John alone?"

PRACTICE Have students complete Blackline Master 29. **Say** *Read each paragraph. Read the pairs of sentences that follow. Label each sentence* cause *or* effect.

CORRECTIVE FEEDBACK

If students incorrectly identify causes and effects, have them circle clue words. Urge them to ask: "Why did this happen?" "What happened because of this?"

Answers: 1. cause, effect; effect, cause   2. effect, cause; effect, cause

Name _____ Date _____ Instructor _____

Cause and Effect

Since Mark wanted to learn about birds, his father bought him a guidebook. Mark wasn't sure how to use it, so his father showed him. In no time, Mark was identifying all kinds of birds.

Because Brenda was making funny faces, her brother John got angry. "Please stop making me laugh," John said. Brenda understood, and left him alone so he could do his homework.

PRACTICE

1. Bobby had a really bad cold, so his mother let him stay home from school. Since he felt so sick, he wasn't happy about having a day off.

_____ Bobby had a really bad cold.

_____ His mother let him stay home from school.

_____ He wasn't happy about having a day off.

_____ He felt so sick.

2. Because it got too dark to play any more, the baseball game was called off. The players wanted to finish it, so they were quite unhappy.

_____ The baseball game was called off.

_____ It got too dark to play any more.

_____ They were quite unhappy.

_____ The players wanted to finish it.

Cause and Effect / C

TEACHING FRAME: BLM 30 Say *Understanding relationships between events helps you understand what you read.* **Say** *A cause is an event that makes another event happen. An effect is an event that results from one or more causes.* Have students repeat.

MODEL Read the first paragraph of the teaching frame together. **Say** *What causes millions of people to move to Florida each year?* Underline *Florida has wonderful warm weather.* **Say** *This is the cause. The effect is that people move there. There's a feeling that Florida has no changes of season. Why?* Underline *The sun shines almost daily.* **Say** *This is the cause. The effect is the feeling that Florida has no changes of season. The clue words* so *and* leading to *show relationships between the events.* Circle those words.

Read the next paragraph. **Ask** *Why do people measure the year in different ways?* Underline this. **Ask** *What clue word relates these events? Which is the cause? Which is the effect?* **Say** *A whole chain of events can cause an effect. Here's a chain. Winters get cold, so some birds fly south to Florida, so Floridians are reminded that summer is turning to autumn.*

CORRECTIVE FEEDBACK

If students have trouble identifying cause and effect, have them ask themselves: "Why did this happen?" "What happened because of this?"

PRACTICE Have students complete Blackline Master 30. **Say** *Read the article. Then complete the chart. List an effect for each cause. List a cause for each effect.*

CORRECTIVE FEEDBACK

If students cannot identify cause and effect, have them reread the article and circle the clue words.

Answers: 1. I decided to try to write one of my own. 2. I couldn't decide what I should write a poem about. 3. Maybe I'd like to write about some kind of animal. 4. This was such an exciting idea.

Part 2
COMPREHENSION

Name _____ Date _____ Instructor _____

Cause and Effect

Florida has wonderful warm weather, so millions of people move there each year. What they don't realize is how shocking the climate can be for someone not used to it. The sun shines almost daily, leading to a feeling that Florida has no changes of season.

Since Florida's climate doesn't have drastic changes, people measure the year's passing in other ways. They notice things that distinguish the seasons. The winters get cold up north, so some birds fly south in the fall. The coming of certain birds reminds Floridians that summer is turning to autumn.

PRACTICE

I love reading poems in school and even at home, so I decided to try to write one of my own. Since I couldn't decide what I should write a poem about, I asked my mother if she had any good ideas for me.

My mother thought for a few minutes, and then had a suggestion. I love going to the zoo, so maybe I'd like to write about some kind of animal. Because this was such an exciting idea, I got started right away on a poem about giraffes.

CAUSE	EFFECT
1. I love reading poems in school and even at home.	
2.	I asked my mother if she had any good ideas for me.
3. I love going to the zoo.	
4.	I got started right away on a poem about giraffes.

Author's Purpose / A

TEACHING FRAME: BLM 31 Say *What do you look for when you read? You're looking for something different from a cook book than you are from a story book. In the same way that you have different reasons for reading, authors have different reasons for writing. The reason an author has for writing a passage is called the author's purpose. Writing that tells or teaches you something, is writing that informs. Writing that tries to convince you to do something or think a certain way, is writing that persuades. And writing that is just for fun, is writing that entertains.* **Ask** *What are the three major author's purposes?*

Read the first paragraph. **Ask** *What was the author's purpose here — to tell you something, convince you of something, or just entertain you?* (It tries to get you to do something). Underline the phrase *come today*. **Say** *Is the author just giving you information about Fun Land, trying to convince you to come to Fun Land, or trying to amuse you with facts about Fun Land? The purpose of the paragraph is to persuade.*

Say *Look for clues to the author's purpose as we read this paragraph.* Read the second paragraph aloud. **Say** *What clues to the author's purpose did you see in the paragraph? Did the paragraph present information? Did the paragraph try to convince you of anything? Did the paragraph try to get you involved in a story or amuse you? What do you think the author's purpose was?*

CORRECTIVE FEEDBACK

If students have trouble identifying the author's purpose, have them ask themselves: "How would the author answer the question *What did you write this for?*"

PRACTICE Have students complete Blackline Master 31. **Say** *Read each paragraph, then identify the author's purpose. Circle the letter of the correct answer.*

CORRECTIVE FEEDBACK

If students are unable to determine the author's purpose, have them ask themselves these questions: "Does the paragraph teach or tell me anything?" "Does the paragraph try to convince me of anything?" "Is the paragraph just for fun?"

Answers: 1. b   2. a

Name _____ Date _____ Instructor _____

Author's Purpose

It's better than ever! All new Fun Land has amazing rides, fabulous food, and great games! So come today! Fun Land: where fun is everything, and everything is fun!

Many family names originally had meanings. A Smith put shoes on horses. Coopers made barrels. Can you guess what people named Baker did? They baked bread, of course!

PRACTICE

1. It was a dark and stormy night. Suddenly, I heard a strange voice coming from the attic: "Is Victor in the house?" it asked. Slowly I climbed the steps. The voice got louder. And louder. "Is Victor in the house?" Finally I reached the top and opened the door. "Is Victor in the house?" the voice asked. It was Victor, my next-door neighbor's parrot! He must have escaped.

    a. to persuade

    b. to entertain

    c. to inform

2. Take a tip from me. Don't go see the new movie, "Fish Cakes." It's silly. The story is pointless. Who ever heard of a fish becoming president? The acting is bad! Rather than go to this movie, have dinner instead. Just make sure it isn't fish.

    a. to persuade

    b. to entertain

    c. to inform

Author's Purpose / B

TEACHING FRAME BLM: 32 Say *The author's purpose is the reason he or she has for writing.* Have students repeat this definition. **Say** *Authors generally have three purposes to write: to inform, to entertain, or to persuade.* **Say** *The author's point of view expresses their feelings towards the subject. A point of view may be positive, negative, or it may express no strong feelings one way or another. Clue words in the text help you determine what the author's point of view is.*

MODEL Read the first paragraph of the teaching frame together. **Say** *I see several clue words that tell me how the author feels.* Circle *terrific* and *fun.* **Ask** *Is the author trying to teach or tell the reader something? If so, his purpose is to inform. Is the author trying to convince the reader to do something? Then his purpose is to persuade. Is the author trying to amuse the reader? If so, his purpose is to entertain. In this case, I don't see any evidence that the author is trying to persuade. I see evidence that the author is trying to inform by listing all of the things he did. The author does this in an amusing way, but I think his main purpose is to inform what camp is like.* **Say** *Now try to determine the author's purpose and point of view in the second paragraph.* Read the paragraph aloud. *What word tells you how the author feels about the subject? Is this point of view positive, negative, or indifferent? How does this point of view affect the author's purpose? What do you think the author's purpose was?*

CORRECTIVE FEEDBACK

If students have trouble identifying the author's purpose, have them ask themselves questions: "Is this paragraph trying to teach or tell the reader something?" "Is it trying to get the reader to think a certain way or do something?" "Is it written just for fun?"

PRACTICE Have students complete Blackline Master 32. **Say** *Read each paragraph. Answer the questions that follow. Circle the letter of the best answer.*

CORRECTIVE FEEDBACK

Tell students who have difficulty identifying the author's purpose and point of view to return to the paragraph and circle clue words.

Answers: 1. b   2. c

Author's Purpose

Dear Mom and Dad, Camp is terrific. I'm having so much fun I can't stand it! Yesterday I played soccer, tennis, baseball, sailed a boat, fixed a bike, and wrote a poem. Love, Evan.

P.S.: The food here is horrible! Please send: bagels, apples, cookies, pizza, anything! I need more books. And most important: I forgot my best friend Teddy bear. Please send him now!

PRACTICE

1. My name is Doberman. I'm a private eye. I'm also a dog. I guess you could say I'm pretty good at sniffing out cases. Anyway, when it comes to solving mysteries, I'm pretty much like your ten fingers. In other words, you can count on me!

   a. to persuade

   b. to entertain

   c. to inform

2. In the late 1800s, the London Music Hall was thought to be the world's best music hall. By the 1930s, people complained that music didn't sound as good as it had in the past. So what happened? Nothing in the hall had changed. But the audience *had* changed. Their simple clothing didn't absorb sound as well as the long flowing dresses and big hats from earlier times. That explained why the music didn't sound as good as it had.

   a. to persuade

   b. to entertain

   c. to inform

Author's Purpose / C

TEACHING FRAME: BLM 33 **Say** *The author's purpose is the reason that he or she has for writing.* **Say** *An author's purpose may be to inform, to persuade, to entertain, or to describe or express.* **Ask** *Who can define the author's purpose?* **Say** *The author's point of view is how the author feels about the topic.* Have students repeat. **Say** *Identifying the author's point of view can help you determine and understand the author's purpose.*

MODEL Read the first paragraph of the teaching chart together. **Say** *As I read, I look for words and clues to the author's feelings about the topic. The author may be positive, negative, or indifferent. In this case, the words* delighted *and* brilliant *tell me that the speaker really likes the comedian.* Circle *delighted* and *brilliant.* *The main purpose of this paragraph seems to be to introduce Pam and give information about her. So, the purpose of this paragraph is to inform.*

Say *Let's read the second paragraph together.* Read the second paragraph. **Say** *Look closely for clues to the author's point of view and purpose for writing. Do you see any clues to the author's point of view? Is she positive or negative toward her topic, or indifferent?* (indifferent) *Rather than express opinions, the author seems much more concerned with telling jokes. What would you say the purpose of this writing is?* (to entertain)

CORRECTIVE FEEDBACK

If students have trouble identifying the author's purpose, have them ask themselves, "What does the author want me to get out of this paragraph — information? An opinion? Or fun?"

PRACTICE Have students complete Blackline Master 33. **Say** *Read the paragraphs. Then write your answers to the questions on the lines provided.*

CORRECTIVE FEEDBACK

If students have trouble identifying the author's purpose and point of view, have them return to the paragraphs and circle clue words that reveal how the author feels about the topic.

Answers: 1. Positive 2. Indifferent 3. persuade 4. entertain

Part 2
COMPREHENSION

Name _____ Date _____ Instructor _____

Author's Purpose

Good evening. Tonight the Laugh Club is delighted bring you Pam Yung, a brilliant new comedian. Pam is from Austin, Texas. She has appeared in movies, on TV, and in many comedy clubs. Please give Pam a warm welcome!

Hi, I'm Pam. I'll be your comic tonight. When folks hear I'm from Texas they ask, "What part?" I tell them, "Why all of me, of course." But seriously, I wish I had time to tell my Texas rope joke. But I guess I'll have to skip it. Good night!

People should vote Yes for the new law that allows dogs to eat in restaurants. Dogs are quiet and well-behaved. My dog Trixie has better manners than most people I see in restaurants. So why shouldn't she be allowed to eat in restaurants? Please vote Yes, and help all dog owners.

What's this I hear about dogs being more polite than people! Think about this: suppose you took a friend to dinner. How would you feel if he or she: stood on the table? licked the plate? ate out of the trash can? Would you think this friend was polite? I don't think so. I don't really care if dogs eat in restaurants. But calling them polite is well — silly!

1. How does the first author feel about dogs eating in restaurants?

_____

2. How does the second author feel about dogs eating in restaurants?

_____

3. The purpose of paragraph 1 is to _____

4. The purpose of paragraph 2 is to _____

Steps in a Process / A

TEACHING FRAME: BLM 34 Ask *How do you make a sandwich? What do you do first? Second? Third?* **Say** *It's important to do the steps in order. You wouldn't spread peanut butter before you get the bread, would you? Writers sometimes explain things in order. If you understand the order of the steps, it will help you understand what the writer is trying to say.*

Read the first paragraph aloud. **Ask** *What did Yoshi do first? Say "First" is a clue word that helps me know the order.* Circle it. *What did Yoshi do second? What clue word tells the order here?* (then) Circle it. **Ask** *What did Yoshi do third?* **Say** *There's no clue word here, right? But I already know the paragraph tells events in order. So I know this step comes third. What did Yoshi do last?* Circle *finally.* **Say** *Here's another clue word. It tells me what happened last.* Go back to the paragraph and number the steps 1, 2, 3, and 4. **Say** *Yoshi got ready for bed in four steps. He could not have changed the order of steps and still got ready for bed correctly.*

Say *Let's look at the next paragraph. Read it silently with me while I read it aloud.* **Ask** *Which three words give you clues about when things happened?* (first, next, last) *Which step does not have a clue word?* (dry them well) *What are all four steps in order, for doing the dishes?*

CORRECTIVE FEEDBACK

If students have trouble ordering the steps, have them circle the clue words and number the steps 1, 2, 3, and 4.

PRACTICE Have students complete Blackline Master 34. **Say** *Read the paragraph. Decide which step comes first, second, and third. Write 1, 2, or 3 before each sentence to show the order of steps. Then do the same for the next paragraph.*

CORRECTIVE FEEDBACK

If students cannot number steps in order, have them circle the clue words *First, Then, Next, Last,* and *Finally* in each paragraph and write the numbers 1, 2, and 3 over the steps.

Answers: 1. 2, 3, 1   2. 1, 3, 2

Name _____ Date _____ Instructor _____

Steps in a Process

Yoshi was tired, so he got ready for bed. First, he took off his clothes. Then, he reached under his pillow. He pulled out his pajamas from underneath. Finally, he put them on. Sweet dreams, Yoshi!

It's not hard to do the dishes. First, wash them with dish washing liquid. Next, rinse them to get the soap off. Dry them well. Last, put them away where they belong. Now they're ready for the next meal.

PRACTICE

1. Cindy saw that it was getting very late. First, she grabbed her books and lunch. Then, she raced out the door. Finally, she ran to the bus stop. She got there just in time!

_____ Cindy raced out the door.
_____ Cindy ran to the bus stop.
_____ Cindy grabbed her books and lunch.

2. Brian was buying new shoes. First, he pointed to a pair he liked. Next, the clerk got the shoes. Last, Brian tried them on. They looked great.

_____ Brian pointed to a pair he liked.
_____ Brian tried them on.
_____ The clerk got the shoes.

Steps in a Process / B

TEACHING FRAME: BLM 35 Say *A process is a series of steps carried out in order.* Have students repeat. **Ask** *How are the steps carried out?* **Say** *Certain words give us clues about steps in a process. Clue words like* first, next, *and* last *tell us when things happen.*

MODEL Read the teaching frame together. **Say** *This paragraph tells about the process of hanging a painting. Since I know it's a process, I'm looking for what happened first, second, and so on. I find clue words that help me keep the events straight.* Circle the words *first, then, last.* **Say** *One of the steps doesn't have a clue word. Still I know when it happened. In this paragraph, Dad and I follow four steps. First, we pick the wall.* Write 1 over that sentence. *Second, I stand on a stool and hold the painting.* Write 2 over that sentence. *Third, Dad had me move it.* Write 3 over that sentence. *Fourth, I marked the spot.* Write 4 over that sentence. **Say** *This process had four steps. It was important to do them in order and not to skip any steps.*

Say *Let's think about the steps as we read the next paragraph.* **Ask** *What process is this about? Find clue words that help you put the steps in order? What are they?* (first, next, then, finally) Circle *these.* **How many steps are there?** (four) **What are they?**

> **CORRECTIVE FEEDBACK**
>
> If students have trouble listing events in order, ask them to number the steps.

PRACTICE Have students complete Blackline Master 35. **Say** *Read each paragraph. Decide what happened first, second, third, and fourth. The first step is given. Fill in the remaining steps in the process.*

> **CORRECTIVE FEEDBACK**
>
> If students cannot identify the steps in a process, have them look for clue words and circle them. Then have them write the numbers of the steps.

Answers: 1. Step 2: She keyed in his address. Step 3: She wrote the note. Step 4: She clicked on the "send" button. 2. Step 2: I toasted them. Step 3: covered them with butter. Step 4: I sprinkled on some cinnamon.

Part 2 COMPREHENSION

Name _____ Date _____ Instructor _____

Steps in a Process

Yesterday, I helped Dad prepare to hang a painting. First, we decided what wall we wanted the painting on. Then, I stood on a stool to hold the painting against that wall. Dad had me move it until it was perfect. Last, I marked the spot with a pencil.

Dad showed me exactly how to hang the painting. First, you find the spot you marked. Next, you hammer a nail into the spot. Then, you hook the hanger of the frame onto the nail. Finally, you adjust the picture until it's even.

PRACTICE

1. Shirley wanted to e-mail a note to her Uncle Dave. First, she clicked on the "write" button. Then she keyed in Uncle Dave's address. She wrote the note. Finally, she clicked on the "send" button.

   Step 1: Shirley clicked on the "write" button.
   Step 2: _____
   Step 3: _____
   Step 4: _____

2. I decided to make cinnamon toast for a snack. First, I got two slices of bread. I toasted them. Then I covered them with butter. Last, I sprinkled on a little bit of cinnamon. Yum!

   Step 1: I got two slices of bread.
   Step 2: _____
   Step 3: _____
   Step 4: _____

Steps in a Process / C

TEACHING FRAME: BLM 36 Say *A process is a series of steps carried out in order.* Have students repeat. **Ask What is a process? Say** *Sometimes, we see time-order words that clue us about the order of the steps in a process. First, next, finally. Clue words tell us the time relationship between the steps.*

MODEL Read the first part of the teaching frame together. **Say** *This paragraph describes the process of pressing a leaf. I see several time-order words that help me understand the process.* Circle *first, then, finally.* **Say** *The first step is to go and pick a leaf.* Write 1 over that sentence. *The second step is to blot the leaf dry.* Write 2 over that sentence. *The last step is to place the leaf between two sheets of tissue paper.* Write 3 over that sentence. *With the time-order words to make the steps clear, I could now do this part of the process easily.*

Say *This paragraph continues the process.* Read the paragraph. **Say** *What clue words do you see?* Circle these. *Not every step has a clue word. Which step doesn't? Can you list the steps in order?* (put the leaf into a book, put something heavy on the book, wait two weeks, remove your leaf)

COMPREHENSION — Part 2

> ### CORRECTIVE FEEDBACK
>
> If students have trouble identifying steps in a process, have them number the steps as they are mentioned in the paragraph.

PRACTICE Have students complete Blackline Master 36. **Say** *Read the paragraph. Think about the steps. Then write the steps in order on the chart.*

> ### CORRECTIVE FEEDBACK
>
> If students cannot identify the order of steps, have them go back and circle the clue words they find. Then have them number the steps as they are mentioned.

Answers: Step 1: We make sure that everyone is in the car. Step 2: We back out of the driveway. Step 3: Somebody remembers that we forgot to lock the door. Step 4: I lock the door. Step 5: We drive for about a mile. Step 6: Dad goes back for his sunglasses. Step 7: We get Dad's sunglasses and a snack for me. Step 8: It starts to rain.

Steps in a Process

Pressed leaves are beautiful, easy to make, and last forever. To press a leaf, you first have to go and pick one. Then, carefully blot it dry with a paper towel. Finally, place the leaf between two sheets of tissue paper.

Now you're ready for the real pressing. After you've placed your leaf between paper, put it into the middle of a fat book. Find something heavy to sit on the book. Next, wait about two weeks. Last, remove your pressed leaf and admire it.

PRACTICE

Whenever my family drives from the city to our beach house, we follow a special procedure. First, we make sure that everyone, including the dog, is in the car. Mom or Dad backs out of the driveway. Then somebody remembers that we forgot to lock the door. The next thing I know, I'm jumping out of the car with my key to take care of that. After I lock the door, we drive for about a mile. At the end of the mile, Dad decides to go back and get his sunglasses. We get Dad's sunglasses and a snack for me. Finally, it starts to rain!

	My Family's Special Procedure
Step 1	
Step 2	
Step 3	
Step 4	
Step 5	
Step 6	
Step 7	
Step 8	

Fact and Nonfact / A

TEACHING FRAME: BLM 37 Say *I'm going to make a statement: I live in the prettiest house in the country. Can you believe that statement? Before you answer, think. Do you know every house in the country? Do you believe my statement? How about this one: I live in a pink house. Can you believe that?* **Say** *You can believe a statement if it can be proven true.*

Have students listen as you read the first paragraph. **Ask** *If you had a watch with you, could you prove that I can ride around the block in less than five minutes?* **Say** *That's a fact.* Underline that sentence. **Ask** *Do you believe that my bike thinks it's a fast horse in a race? Could you prove that?* Circle that sentence. *So that is not a fact. Could you prove that my bike is the most beautiful bike in the world? That is not a fact.* Circle the sentence. *Now find one more fact in the paragraph.* Underline the last sentence. **Say** *All you'd have to do is look at my bike to prove that it's shiny and red. That's a fact.*

Say *Now let's read the second paragraph and look for facts.* Read the paragraph. **Ask** *Could you prove that I drew a forest scene with trees and birds.* Underline that sentence. *This is a fact. You could prove it by looking at my drawing. Could you prove that the trees were green and the birds were yellow?* Underline that sentence. **Say** *That's a fact. Could you prove that the trees are the best trees anybody ever drew?* Circle that sentence. **Say** *People say this kind of thing all the time, but it's not a fact. Could you prove that the birds are happy?* Circle that sentence.

> **CORRECTIVE FEEDBACK**
>
> If students have trouble identifying facts, have them ask themselves, "Do I believe this? How could I prove it?"

PRACTICE Have students complete Blackline Master 37. **Say** *Read each paragraph. Then answer the question. Circle the letter of the correct answer.*

> **CORRECTIVE FEEDBACK**
>
> If students cannot identify facts, have them reread the paragraph, underlining facts and circling nonfacts.

Answers: 1. b   2. c

Name _____ Date _____ Instructor _____

Fact and Nonfact

I love riding my bike. I can ride around the block in less than five minutes. My bike thinks that it's a fast horse in a race. My bike is the most beautiful bike in the world. It's shiny and red.

I drew a forest scene, with trees and birds. I colored the trees green and the birds yellow. The trees are the best trees anybody ever drew. The birds are happy to be in my drawing.

PRACTICE

1. An elephant is the most interesting animal. It is huge, and it has a trunk. An elephant thinks it's the king of wherever it goes.

Which sentence is a fact?

a. An elephant is the most interesting animal.

b. An elephant is huge, and it has a trunk.

c. An elephant thinks it's the king of wherever it goes.

2. Everybody loves listening to the radio. It's silly to watch TV instead. I listened to music this morning while I got dressed.

Which sentence is a fact?

a. Everybody loves listening to the radio.

b. It's silly to watch TV instead.

c. I listened to music this morning while I get dressed.

Fact and Nonfact / B

TEACHING FRAME: BLM 38 Say *A statement of fact is a statement that can be proved.* **Say** *A statement of nonfact is a statement that cannot be proved.* Have students repeat these definitions. **Say** *Just because an author says something, doesn't make it automatically true. You have to decide for yourself if what you are reading is believable.*

MODEL Read the first paragraph together. **Say** *I'm going to decide if each sentence is a fact or a nonfact. The first sentence says that the museum is having a show of paintings about flowers. I could prove that by going to the museum myself or calling them on the phone to ask about it. That's a fact.* Underline that sentence. *The second sentence says that some of the art really spoke to me. I couldn't prove it. It's a nonfact.* Circle that sentence. **Say** *The third statement could be proven by looking for that painting. It's a fact.* Underline the sentence. **Ask** *How could I prove the fourth sentence? There's no way. It's just what the writer thinks. It's a nonfact.* Circle the sentence. **Say** *This writer made an interesting paragraph by mixing facts and nonfacts.*

Say *Now let's look for facts and nonfacts in the next paragraph.* **Ask** *Is the first sentence a fact or a nonfact? How do you know?* Underline that sentence. **Ask** *Is the second sentence a fact or a nonfact? How do you know?* Circle that sentence. **Ask** *What other facts and nonfacts do you see?*

CORRECTIVE FEEDBACK

If students have trouble distinguishing fact from nonfact, have them ask themselves: "Do I believe this? How could I prove it?"

PRACTICE Have students complete Blackline Master 38. **Say** *Read each paragraph. Then label each statement* **fact** *or* **nonfact.**

CORRECTIVE FEEDBACK

If students cannot distinguish fact from nonfact, have them reread each sentence, asking themselves "How could I prove this?"

Answers: 1. nonfact, fact, nonfact, fact   2. fact, nonfact, nonfact, fact

Name _____ Date _____ Instructor _____

Fact and Nonfact

The museum is having a special show of paintings about flowers. Some of the art really spoke to me. One painting shows a woman sitting next to a big vase of flowers. They're the most beautiful flowers anybody ever saw.

A big picture at the museum shows some water lilies. It probably took the artist a hundred years to paint it. Anybody who misses this show is foolish. And it's free admission if you're a student!

PRACTICE

1. My father is the world's best cook. He makes a stew every Monday. He must know a million different kinds of stew. Today he made one with only vegetables.

   _____ He is the world's best cook.

   _____ He makes a stew every Monday.

   _____ He knows a million different kinds.

   _____ Today he made one with only vegetables.

2. Yesterday, Ben and Marcie played checkers. Neither of them breathed while they played. The whole world knows Marcie's a better player. But Ben won the game.

   _____ Ben and Marcie played checkers.

   _____ Neither of them breathed.

   _____ The whole world knows Marcie's better.

   _____ Ben won the game.

Fact and Nonfact / C

TEACHING FRAME: BLM 39 Say *Authors often mix facts and nonfacts to make their writing interesting. It's important to be able to tell the difference.* **Say** *A statement of fact is a statement that can be proved scientifically.* Have students repeat. **Say** *Scientifically means by direct observation or by research. A statement of nonfact is a statement that cannot be proved scientifically.* Have students repeat. **Ask** *What's the difference between a statement of fact and a statement of nonfact?*

MODEL Read the first paragraph of the teaching frame together. **Say** *This paragraph is about the piano. I'm going to look at each sentence to see if it's a fact or a nonfact. I could easily prove the piano has 88 keys by looking it up in a book or by counting. That's a fact.* Underline that sentence. **Say** *I don't believe the piano cries out. I certainly couldn't prove it from my own observations or research. It's a nonfact.* Circle that sentence. **Say** *If I asked an expert or read about it in a book, I could find out how a piano works. I can prove that the hammer strikes a tuned string. It's a fact.* Underline that sentence. **Say** *The string doesn't really say ouch! I can't prove it. It's a nonfact.* Circle that sentence.

> **CORRECTIVE FEEDBACK**
>
> If students have trouble distinguishing fact from nonfact, have them ask themselves: "Is this believable? How could I prove it?"

PRACTICE Have students complete Blackline Master 39. **Say** *Read the article. Then complete the chart. Find five facts and five nonfacts.*

> **CORRECTIVE FEEDBACK**
>
> If students cannot distinguish fact from nonfact, have them ask themselves "Can I prove it?" underline the sentences that could be proved and circle the sentences that could never be proved.

Answers: Facts: Sentences; 1, 3, 5, 7, 8; Nonfacts: Sentences; 2, 4, 6, 9, 10

Name _____ Date _____ Instructor _____

Fact and Nonfact

The piano is a musical instrument that has **88** keys. It cries out to be played. Every time you hit a key, it makes a hammer inside the piano strike a tuned string. The note you hear is the string saying "ouch!"

The piano was invented around 1709 in Italy. That makes it almost 300 years old! There's nowhere in the universe where you can't find a piano today. It has stayed popular this long because everybody loves its sound.

PRACTICE

Fingerprints were first used in China over a thousand years ago. People must have enjoyed pressing their inky thumbs onto certain documents. Japan had a similar law. Someone in Japan probably got the idea on a trip to China.

There are four basic kinds of fingerprints. Four is a nice even number, so they're easy to remember. "Loops" and "arches" look like different types of curves. "Whorls" appear to the eye as spirals running around a point. "Accidentals" are the silliest kind of fingerprints. You can almost hear them saying "We wish we were loops."

FACTS	NONFACTS

Make Judgments and Decisions / A

TEACHING FRAME BLM 40 Say *Suppose you promised to fold the laundry for your dad after school. But a friend comes over and asks you to play hockey. You are faced with three choices: fold the clothes, play hockey, or call your dad and ask if it would be okay to fold the clothes later. Which decision should you make?* Ask students to think about the consequences of each decision. **Say** *You need to make decisions all the time. So do characters in stories. They try to make the right decision, but sometimes a decision doesn't work out.*

Read the first paragraph aloud. **Say** *What does Fran want to do? Why can't she do it? What choices does Fran have?* Circle the words *movie* and *skate*. **Say** *Each choice has its strong and weak points. If Fran goes to the movie, she is keeping her promise. If Fran skates, she is doing what she really wants. If Fran tries to convince Polly to skate, she can skate without betraying a friend. What should Fran do? Why should she make this choice?*

Say *Think about the choices the character can make as I read this second paragraph.* Read the paragraph aloud. **Say** *What problem does Tim face?* Circle the phrase *hated the Comets*. **Ask** *What choices does Tim have? What should Tim do? Why do you think he should make this choice?*

> ### CORRECTIVE FEEDBACK
>
> If students have trouble making decisions, suggest that they make a chart that outlines the pro's and con's of each choice.

PRACTICE Have students complete Blackline Master 40. **Say** *Read each paragraph, then answer the question. Write the best decision on the line provided.*

> ### CORRECTIVE FEEDBACK
>
> If students are unable to make reasonable decisions, ask them to make a list of reasons why they made their choice. Their failure to support their decisions may lead them to choosing a different option.

Answers: 1. She shouldn't make the call. 2. He should not copy the homework. It is dishonest.

Name _____ Date _____ Instructor _____

Make Judgments and Decisions

Fran desperately wanted to try her new skates. But when Polly called, Fran agreed to go to a movie. A moment later Jen called and asked Fran to skate. Fran should . . .

Tim eagerly opened his gift from Aunt Ida. It was a "Comets" cap. The Comets were not Tim's favorite team. In fact, he hated the Comets. Tim should . . .

PRACTICE

1. Morgan was baby-sitting for the Martins. She promised that she would not tie up the phone line. Then, Morgan saw that her favorite musical group was on TV. She really wanted to call Erica and tell her. Would it hurt to just make one phone call?

   What should Morgan do?

   _____

2. Steve did his Math homework last night. Then, just before class, Steve realized that he had left his homework at home. "You can copy my homework," Lucy said. It wasn't wrong because Steve actually *had* done the homework himself.

   What should Steve do?

   _____

Make Judgments and Decisions / B

TEACHING FRAME: BLM 41 **Say** *Making judgments and decisions means using what you know and believe to make good choices in situations that involve people, events, and ideas.* Have students repeat this definition. **Say** *Use information in the story, common sense, and your own feelings and opinions to decide whether characters in the story make good choices.*

MODEL Read the first paragraph of the teaching frame together. **Say** *The problem Simon faces is what to do about his team. He would like to organize a good team. But he doesn't want to disappoint his best friend P.J.* Underline the phrase *dreadful hockey player.* **Say** *The reason not to invite P.J. to play is that it may make Simon's team worse. The reason to include P.J. is that he is Simon's best friend.* Underline the last sentence. **Say** *Loyalty to a friend is more important than winning hockey games, so Simon's decision seems like a good one.*

Say *Think about the decision the character makes as you read this paragraph.* Read the second paragraph aloud. **Ask** *What problem does Simon face?* Underline the words *shot, hero, passed,* and *win.* **Say** *What reason does Simon have for shooting? What reason does he have for passing in this situation? What decision does Simon make?* Underline the final sentence. **What is your opinion of Simon's decision? Is it a good one? Explain.**

> ### CORRECTIVE FEEDBACK
>
> If students have trouble making judgments and decisions, have them make a chart that shows the consequences of each choice he can make.

PRACTICE Have students complete Blackline Master 41. **Say** *Read each paragraph, then answer the questions.*

> ### CORRECTIVE FEEDBACK
>
> Tell students who have trouble making judgments and decisions to make a diagram that looks like a see-saw. Put evidence for one choice on one side of the see-saw, and evidence for the other choice on the other side. Then "weigh" the two sides and choose the side that has more "weight."

Answers: 1. a. 2. Answers will vary.

Name _____ Date _____ Instructor _____

Make Judgments and Decisions

Simon was organizing a hockey team. He got Mike, Eva, and Dov to play. Now his best friend P.J. wanted to play. P.J. was a dreadful hockey player! Simon finally decided to let P.J. play.

Simon skated toward the goal. Three players came up to guard him. If Simon shot, he could be a hero. If he passed to a teammate, his team was more likely to win. Simon decided to pass.

Carla was at the lake with her mom and her older brother Billy. Billy went off by himself and promised to meet the other two at 4 o'clock at the boat house. At four, Carla and her mom waited, but Billy didn't show up.

"You wait here," Carla's mom said. "Don't go anywhere. I'm going to look for Billy at the beach." Five minutes later Billy showed up. "Let's go to the beach to find mom," Billy said. "She'll be looking all over for me." "But she told me to wait here," Carla said. Finally, Carla gave in and went to the beach with her brother to look for her mom.

1 What is one reason to go with Billy?

   a. to save her mom the time and trouble of looking for Billy

   b. to make sure he doesn't get lonely

   c. that's what her mom would have wanted

2. What decision did Carla make? _____

Make Judgments and Decisions / C

TEACHING FRAME: BLM 42 Say *When you make judgments and decisions, you determine how to react to people, events, and ideas based on your beliefs, values, and your best understanding of the situation.* Have students repeat the definition. **Say** *When you read, you constantly make judgments and decisions about the actions that characters take.*

MODEL Read the first paragraph of the teaching frame together. **Say** *Ahmet's problem is that he needs to decide whether or not to hold his uncle to his promise.* Underline the uncle's words. **Say** *Here is the promise the uncle makes.* Now underline the phrase *uncle's jaw dropped* in the second sentence. **Say** *This shows that he does not really want to keep his promise. Ahmet ignores his uncle's feelings and decides to get the expensive sneakers anyway.* Underline the last sentence. **Say** *I understand why Ahmet made this decision, the sneakers are important to him, but I think it is a selfish decision. I would buy less expensive sneakers.*

Say *As we read the second paragraph, think about the decision that Ahmet makes.* Read the second paragraph. **Ask** *What problem does Ahmet face here? What choices does Ahmet have? What does Ahmet decide, and why?* Underline the final sentence. **Ask** *What do you think of Ahmet's decision, was it a good one? Why?*

CORRECTIVE FEEDBACK

If students have trouble making judgments and decisions, have them consider the decision from the *other person's* point of view and ask: "Does this decision hurt the other person?" "Does it help the other person?" "Is it more important to the other person than it is to you?"

PRACTICE Have students complete Blackline Master 42. **Say** *Read each paragraph, then answer the questions.*

CORRECTIVE FEEDBACK

Help students who have trouble making judgments and decisions to make a diagram that shows how each choice affects each major character in the story. Have them base their decisions on the choices that are best for all involved.

Answers: 1. b 2. To sell pizza 3. Answers will vary.

Name _____ Date _____ Instructor _____

Make Judgments and Decisions

At the sporting goods store, Ahmet's uncle said, "Pick any sneakers you like." When Ahmet chose X54's that cost $145, his uncle's jaw dropped. Should he hold his uncle to his pledge? Or get less expensive shoes? Ahmet bought the X54's.

Ahmet's X54 shoes turned out not to fit. Ahmet tried to replace them, but the store had no shoes in his size. "Here's a refund," said the clerk. He counted out $160. "That's too much," Ahmet thought. He refused to keep the extra money.

PRACTICE

Katie was at Pizza Land, picking up a pizza. Just as she began to walk out the door, a man stopped her. "Would you sell me your pizza?" he said. "I'm late. I don't have the time to order my own pizza. I'll give you thirty dollars for it."

Katie thought about the situation. Her family was waiting at home. Her brother might be late to soccer practice if she had to wait for a new pizza. On the other hand, she could get three pizzas for thirty dollars! "I'll take the money," she told the man.

1. What is one reason to keep the pizza?

   a. You shouldn't give away something that you earned

   b. She didn't want to make her brother late.

   c. She would be cheating the man out of his money.

2. What decision did Katie make? _____

3. What do you think of this decision? _____

Important and Unimportant Information / A

TEACHING FRAME: BLM 43 Say *You can probably think of many facts about yourself. Do you prefer apples or oranges? Who is your best friend? Do you own a pet at home? Imagine that I asked you to tell me three important facts about you. You'd want to tell me something that I really needed to know about you.* **Say** *When you read, you want to figure out which information is important.*

Have students listen as you read the first paragraph. **Ask** *What is the main idea of this paragraph?* Circle that sentence. **Say** *Is it important to know that they can fly? Does that help you understand the main idea?* Underline that sentence. *Is it important to know that they can swim?* Underline that sentence. *Is it important that lots of people think ducks are cute? That's interesting, but does it help you understand the main idea? Is it important to the main idea to know that the author loves to watch them? These last two sentences are not important. They don't help you understand the main idea.*

Say *Let's read the next paragraph and look for important information.* Read the paragraph. **Ask** *What is the main idea of this paragraph?* Circle that sentence. **Ask** *Which sentences support this main idea? So which information is important?* Underline those sentences.

CORRECTIVE FEEDBACK

If students have trouble identifying important information, ask them to imagine that they're studying for a test on this topic. Have them ask themselves, "Which facts would I need to know?"

PRACTICE Have students complete Blackline Master 43. **Say** *Read each paragraph. Then answer the question. Circle the letter of the correct answer.*

CORRECTIVE FEEDBACK

If students cannot identify important information, have them reread each paragraph and underline <u>only</u> those details that help them understand the main idea.

Answers: 1. a   2. b

Name _____ Date _____ Instructor _____

Important and Unimportant Information

Ducks travel in two ways. They can fly in the air just like most other birds. They can also swim in the water. Lots of people think ducks are cute. I love to watch them.

Kevin is just like his mother. Everybody who knows them says so. The both like to dance to music on the radio. They also both love to tell jokes. Kevin's father, though, doesn't care for dancing.

PRACTICE

1. A movie camera doesn't really take movies. It takes lots of still pictures very quickly. I love to go to the movies. Grandpa and I went to see a funny one last week.

Which information is important?

    a. It takes lots of still pictures very quickly.

    b. I love to go to the movies.

    c. Grandpa and I went to see a funny one last week.

2. A fable is a story with animals that act like people. It's probably my favorite kind of story. Fables usually teach some lesson. I like the ones with pictures of bears.

Which information is important?

    a. It's probably my favorite kind of story.

    b. Fables usually teach some lesson.

    c. I like the ones with pictures of bears.

Important and Unimportant Information / B

TEACHING FRAME: BLM 44 Say *Important information is information that directly supports the main idea. Unimportant information is information that could be omitted without taking away from the main idea.* Have students repeat. **Say** *When you read, you need to determine which details are important and which aren't. This helps you understand what you read.*

MODEL Read the first paragraph on the teaching frame together. **Say** *This paragraph is about hurricanes. The main idea seems to be in the first sentence, that a hurricane forms in a special way.* Circle that sentence. *Let's look for sentences that support that main idea. They'll be the important ones. The second sentence is probably true, but it could be left out. It doesn't tell us how a hurricane forms. The third and fifth sentences explain more about how a hurricane forms. They give important information that supports the main idea.* Underline those sentences. *What about the sentence that tells me that Africa is far away? It's nice to know, but it doesn't support the main idea about hurricanes. The sentence about Africa is unimportant.*

Say *Let's see what's important in the next paragraph.* Read the paragraph aloud. **Ask** *What is the main idea?* Circle that sentence. **Ask** *Which sentences support this main idea?* Underline those sentences. *Which sentences could be left out without taking away from the main idea?*

CORRECTIVE FEEDBACK

If students have trouble telling important from unimportant information, have them reread the paragraph and underline sentences that don't help them understand the main idea.

PRACTICE: Have students complete Blackline Master 44. **Say** *Read each paragraph. Then label each statement* **I** *for important or* **U** *for unimportant.*

CORRECTIVE FEEDBACK

If students cannot label information important or unimportant, guide them to find and circle the main idea sentence first then find statements that support it.

Answers: 1. I, U, I, U 2. U, I, I, U

Name _____ Date _____ Instructor _____

Important and Unimportant Information

> A hurricane forms in a special way. Hurricanes are awesome. They begin as a patch of thunderstorms over western Africa. Africa is far from the United States. The patch of storms moves over the Atlantic ocean and is then called a wave.
>
> Over the ocean, the wave changes. If the water is hot enough, the wave gets stronger. It becomes a pinwheel and then turns into a hurricane. You've probably seen pictures of this on TV. There are good books about it, too.

PRACTICE

1. There are lots of things to do in New York City. The city has great museums, zoos, and parks. Going to the zoo is really fun. The city also has many wonderful restaurants. People in cities eat out more often than other people.

   _____ New York has great museums, zoos and parks.

   _____ Going to the zoo is really fun.

   _____ New York has many wonderful restaurants.

   _____ People in cities eat out more often than other people.

2. Canada is a very large country. You should visit it if you want to have a great time. In area, it is the second largest nation in the world. It's almost 3,500 miles long from east to west. Canada can get very cold, so bring a coat!

   _____ You really should visit Canada.

   _____ It's the second largest nation.

   _____ It's almost 3,500 mile long.

   _____ Canada can get very cold.

Important and Unimportant Information / C

TEACHING FRAME: BLM 45 Say *Important information is information that directly supports the main idea.* **Say** *Unimportant information is information that could be left out without affecting the main idea.* Have students repeat. **Say** *As you read, you need to determine which details are important. They will help you remember what you read.*

MODEL Read the first paragraph of the teaching frame together. **Say** *This paragraph is about puppets. The main idea is in the second sentence, that there are several kinds of puppets.* Circle it. *Which sentences directly support this main idea? The first sentence doesn't, even though it may be true. The sentence about hand puppets and the sentence about string puppets give examples of kinds of puppets. Those sentences have important information that supports the main idea.* Underline them. *The last sentence is an unimportant statement by the author and could be left out. If I were learning about puppets, I'd want to remember sentences 3 and 4.*

Say *Now let's look at the next paragraph and analyze it for important information.* Read the paragraph. **Ask** *What's the main idea?* Circle that sentence. *Which sentences best support that main idea?* Underline those sentences as they are mentioned. **Ask** *Why aren't the other sentences important?*

CORRECTIVE FEEDBACK

If students have trouble telling important from unimportant information, have them make a list of facts that taught them something about puppets.

PRACTICE Have students complete Blackline Master 45. **Say** *Read the article. Circle the main idea sentence in each paragraph. Then list the other sentences where they belong on the chart.*

CORRECTIVE FEEDBACK

If students cannot distinguish important from unimportant information, have them list each statement and check off only those that are about the alphabet.

Answers: Main Idea, paragraph 1: sentence 3.   Main Idea, paragraph 2: sentence 1. Important Information: sentences 3, 7, 9   Unimportant Information: sentences 1, 2, 5, 8

Name _____ Date _____ Instructor _____

Important and Unimportant Information

Children all over the world love puppet shows. There are several different kinds of puppets. Hand puppets are like figures attached to gloves. String puppets look like dolls with wires attached. Maybe you own a few puppets yourself.

Rod puppets can be simple or complicated. The simplest rod puppet is a little cut-out figure on one stick. The figure could be an animal. More complicated rod puppets are life-size and need a few people to work them. They'll make you say, "Wow!"

PRACTICE

You probably take the alphabet for granted. Do you know what an alphabet is? An alphabet is a set of symbols used for writing. The symbols stand for sounds we make when we speak. Most of us speak hundreds of times a day.

Alphabets — and words made from them — can be written in many ways. Our alphabet and our words are read from left to right. That makes the most sense to us because it's what we're used to. Arabic and Hebrew alphabets (and words) are written from right to left.

IMPORTANT INFORMATION	UNIMPORTANT INFORMATION

Recognize Techniques of Persuasion / A

TEACHING FRAME: BLM 46 Say *Suppose you want to buy a bike. What could you learn from reading an ad? Suppose the ad says, "We have the best bikes!" Would you hurry to that shop? Why or why not?* **Say** *The purpose of an ad is to sell something. They are trying to persuade you.*

Read the first paragraph together. **Say** *Like most ads, this one wants you to buy something.* Circle *Krispy Krisp* in the first sentence. *In sentence one, they tell us that everyone else loves it. Can they prove that? In sentence two, they say it is also delicious, but that's their opinion. They also tell me the ingredients, and it's good for me. This information contains facts, so I may use those facts to decide if I should try the cereal.*

Say *Now read the second paragraph as I read it aloud. Ask yourself what the writer wants you to do or think. Look for examples of techniques of persuasion.* Read the paragraph. **Ask** *Which sentence tells me how I should act or think? Which sentences use techniques of persuasion to convince me to attend the school?* Circle those sentences. **Ask** *Which sentences have facts that might help me decide if I'm interested in Buzzard Falls School?*

CORRECTIVE FEEDBACK

If students still have trouble identifying techniques of persuasion, have them ask themselves, "What does this writing want me to do or think?" "What information here will help me make up my own mind about this topic?"

PRACTICE Have students complete Blackline Master 46. **Say** *Read each paragraph. Then choose the statement that tells what the author wants you to do or think. Circle the best answer.*

CORRECTIVE FEEDBACK

If students cannot recognize persuasive language, have them review the paragraphs sentence by sentence and underline words or phrases that tell them to act or think a certain way.

Answers: 1. c 2. b

Name _____ Date _____ Instructor _____

Recognize Techniques of Persuasion

Everyone loves Krispy Krisp cereal! It's delicious, and it's good for you, too! Krispy Krisp is made of corn and rice. Corn and rice are part of a balanced diet. Krispy Krisp contains Vitamins A, B12, C, and D. Buy it today!

Buzzard Falls School is having an open house on Wednesday. Buzzard Falls is the school of champions. Our sports program is the best in the state! Most of our seniors go right on to college. Come join our winning team at the Buzzard Falls open house!

PRACTICE

1. Come to Darla's Gift Shop for your Valentine's present. Only Darla's has one-of-a-kind, handmade gifts for your special someone. Our rings are made by a local silversmith. Our fancy baskets are on sale this week for $10 each.

    a. Come to Darla's Gift Shop for your Valentine's present.

    b. Our rings are made by a local silversmith.

    c. Our fancy baskets are on sale this week for $10 each.

2. Have you visited Liza's Log Homes? We have new model houses in many styles! You'll find your dream house in Liza's plan book. Our logs are cut from hemlock and pine. Don't miss our special offers in May!

    a. We have new model houses in many styles!

    b. You'll find your dream house in Liza's plan book.

    c. Our logs are cut from hemlock and pine.

Recognize Techniques of Persuasion / B

TEACHING FRAME: BLM 47 Say *Some persuasive writing is meant to convince you to act or think a certain way. Generalizations imply that something is true for everyone or in all cases.* Have students repeat. **Say** *Arguments are statements that may or may not be true.* Have students repeat.

MODEL Read the first paragraph together. **Say** *The paragraph begins with an invitation to buy the Fido First program. Sentence 2 refers to pet owners everywhere. This is a generalization.* Underline sentence 2. **Say** *Sentence 3 states that Fido First is the best program. This is an opinion.* Underline sentence 3. **Say** *The last sentence uses the word* all, *which is a generalization.* Underline sentence 4. *Three sentences use persuasive language.*

Say *Let's apply what you know about techniques of persuasion.* Read the paragraph. **Say** *Look at sentence 2. Does it imply that something is true for all people? So which technique is used in sentence 2?* Write G over sentence 2. *What kind of argument is presented in sentence 3?* Write O over sentence 3. *Does sentence 4 contain an opinion or a fact?*

CORRECTIVE FEEDBACK

If students have trouble recognizing techniques of persuasion, ask them *"Which sentence makes claim for large groups of people?" "Which sentence states an argument that cannot be tested for truth?"*

PRACTICE Have students complete Blackline Master 47. **Say** *Decide whether the sentence is a generalization, an opinion, or a fact. Circle the answer.*

CORRECTIVE FEEDBACK

If students cannot recognize techniques of persuasion, have them analyze each paragraph sentence by sentence, asking themselves, "Does it imply that something is true for everyone?" "Does it state an argument that may or may not be true at all?"

Answers: 1. a   2. b

Name _____ Date _____ Instructor _____

Recognize Techniques of Persuasion

> Before you give up on training your new puppy, try Fido First. Pet owners everywhere believe that Fido First gets great results fast. Fido First uses only the best, most effective techniques. Dogs of all shapes and sizes agree — Fido First works!
>
> We need to keep businesses downtown and away from the mall. All small towns need a thriving downtown. A mix of housing and business is the best formula. The town of Danville attracted twice as many visitors to its downtown area after the mall closed. Don't let small town America die out!

PRACTICE

1. <u>All across the country, police chiefs and sheriffs have instructed local residents to install alarm systems in their homes.</u> Today, home security experts agree that Second-Story Alarms are the best around.

   a. generalization

   b. opinion

   c. fact

2. Buttermilk Falls is a lovely, peaceful area for swimmers and hikers. <u>The last thing we need is a noisy stadium right across the road.</u> Everything that we love and appreciate about this historic site will be destroyed.

   a. generalization

   b. opinion

   c. fact

Recognize Techniques of Persuasion / C

TEACHING FRAME: BLM 48 Say *Persuasive writing is meant to convince a reader to act or think a certain way.* Have students repeat. **Say** *Generalizations suggest that something is true for everyone. Arguments from tradition appeal to people who hold on to the past. Arguments from an authority are claims from unknown experts. Oversimplifications present simple solutions to complicated problems.* **Ask** *Who can define these techniques of persuasion?*

MODEL Read the first part of the teaching frame together. **Say** *The first sentence tells me that the purpose is to get people to join the Committee for Smaller Schools. Sentence 2 is clearly an oversimplification.* Write O over sentence 2. *Sentence 3 refers to unnamed studies, which makes this an argument from an authority.* Write A over sentence 3. *Sentence 4 uses the word everyone, which is a generalization.* Write G over sentence 4.

Say *Find the techniques of persuasion that appear in the next paragraph. Read the paragraph.* **Say** *Who would respond to sentences 1 and 2? What would you call this technique?* Write A over sentences 1 and 2. **Ask** *Can you find an example of oversimplification in this paragraph? Where is it?* Write O over sentence 4. **Ask** *What technique is used in sentence 3? How do you know?*

CORRECTIVE FEEDBACK

If students have trouble recognizing techniques of persuasion, ask them to repeat the definitions of each technique.

PRACTICE Have students complete Blackline Master 48. **Say** *Read the paragraph. Find the techniques of persuasion. Write the sentence on the chart.*

CORRECTIVE FEEDBACK

If students cannot recognize techniques of persuasion, have them reread each sentence and ask themselves: "Does this suggest that something is true for everyone?" "Does this refer to unnamed experts?"

Answers: 1. sentence 2   2. Sentence 5   3. Sentence 3   4. Sentence 4

Name _____ Date _____ Instructor _____

Recognize Techniques of Persuasion

Please join the Committee for Smaller Schools. Smaller schools will cure all our problems. Studies show that smaller schools are safe, and they allow students to thrive. Everyone prefers smaller schools — students, teachers, and parents.

Do you remember walking on sunny mornings to your neighborhood school? We need to bring back that old-time feeling! Government officials say that smaller schools are the backbones of our communities. Smaller schools lead to smarter students leading happier lives.

PRACTICE

Do you wake up with a stiff neck every morning? The chair you sit in all day is the problem. Doctors and chiropractors know that changing your chair can help. Today's modern office chairs are the worst. Everyone needs an Ace's Easy Office Chair.

1. Oversimplification:
2. Generalization:
3. Dubious Authority:
4. Argument from Tradition:

Evaluate Evidence and Sources / A

TEACHING FRAME BLM 49 Say *Suppose I told you that I was a hero. What would make you believe me?* (true stories of heroic action; awards or trophies) *Sometimes we need to decide if a statement is true or false. We look for evidence, or facts, to support the statement.* Ask students to read the first paragraph with you. **Say** *In this paragraph, the main idea is presented in the first sentence.* Circle that sentence. **Say** *In order to believe that Winter Creek needs a clean-up, see which sentences answer the question "Why does the creek need a clean-up?" Those sentences will be evidence. Sentence 2 is a fact, but it doesn't really tell why the creek needs to be cleaned up. Sentence 3 states that run-off has polluted the creek. It is evidence.* Underline sentence 3. **Sentence 4 tells that we can see the trash. That is also evidence.** Underline sentence 4. **Say** *So sentences 3 and 4, which give examples of pollution, support the idea that the creek needs a clean-up.*

Say *Now read the second paragraph as I read it aloud. Think about the main idea.* Read the paragraph. **Ask** *What is the main idea?* Circle sentence 1. **Ask** *Which sentences give evidence to support that main idea?* Underline sentences 2, 4, 5. **Say** *All of these sentences are evidence that the author's grandfather was a great man.*

CORRECTIVE FEEDBACK

If students have trouble identifying which sentences provide evidence, have them ask themselves, "Why was Grandfather a great citizen?"

PRACTICE Have students complete Blackline Master 49. **Say** *Read the first sentence. This is the main idea for a paragraph. Then choose the sentence that gives evidence to support that main idea. Circle the letter of the correct answer.*

CORRECTIVE FEEDBACK

If students cannot identify evidence, have them use the main idea to ask a question: "Why is rock 'n roll related to rhythm and blues?" "Why do we need to get the deer out of the village?"

Answers: 1. a   2. b

Name _____ Date _____ Instructor _____

Evaluate Evidence and Sources

Winter Creek needs a clean-up. The creek has wound through our countryside for ages. In the 1980s, it became polluted from farm run-off. Today, the farms are gone, but you can still see the trash along the creek banks. The county should get a grant to clean it up.

My grandfather was a great man. He worked down south to gain voting rights in the 1960s. He later moved to Chicago. He was elected to the city council three times. He won many awards for his work. He finally retired in 1990.

PRACTICE

1. Our radio station should play more music from the past.

   a. Many people still like to listen to the "golden oldies."

   b. My parents like to dance to the songs of Fats Domino.

   c. You can dance to many of today's top hits.

2. We need to get the deer out of our town.

   a. Deer are big, peaceful animals.

   b. Even so, they eat from our gardens and ruin our trees.

   c. The Town Council will talk about the subject on June 3.

Evaluate Evidence and Sources / B

TEACHING FRAME: BLM 50 Say *Evidence means facts that support the main idea of a paragraph.* Have students repeat. **Say** *Reliable sources include historical records, news reports, and encyclopedias. Unreliable sources include personal opinions, ads, and hearsay or rumors.* Have students repeat. **Say** *By evaluating the sources of evidence, you can determine how believable the main ideas are.*

MODEL Read the first paragraph together. **Say** *The paragraph begins with a main idea.* Circle the first sentence. *The first source of evidence is Coast Guard officers on the scene of the oil spill. This is a reliable source.* Underline sentence 2. Continue *The second source of evidence is TV broadcasts from the scene. This is also reliable.* Underline sentence 3. **Say** *The third source of evidence is the author's cousin, who heard from some unnamed person that whales in Japan had oil on their coats. This is what is called hearsay or rumor.*

Read the next paragraph. **Say** *What is the main idea? Read sentence 2. Does it refer to a reliable source? How about sentence 3?* **Say** *A made-for-TV movie is likely to be fictional. It is not a reliable source. Try sentence 4. Yes, a Department of Energy report is accurate.*

CORRECTIVE FEEDBACK

If students have trouble evaluating sources of evidence, ask them *"Is the source knowledgeable on the subject?" "Does the source provide facts and not just opinions?" "Did the source have direct access to the information?"*

PRACTICE Have students complete Blackline Master 50. **Say** *Choose the source that is most reliable. Circle the correct answer.*

CORRECTIVE FEEDBACK

If students cannot evaluate sources of evidence, **ask** *Which source is most knowledgeable? Which source provides more facts than opinions?*

Answers: 1. a   2. b

Part 2
COMPREHENSION

Name _____ Date _____ Instructor _____

Evaluate Evidence and Sources

Oil spills are a disaster for plants and animals. Coast Guard officers on the scene reported thousands of dead seabirds. Television broadcasts showed seals and otters covered with oil. My cousin heard that whales in Japan showed up with oily coats.

Although prevention has been improved, oil spills still happen. I read in the newspaper about a spill near Mexico. A recent TV movie showed a spill in Alaska. An study from the Department of Energy reported four small spills in a six-month period.

PRACTICE

1. **TOPIC:** Wolves of the Arctic

   EVIDENCE: The wolves are very loyal to the pack.

   SOURCE:

   a. an ancient Inuit folktale

   b. a study by Canadian biologists

   c. a movie about an Arctic explorer

2. **TOPIC:** George Washington

   EVIDENCE: The first U.S. president had wooden teeth.

   SOURCE:

   a. a bill from Washington's doctor at the time

   b. a letter from Washington's great-great-great nephew

   c. a student's history report on the Internet

Evaluate Evidence and Sources / C

TEACHING FRAME: BLM 51 Say *Evidence means facts that support the main idea. Look for evidence that supports the ideas. Consider the sources of that evidence to determine whether the ideas are believable. Reliable sources include historical records, news reports, and encyclopedias. Unreliable sources include personal opinions, advertisements, and hearsay.* Have students repeat. **Ask** *Who can give some examples of reliable sources?*

MODEL Read the first part of the teaching frame together. **Say** *The first sentence gives the main idea.* Circle sentence 1. *The other sentences give evidence that supports that main idea. In sentence 2, the source of the evidence is a report from the state. I would call that a reliable source.* Underline sentence 2. *In sentence 3, the source of the evidence is parents. I don't think many parents are experts on testing, so I won't consider this a reliable source. Finally, in sentence 4, the source of the evidence is the superintendent. He or she has access to the information. This is a reliable source.* Underline sentence 4.

Read the next paragraph. **Ask** *What is the main idea?* Circle that sentence. *What is the source of the evidence in sentence 2? Is that a reliable source? Why or why not?* Underline sentence 2. *Is the source in sentence 3 reliable? Why or why not?* Underline sentence 3. *How about sentence 4?*

CORRECTIVE FEEDBACK

If students have trouble analyzing sources of evidence, remind them of the reliable and unreliable sources they identified at the start of the lesson.

PRACTICE Have students complete Blackline Master 51. **Say** *Read each paragraph and the information about the source. Then answer the question.*

CORRECTIVE FEEDBACK

If students cannot evaluate sources of evidence, have them ask themselves, "Is this source an expert?" "Is this source impartial and unbiased?"

Answers: 1. Yes

Part 2

COMPREHENSION

Evaluate Evidence and Sources

Test scores at our school are too low. The annual "Report on Our Schools" from the state shows that the average scores for schools our size are five to ten points higher than ours. Parents are complaining that the scores aren't where they should be. Even our superintendent admits that our scores have dropped in past years.

There are several ways to improve our test scores. The Commissioner of Education wrote an editorial in the newspaper listing a five-point plan for improving achievement. Our principal received a brochure from the state university's Department of Education with ideas for test preparation. We saw an ad on TV for a math kit that's guaranteed to help.

PRACTICE

1. The Teeburg Spelling Bee has been held annually since 1865. That year, it was won by Jebediah Morton, son of the founder of the Morton China Works. The Spelling Bee was open only to boys at first. Girls started competing in the 1880s and quickly showed their skill. Miss Agatha Mills, daughter of the mayor, won in 1884 and then again in 1885.

   Source: a radio interview with Dr. Elizabeth Crown, history professor at Teeburg College and Teeburg Town Historian

   Is the source reliable? Why or why not? _____

   _____

   _____

Vocabulary Strategies

Context Clues / A

TEACHING FRAME: BLM 52 Say *Detectives figure out mysteries by looking for pieces of information.* **Ask** *Do you know what those pieces of information are called?* (clues) **Say** *Sometimes, readers need to figure out something, too.* **Ask** *What would they look for?* (clues) *Here's a reader's mystery. Read the first sentence aloud.* **Ask** *What does* **ring** *mean?* **Say** *It could be a piece of jewelry, or what a bell does to make a sound. The only way I can decide is to look for clues in the sentence.* **Ask** *Which* **ring** *is it?* (what a bell does) *What clues did you find?* (heard, telephone) Underline those words.

Say *Now let's look for clues in the next sentence.* Read it aloud. **Say** *I need to find the meaning of* **right.** *It has two meanings.* **Right** *means correct, but it also means a direction. Which kind is this?* (a direction) *Do you see any clue words that helped you figure that out?* (looked, left) Underline those words.

> **CORRECTIVE FEEDBACK**
>
> If students have trouble identifying context clues, have them read each sentence carefully to eliminate words that do not offer clues.

PRACTICE Have students complete Blackline Master 52. **Say** *Read each definition. Then read each sentence below it. Write the letter of the underlined clue that helps you define the word in bold print.*

> **CORRECTIVE FEEDBACK**
>
> If students cannot find the clues, ask them to read the definition of the underlined word aloud. Then ask them if they see a word from that definition in the sentence.

Answers: 1. c 2. b 3. a

Name _____ Date _____ Instructor _____

Context Clues

> As soon as I heard the telephone ring, I answered it.
>
> I look to the left and to the right before crossing a street.

PRACTICE

1. **carpenter:** a person who makes things out of wood
   Jo <u>asked</u> a **carpenter** to build her a new <u>table</u> made of <u>wood</u>.

      a   **b**   **c**

2. **tepee:** a Native American tent made of animal skins
   The <u>man</u> pointed to his <u>tent</u> and said, "<u>This</u> is my **tepee**."

      a   **b**   **c**

3. **emu:** a large bird that can't fly
   I had never seen a <u>bird</u> like an **emu** until I <u>went</u> to the <u>zoo</u>.

           a   **b**   **c**

Context Clues / B

TEACHING FRAME: BLM 53 Say *Context clues are words or sentences that help you figure out the meaning of an unknown word.* Have students repeat. **Ask** *Who can tell me the definition of context clues?*

MODEL Read the first sentence on the teaching frame together. Model looking for context clues. **Say** *I've never seen the word* dispute *before, but there are clues in the sentence. A small dispute is something that could grow into a big argument. So I can figure out that a small dispute must be a small argument. The context clues tell me that* dispute *means* argument. Circle *argument.*

Say *Let's see if we can find context clues in the second sentence. I don't know what* inquired *means. But in the next sentence I see a context clue.* **Ask** *Who can find the context clue?* (asked) **Say** *Right.* Inquired *means* asked. Circle *asked.*

CORRECTIVE FEEDBACK

If students have trouble locating context clues, have them look at each word in the sentence and, by process of elimination, cross out words that do not give clues.

PRACTICE Have students complete Blackline Master 53. **Say** *Read the sentences and use the context clues to help you figure out what each underlined word means. Circle the best definition for the word.*

CORRECTIVE FEEDBACK

If students have trouble selecting the correct definition, ask them to imagine what the sentence might mean using each of the definitions in turn.

Answers: 1. a   2. b   3. b   4. c   5. a   6. c

Context Clues

My friend and I settled our small dispute before it grew into a big argument.

I inquired about our homework. "When do we have to hand it in?" I asked.

PRACTICE

1. My favorite <u>condiment</u> is mustard, but I also like ketchup.

    a. something to flavor food   **b.** kind of meat   **c.** fruit

2. Wendy had to <u>guffaw</u> when she heard the funny joke.

    a. fall asleep   **b.** laugh loudly   **c.** paint a picture

3. Watching the mother kangaroo caring for her <u>joey</u> reminded me of watching Mom take care of my little sister.

    a. small girl   **b.** baby kangaroo   **c.** tiny toy

4. My cold was not too bad, so I was able to go to school even with my <u>ailment</u>.

    a. visitor   **b.** new dress   **c.** sickness

5. Lenny is a great artist. You should see his pencil <u>sketch</u> of our house.

    a. drawing   **b.** box   **c.** pen

6. If I stay up too late, I get <u>weary</u> and start to yawn.

    a. happy   **b.** silly   **c.** tired

Context Clues / C

TEACHING FRAME: BLM 54 Say *Context clues are words or sentences that help you figure out the meaning of an unknown word.* Have students repeat. **Ask** *Who can tell me the definition of context clues?*

MODEL Read the first sentence on the teaching frame together. Model looking for context clues. **Say** *I don't know what the word* **wafted** *means, but I do see some context clues. The sentence says that the leaf was* **carried lightly through the air.** *I can make a good guess that* **wafted** *must mean* **carried lightly through the air.** Underline *carried lightly through the air.*

Say *Let's look in the next sentence for context clues. I've never seen this word* **appreciated** *before.* **Ask** *Can you find a context clue?* (was thankful for) Underline it. *So what does* **appreciated** *mean?* (was thankful for)

CORRECTIVE FEEDBACK

If students have trouble locating context clues, have them read the sentence carefully. Have them eliminate words that do not offer context clues.

PRACTICE Have students complete Blackline Master 54. **Say** *Read the sentences. Look at each underlined word and use the context clues to help you define it. Then circle the best definition.*

CORRECTIVE FEEDBACK

If students have trouble selecting the correct definition, have them substitute each answer choice for the underlined phrase in the sentence. Then have them eliminate the choices that do not make sense.

Answers: 1. c 2. a 3. b 4. c 5. b 6. b

Name _____ Date _____ Instructor _____

Context Clues

The leaf wafted by, and was carried lightly through the air past my window.

I appreciated the present from my Aunt Rose, and told her I was thankful for it.

PRACTICE

1. Jennie <u>apologized</u> to her friend for hurting his feelings.

    a. took a walk   **b.** read a book   **c.** said she was sorry

2. The policeman <u>pursued</u> the criminal and finally caught him.

    a. chased   **b.** loved   **c.** shouted

3. Books are very <u>flammable</u>, so keep them away from the fireplace.

    a. hard to understand   **b.** easy to burn   **c.** fun to read

4. I fell and cut my knee. A few drops of my blood colored the ground <u>scarlet</u>.

    a. yellow   **b.** blue   **c.** red

5. When the band at the party played, my parents got up and did the <u>tango</u>.

    a. a kind of speech   **b.** a kind of dance   **c.** a kind of game

6. Because Paul was wearing a helmet, he came away from the accident without serious <u>injury</u>.

    a. boredom   **b.** harm   **c.** travel

Inflectional Endings / A

TEACHING FRAME: BLM 55 **Say** *Listen as I say the following three sentences. Think about the verb in each sentence. We paint a picture. We painted a picture. We are painting a picture. Which sentence tells about the past?* Repeat the sentences if needed. (the second) *We add endings to verbs, action words, to show a change in tense or a change in number. We add -ed to change a verb from present to past tense. We add -s or -es to show that a subject is singular. We add -ing when we use the verb with a helping form of be. Sometimes adding an ending means changing the spelling of a word. For verbs that end in a consonant and y, change y to i before adding -es or -ed. For words that end in a vowel and a consonant, double that consonant before adding the ending.* Now read the first sentence pair aloud. **Ask** *Which verb has an ending?* (likes) *Why is the ending added?* (to show that the subject is singular)

Say *Now try the second pair of sentences.* Read the sentence pair. **Ask** *Which verb has an ending?* (dropped) *Why is the ending added?* (to show that the action happened in the past) *What spelling change took place?* (The consonant was doubled before the ending was added.)

> **CORRECTIVE FEEDBACK**
>
> If students have difficulty identifying the meaning of inflectional endings, review the possibilities: -*ed* changes a verb from present to past tense; -*s* or -*es* shows that a subject is singular; -*ing* works with a helping form of *be*.

PRACTICE Have students complete Blackline Master 55. **Say** *Complete the chart with the correct forms of each verb.*

> **CORRECTIVE FEEDBACK**
>
> If students cannot add inflectional endings, review the spelling rules above. Write examples of each rule on the board, so students can use them as reference.

Answers: 1. plays, played, playing 2. trips, tripped, tripping 3. fries, fried, frying

Name _____ Date _____ Instructor _____

Inflectional Endings

My brothers like snow cones.

My brother likes snow cones.

I drop my cone.

I dropped my cone.

PRACTICE

VERB	ADD -s OR -es	ADD -ed	ADD -ing
1. play			
2. trip			
3. fry			

© Macmillan/McGraw-Hill School Division

Inflectional Endings / B

TEACHING FRAME: BLM 56 Say *We add inflectional endings to verbs to show a change in tense or a change in number.* Have students repeat. **Say** *We add -ed to change a verb from present to past tense. We add -s or -es to show that a subject is singular. We add -ing when we use the verb with a helping form of* be. *Sometimes adding an ending means changing the spelling of a word. For verbs that end in a consonant and* y, *change* y *to* i *before adding -es or -ed. For words that end in a vowel and a consonant, double that consonant before adding the ending.*

MODEL Read the first sentence pair on the teaching frame together. Model analyzing inflectional endings. **Say** *The second sentence has a verb with an inflectional ending—checks. The ending -s is added to show that the subject of the sentence,* doctor, *is singular.*

Say *Now look at the second sentence pair.* Read the sentence pair aloud. **Ask** *Which verb has an inflectional ending?* (replied) *Why was the ending added?* (to show that the action happened in the past) *What spelling change was made?* (Changed *y* to *i* before adding *-ed*)

> ## CORRECTIVE FEEDBACK
>
> If students have difficulty identifying the meanings of inflectional endings, review the possibilities: *-ed* changes a verb from present to past tense; *-s* or *-es* shows that a subject is singular; *-ing* works with a helping form of *be*.

PRACTICE Have students complete Blackline Master 56. **Say** *Add an inflectional ending to the word in bold print and then write the new word in the sentence.*

> ## CORRECTIVE FEEDBACK
>
> If students cannot add inflectional endings, review the spelling rules above.

Answers: 1. *washed* 2. *carrying* 3. *plays* 4. *mopped* 5. *tries*

Name _____ Date _____ Instructor _____

Inflectional Endings

The doctors check our ears.

The doctor checks our ears.

Nurses reply to our questions.

Nurses replied to our questions.

PRACTICE

Inflectional Endings: -s, -es, -ed, -ing

wash **1.** Yesterday, the rain _____ away my wagon.

carry **2.** The puppy is _____ a newspaper.

play **3.** George _____ baseball every Saturday morning.

mop **4.** Last week I _____ the whole basement.

try **5.** Luisa always _____ her very best.

Inflectional Endings / C

TEACHING FRAME: BLM 57 Say *We add inflectional endings to verbs to show a change in tense or a change in number.* Have students repeat. **Ask** *Why do we add inflectional endings?* **Say** *We add -ed to change a verb from present to past tense. We add -s or -es to show that a subject is singular. We add -ing when we use the verb with a helping form of* be. *Sometimes adding an ending means changing the spelling of a word. For verbs that end in a consonant and y, change y to i before adding -es or -ed. For one-syllable verbs that end in a vowel and a consonant, double that consonant before adding the ending. For verbs that end in -e, drop the -e before adding the ending -ed, -es, or -ing. For verbs that end in s, ss, x, z, zz, sh, or ch, add an -es ending rather than an -s ending.*

MODEL Direct students' attention to the first pair of sentences. Model analyzing inflectional endings. **Say** *The second sentence contains a verb with an inflectional ending. The ending -ed is added to show that the action happened in the past. Because the verb trot ends in a vowel and a consonant, the consonant is doubled before the ending is added.*

Say *Now look at the next sentence pair.* Read the sentence pair aloud. **Ask** *Which verb has an inflectional ending?* (whinnies) *Why is the ending added?* (to show that the subject of the sentence is singular) *What spelling change is needed?* (Change *y* to *i* and add -es)

> ### CORRECTIVE FEEDBACK
> If students have difficulty identifying spelling changes, review the choices above.

PRACTICE Have students complete Blackline Master 57. **Say** *Add an inflectional ending to the word in bold print and then write the new word in the sentence.*

> ### CORRECTIVE FEEDBACK
> If students choose the wrong inflectional ending, have them look for clues in the sentence and ask themselves: "Does the sentence express action in the past?" "Is the subject of the sentence singular?" "Does the verb have a helping verb?"

Answers: 1. grabbed 2. collecting 3. fixes 4. touches 5. married 6. hoping

Part 2 VOCABULARY

Name _____ Date _____ Instructor _____

Inflectional Endings

> Two black horses trot in the field.
>
> Two black horses trotted in the field.
>
> The horses whinny with delight.
>
> The horse whinnies with delight.

PRACTICE

Inflectional Endings: -s, -es, -ed, -ing

---

grab   **1.**   The dog _____ the ball and ran away.

collect 2.   Our club was _____ cans and bottles.

fix   **3.**   Mary always _____ her bike herself.

touch 4.   Omar _____ the base and heads for home.

marry 5.   Last year my cousin _____ a police officer.

hope   6.   He is _____ for a good grade on his test.

Compound Words / A

TEACHING FRAME: BLM 58 Say *What is a candle?* (a wax stick that can be lit) **Ask** *What is* **light?** (brightness) *If I put the two words together,* **candle** *and* **light,** *I make a new word. What word is it?* (candlelight) *What is* **candlelight?** (the brightness created by a candle) Have students listen as you read the sentence. **Ask** *Which word in this sentence is made of two words put together?* (oversleep) *What are the two words that make up* **oversleep?** (over and sleep) *What does* **over** *mean?* (on top of or more than) *What is* **sleep?** (rest in bed) **Say** *So to* **oversleep** *is to sleep more than you normally would.* Draw a vertical line to separate the words *over* and *sleep* in the word *oversleep.* **Say** *We call words that are made of two or more words put together* **compound** *words.*

Say *Now look for another compound word as I read the next sentence.* Read the sentence aloud. **Ask** *Which word in the sentence is a compound word that is made of two words put together?* (downstairs) *What two words make up the word* **downstairs?** (down and stairs) Underline *downstairs.* **Ask** *What is* **down?** (a direction that moves from high to low) *What are* **stairs?** (steps) **Say** *So* **downstairs** *is the place where you go when you walk down the steps.*

CORRECTIVE FEEDBACK

If students have trouble identifying and breaking down compound words, have them draw a vertical line to separate each word in a compound word.

PRACTICE Have students complete Blackline Master 58. **Say** *Read each sentence and look closely at the underlined words. Find the compound word. Circle the letter of the correct answer.*

CORRECTIVE FEEDBACK

If students mistake words with affixes for compound words, make a list of affixes and display it for students to see. Tell students that words that use these prefixes and suffixes are not compound words.

Answers: 1. a   2. a   3. c

Part 2
VOCABULARY

Compound Words

On Sundays, I can oversleep until ten o'clock.

Paul ran downstairs to the garden.

PRACTICE

1. Jeff tried to <u>download</u> a <u>computer</u> <u>program</u>.

           a   **b**   **c**

2. <u>Moonbeams</u> danced <u>softly</u> on the <u>shimmering</u> water.

   a   **b**   **c**

3. In <u>tennis</u>, Nita <u>normally</u> hits her shots with <u>underspin</u>.

   a   **b**   **c**

Compound Words / B

TEACHING FRAME: BLM 59 Say *A compound word is a new word that is formed by joining two smaller words together.* Have students repeat this definition. Then **say** *A compound word often combines the meanings of the smaller words it is made of.*

MODEL Read the first sentence of the teaching frame together and model how to identify compound words. **Say** *I notice two long words in this sentence. The first word is* **doghouse.** Underline the word *doghouse.* **Say Doghouse** *is made of two words,* **dog,** *an animal, and* **house,** *a place to live.* Draw a vertical line to separate *dog* and *house.* **Explain** *The compound word* **doghouse** *means a place for a dog to live. The other compound word I see is* **skylight.** Underline the word *skylight.* **Say Skylight** *is made of the words* **sky,** *which means the open space above, and* **light,** *which means* **brightness.** Draw a vertical line between *sky* and *light.* **Say** *So* **skylight** *means an open space above that lets in brightness.*

Ask *Which words in the second sentence are made of two smaller words?* (sunlight and doorway) Underline the two words. **Ask** *What are the two words that make up each of the compound words?* (sun and light, door and way) Draw vertical lines to separate the compound words.

> **CORRECTIVE FEEDBACK**
>
> If students have trouble dividing compound words into their component words, have them define each component word separately.

PRACTICE Have students complete Blackline Master 59. **Say** *Underline two compound words in each sentence. Then draw a line to divide each word.*

> **CORRECTIVE FEEDBACK**
>
> Give students who have trouble understanding compound words a chance to make their own words. Start with the component words, then ask students to put them together. Have them define the compound words that they made.

Answers: 1. high/way, over/pass 2. book/mark, story/book 3. dinner/time, chop/sticks 4. row/boat, water/fall 5. back/hand, over/power

160 | Compound Words / B | Skills Intervention — Book C

Name _____ Date _____ Instructor _____

Compound Words

> We built a fancy doghouse with a skylight.
>
> Sunlight streams in through the doorway.

PRACTICE

1. The highway had a large overpass.

2. I put a bookmark in the storybook.

3. At dinnertime, I ate with chopsticks.

4. We took the rowboat to the edge of the waterfall.

5. Her backhand shots did not overpower me.

Compound Words / C

TEACHING FRAME: BLM 60 Say *A compound word is a new word that is formed when two smaller words are joined.* Have students repeat the definition. **Say** *The meaning of a compound word is often related to the meanings of the words that it is formed from.*

MODEL Read the first sentence on the teaching frame together. **Say** *This first sentence has some longer words. The first long word is* highlight. *I can break up this word into two smaller words,* high *and* light. Underline *highlight* and draw a vertical line to separate its component words. **Say** High *means* up above *and* light *is a thing that shines. So the compound word* highlight *means something that shines above other things. Next I see the word* bedroom. Underline the word bedroom. *I can split* bedroom *into* bed *and* room, *two words.* Bedroom *is a compound word. Since* bed *is a place to sleep and* room *is a space, I can infer* bedroom *means a space for sleeping.* Draw a vertical line through the component words of *bedroom.*

Say *Now, as you read the next sentence, notice compound words.* Read the sentence aloud. **Ask** *Is* halftime *a compound word?* (yes) *What two words make up* halftime? (half and time) Underline this word and draw a vertical line to divide its two word parts. **Ask** *What other compound words do you see?* (football) *What smaller words make up this word?* (foot and ball) Underline that word and draw a vertical line to divide it.

> **CORRECTIVE FEEDBACK**
>
> If students have trouble identifying compound words, have them define the component words that make up each compound word.

PRACTICE Have students complete Blackline Master 60. **Say** *Read each set of small words. Then circle the letter beside the real compound word.*

> **CORRECTIVE FEEDBACK**
>
> If students cannot identify compound words, have them try to use each word choice in a sentence.

Answers: 1. b 2. a 3. c 4. b 5. a

Compound Words

The highlight of the house was the master bedroom.

At halftime, the football game was tied.

PRACTICE

1. table   under   cloth
   a. undertable   **b.** tablecloth   **c.** undercloth

2. boat   speed   water
   a. speedboat   **b.** speedwater   **c.** waterboat

3. time   first   show
   a. firstshow   **b.** timeshow   **c.** showtime

4. washer   straw   dish
   a. strawwasher   **b.** dishwasher   **c.** dishstraw

5. power   cow   horse
   a. horsepower   **b.** powercow   **c.** horsecow

Antonyms and Synonyms / A

TEACHING FRAME: BLM 61 Act out looking up and down and **say *I am looking upward. I am looking downward. I just looked in opposite directions. Upward and downward *are opposites, or antonyms. Now watch me again.** Act out and **say *I am gazing upward. I am gazing downward.* Ask *What word did I use before that means almost the same thing as gazing?*** (looking) **Gazing and looking are synonyms. They mean almost the same thing. Now listen as I read the first sentence.** Read the first sentence aloud. **Ask *Which word is underlined?*** (frowning) ***Why would you frown?*** (because you're sad) ***What word in the sentence means the opposite of frowning?*** (smiling) Underline it. **Ask *So what are the antonyms in this sentence?*** (frowning and smiling)

Say *Now let's read the next sentence.* Read it aloud. **Ask *Which word is underlined?*** (cold) ***Somewhere in the sentence, there's another word that means almost the same as cold. What is it?*** (frozen) Circle it. **Ask *So what are the synonyms in this sentence?*** (cold and frozen)

CORRECTIVE FEEDBACK

If students have trouble identifying synonyms and antonyms, have them ask themselves: "Which words mean almost the same thing?" "Which words mean the opposite?"

PRACTICE Have students complete Blackline Master 61. **Say *Read each sentence. Find an antonym and a synonym for each underlined word. Circle the letters of the correct answers.***

CORRECTIVE FEEDBACK

If students cannot identify antonyms and synonyms, have them begin by acting out the underlined words.

Answers: 1. c, b   2. a, b

Name _____ Date _____ Instructor _____

Antonyms and Synonyms

On Monday I was <u>frowning</u>, but today I'm smiling.

My hands were <u>cold</u> and my nose was frozen.

PRACTICE

1. The <u>fast</u> rabbit hopped through the garden.

ANTONYM

a. quick   **b.** great   **c.** slow

SYNONYM

a. fat   **b.** speedy   **c.** silly

2. Suddenly, the baby started laughing <u>loudly</u>.

ANTONYM

a. softly   **b.** nicely   **c.** hugely

SYNONYM

a. happily   **b.** noisily   **c.** smartly

Antonyms and Synonyms / B

TEACHING FRAME: BLM 62 Say *Antonyms are words with opposite meanings.* Have students repeat. **Say** *Synonyms are words with the same or almost the same meanings.* Have students repeat. **Say** *To make their writing more interesting, authors often use antonyms and synonyms.*

MODEL Read the first sentence on the teaching frame together. Model identifying antonyms and synonyms. **Say** *There are two words in this sentence with opposite meanings. Stood means the opposite of what?* (sat) **Stood** *and* **sat** *are antonyms.* Circle them. **Say** *There are also two words in this sentence with almost the same meanings. Started and what?* (began) **Started** *and* **began** *mean the same thing. These words are synonyms.* Underline those words. **Say** *If I get confused about the meaning of synonyms and antonyms, I just think,* syn- *means* same, *and* anti- *means* opposite. *Another way to remember is that* syn- *and* same *both start with* s.

Say *Let's read the next sentence and look for antonyms and synonyms.* Read the sentence aloud. **Ask** *Which two words are antonyms?* (man, woman) Circle those words. **Ask** *Which two words are synonyms?* (skinny, thin) Underline those words.

CORRECTIVE FEEDBACK

If students have trouble identifying antonyms and synonyms, have them look at each word in the sentence and ask themselves: "Is there another word that has the opposite meaning?" "Is there a word that has the same or similar meaning?"

PRACTICE Have students complete Blackline Master 62. **Say** *Read each sentence. Find an antonym and a synonym for each underlined word. Circle the letters of the correct answers.*

CORRECTIVE FEEDBACK

If students cannot identify antonyms and synonyms, have them try each answer choice in the sentence and talk about how the meaning changes.

Answers: 1. c, a 2. b, a 3. c, c

Name _____ Date _____ Instructor _____

Antonyms and Synonyms

We stood when the national anthem started, but sat when the game began.

The skinny man walked with the thin woman.

PRACTICE

1. The little boy <u>laughed</u> when his mother tickled him.

ANTONYM

a. chuckled   **b.** yawned   **c.** cried

SYNONYM

a. giggled   **b.** squirmed   **c.** wept

2. My homework was very <u>difficult</u>.

ANTONYM

a. long   **b.** simple   **c.** pleasant

SYNONYM

a. hard   **b.** dangerous   **c.** easy

3. The feather floated <u>lightly</u> to the ground.

ANTONYM

a. faintly   **b.** narrowly   **c.** heavily

SYNONYM

a. happily   **b.** quickly   **c.** softly

Antonyms and Synonyms / C

TEACHING FRAME: BLM 63 Say *Antonyms are words with opposite meanings.* Ask students to repeat. **Say** *Synonyms are words with the same or almost the same meanings.* Ask students to repeat. **Ask** *Who can define* antonym *and give an example? Who can define* synonym *and give an example?*

MODEL Read the first sentence on the teaching frame together. Model identifying antonyms and synonyms. **Say** *Let's look for antonyms and synonyms. But which is which? If I think about word parts, I can always remember. Anti- means opposite. Syn- means same. This sentence has a pair of antonyms. Slim is the opposite of weighty.* Circle those words. **Say** *The writer used antonyms to set up a contrast. There's also a pair of synonyms. A* book *and a* volume *mean the same.* Underline those words. **Say** *Repeating the same word could get boring for the reader, so the writer used synonyms.*

Say *Now, watch for antonyms and synonyms in this next sentence.* Read the sentence aloud. **Ask** *Which two words are antonyms?* (inside and outside) Circle those words. **Ask** *Which two words are synonyms?* (greasy and oily) Underline those words.

> **CORRECTIVE FEEDBACK**
>
> If students have trouble identifying antonyms and synonyms, have them check the sentence word by word, and look for opposite and similar meanings.

PRACTICE Have students complete Blackline Master 63. **Say** *In sentences 1–3, complete each sentence with an antonym for the underlined word. In sentences 4–6, complete each sentence with a synonym for the underlined word.*

> **CORRECTIVE FEEDBACK**
>
> If students mix up antonyms and synonyms, remind them of the meanings of *anti-* and *syn-*. Note that there is more than one correct answer for each item.

Possible Answers: 1. shouted or yelled 2. pretty or beautiful 3. today or tomorrow 4. below or under 5. hi or howdy 6. walked or sauntered

Name _____ Date _____ Instructor _____

Antonyms and Synonyms

This slim book had as much information as that weighty volume.

Greasy, oily stains were inside and outside the mechanic's shirt.

PRACTICE

ANTONYMS

1. The more the boy <u>whispered,</u> the more the girl _____.

2. I think the picture is <u>ugly,</u> but Bob thinks it's _____.

3. We were sad <u>yesterday</u>, but we'll be happy _____.

SYNONYMS

4. I looked for my ball <u>beneath</u> the couch and _____ the chair.

5. Doris said <u>hello</u> to me and I said _____ back.

6. I <u>strolled</u> down the block and _____ right up to my building.

Suffixes / A

TEACHING FRAME: BLM 64 Say *Sometimes you can say the same thing in two different ways, just by changing a few words. Listen. This drink is too full of sugar. This drink is too sugary.* **Ask** *Which one word in the second sentence means full of sugar?* (sugary) *In that word, the base word is sugar. We can add the ending -y to the base word to make a new word that means full of sugar. The ending -y is called a suffix.* Read the first sentence aloud. **Say** *This sentence contains a base word and the same base word with a suffix. What's the base word?* (quick) Underline *quick.* **Ask** *What is the word with a suffix?* (quickly) Underline *quickly.* **Ask** *What's the suffix?* (-ly) Circle the suffix. **Say** *The suffix -ly means in a certain manner. You find out what manner by looking at the base word. So what does quickly mean?* (in a quick manner) *You can pull* quickly *apart to form a base word and a suffix.*

Say *Let's try another base word and a different suffix.* Read the next sentence. **Ask** *Which word is the base word?* (adore) Underline *adore.* *Which word has a suffix?* (adorable) Underline a*dorable.* **Ask** *What is the suffix?* (-able) Circle the suffix. **Say** *The suffix -able means able to be.* **Ask** *What does adorable mean?* (able to be adored)

CORRECTIVE FEEDBACK

If students have trouble recognizing suffixes, have them ask themselves: " Do I see a word that can be pulled apart into a base word and an ending?"

PRACTICE Have students complete Blackline Master 64. **Say** *Read each base word and the meaning under it. Circle the letter of the suffix that will add that meaning to the base word. Then, write the new word on the line.*

CORRECTIVE FEEDBACK

If students cannot use suffixes correctly, review the meanings of the suffixes *-y, -ly, and -able.*

Answers: 1. c, singable 2. a, soapy 3. b, quietly

Suffixes

Quick rabbits jump quickly through the forest.

Who doesn't adore an adorable puppy?

PRACTICE

1. Base Word: sing
   Meaning for New Word: able to be sung
   Suffix:

   a. -y   **b.** -ly   **c.** -able

   _____

2. Base Word: soap
   Meaning for New Word: full of soap
   Suffix:

   a. -y   **b.** -ly   **c.** -able

   _____

3. Base Word: quiet
   Meaning for New Word: in a quiet manner
   Suffix:

   a. -y   **b.** -ly   **c.** -able

   _____

Suffixes / B

TEACHING FRAME: BLM 65 Say *A suffix is a word part added to the end of a base word to change its meaning.* Have students repeat this definition. **Say** *Different suffixes mean different things. If you understand the meaning of a base word and you also understand the meaning of a suffix, you can understand a whole new word: the base word with a suffix at the end.*

MODEL Read the first sentence on the teaching frame together. Model recognizing suffixes. **Say** *I see only one word with an ending in this sentence. The word "thunderous" is made up of the base word thunder and the suffix -ous. It must be related to thunder, but now it has a different meaning.* Underline *thunder* and *thunderous*. Circle the suffix. **Say** *The suffix -ous means* **full of.** *That helps me understand the meaning of* **thunderous.** *It must mean* **full of thunder.**

Say *Let's look at the next sentence and find a word with a suffix. Read the sentence aloud.* **Ask** *Which word has a suffix?* (careful) *Underline careful.* **Ask** *What is the suffix?* (-ful) Circle the suffix. **Ask** *Which word in the sentence is careful related to?* (care) Underline *care.* **Say** *If the suffix -ful means full of, what does careful mean?* (full of care)

CORRECTIVE FEEDBACK

If students have trouble recognizing words with suffixes, ask them to look for base words within longer words.

PRACTICE Have students complete Blackline Master 65. **Say** *Add the base word and suffix together to form a new word, and write it on the line. Then write the meaning of the new word you made.*

CORRECTIVE FEEDBACK

If students have trouble making words with suffixes, have them underline the base word and circle the suffix before they begin to write.

Answers: 1. artful, art 2. thunderous, thunder 3. gladly, glad 4. lemony, lemon 5. countable, counted

Suffixes

The thunder will roar with a thunderous sound.

I need to take care when I promise I'll be careful.

PRACTICE

1. art + ful = _____ = full of _____

2. thunder + ous = _____ = full of _____

3. glad + ly = _____ = in a _____ manner

4. lemon + y = _____ = full of _____

5. count + able = _____ = able to be _____

Suffixes / C

TEACHING FRAME: BLM 66 **Say** *A suffix is a word part added to the end of a base word to change its meaning.* Have students repeat. **Ask** *Who can give me an example of a word with a suffix?* **Say** *If you want to increase your vocabulary, understanding the meanings of base words and suffixes is very useful.*

MODEL Read the first sentence on the teaching frame together. Model identifying words with suffixes. **Say** *I know a suffix will usually add a syllable, so I'm going to start by looking for two-syllable words. Then I'll find a base word and an ending. The first word is* **thoughtless.** Underline *thoughtless.* **Say** *I can find the base word* **thought** *and the suffix* **-less.** Circle the suffix. **Say** *I know that the suffix* **-less** *means* **without,** *so I know that* **thoughtless** *means* **without thought.** *Now here's* **speaker.** Underline *speaker.* **Say** *This word contains* **speak,** *which is a base word and* **-er,** *which is a suffix.* Circle the suffix. **Say** *Since I know that* **-er** *means a person who does something, I know that a* **speaker** *is a person who speaks.*

Say *Let's find suffixes in the next sentence.* Read the sentence aloud. **Ask** *What's the first word with a suffix?* (nervous) *What is the suffix?* (-ous) Underline *nervous* and circle the suffix. **Say** *In this case, the base word is* **nerve,** *but when the suffix is added, the* **e** *is dropped. If* **-ous** *means* **full of,** *what does* **nervous** *mean?* (full of nerves) **Ask** *Do you see any other words with suffixes?* (sailor) **Ask** *What is the suffix?* (-or) Circle the suffix.

> **CORRECTIVE FEEDBACK**
>
> If students have trouble defining words with suffixes, have them first find the base word. If needed, review the definitions of each suffix.

PRACTICE Have students complete Blackline Master 66. **Say** *Read each meaning. Then use the list of suffixes to write a word that has that meaning.*

> **CORRECTIVE FEEDBACK**
>
> If students cannot build words with suffixes, have them identify the base word, then add each suffix and discuss the meaning of the new word.

Answers: 1. *nicely* 2. *traveler* 3. *bendable* 4. *hopeful* 5. *shapeless* 6. *agreement*

Suffixes

A thoughtless speaker can say things that hurt.

A nervous sailor can still be taught.

PRACTICE

Suffixes:	-ly	-er	-able	-less	-ment	-ful

1. in a **nice** manner = _____

2. a person who **travels** = _____

3. able to **bend** = _____

4. full of **hope** = _____

5. without **shape** = _____

6. result of **agreeing** = _____

Prefixes / A

TEACHING FRAME: BLM 67 **Say** *Listen to these two sentences: I am worried about my homework. I am unworried about my homework.* **Ask** *Are those sentences about the same feeling or opposite feelings?* (opposite) *Which word did you hear that meant the opposite of worried?* (unworried) *In that word,* worried *is called the base word. A special beginning is added to the base word to make a new word that means the opposite of. That beginning is un-. A beginning like un- that changes the meaning of a base word is called a prefix. Now listen as I read the first sentence.* Read it aloud. **Say** *This sentence contains a base word and the same base word with a prefix. What's the base word?* (read) Underline *read.* **Ask** *What's the word with a prefix?* (reread). Underline *reread.* **Ask** *What do you think the prefix is?* (re-) Circle it. **Say** *Re- is a prefix that means* again. *So what does reread mean?* (read again)

Say *Now let's look at the next sentence.* Read it aloud. **Ask** *Which word is the base word?* (sure) Underline *sure.* **Ask** *Which word has a prefix?* (unsure) Underline *unsure.* **Ask** *What's the prefix?* (un-) Circle it. **Ask** *What does unsure mean?* (the opposite of sure)

CORRECTIVE FEEDBACK

If students have trouble recognizing prefixes, have them ask themselves: "Do I see a word that can be divided into a base word and a special beginning?"

PRACTICE Have students complete Blackline Master 67. **Say** *Read each base word and meaning. Circle the prefix you'll need to use to get the meaning. Then use the base word and the prefix to write a new word that has the meaning.*

CORRECTIVE FEEDBACK

If students cannot use prefixes correctly, review the meanings of the prefixes *re-* and *un-*.

Answers: 1. a, unaware 2. b, reopen 3. a, unworried

Name _____ Date _____ Instructor _____

Prefixes

When I read a book I really like, I want to reread it right away.

Sam is sure he will like the movie, but he's unsure whether Tom will.

PRACTICE

1. Base Word: aware
Meaning for New Word: the opposite of aware
Prefix: (a) un   (b) re

_____

2. Base Word: open
Meaning for New Word: to open again
Prefix: (a) un   (b) re

_____

3. Base Word: worried
Meaning for New Word: the opposite of worried
Prefix: (a) un   (b) re

_____

Prefixes / B

TEACHING FRAME: BLM 68 Say *A prefix is a word part added before the beginning of a base word to change its meaning.* Ask students to repeat. **Say** *Different prefixes have different meanings. Understanding the meaning of a prefix helps you understand the meaning of a word with a prefix.*

MODEL Read the first sentence on the teaching frame together. **Say** *I see a base word that appears twice in this sentence, the word agree. The word* **disagree** *is made up of the base word* agree *and the prefix* dis-. *If I know that* **dis-** *means* not, *I can tell what* **disagree** *means. What does it mean?* (not agree) **Disagree** *is related to* agree, *but the prefix changes the meaning.* Underline *agree* and *disagree* and circle the prefix. **Say** *Knowing the prefix and the base word lets me figure out the meaning of a new word I may not have seen before.*

Say *Let's look for a word with a prefix in this next sentence.* Read the sentence aloud. **Ask** *Which word has a prefix?* (recheck) Underline *recheck.* **Ask** *What's the prefix?* (re-) Circle it. **Ask** *Which word in the sentence is* **recheck** *related to?* (check) Underline *check.* **Say** *The prefix* re- *means* again. *So what does* **recheck** *mean?* (check again)

> **CORRECTIVE FEEDBACK**
>
> If students have trouble defining words with prefixes, ask them to define the base word and the prefix separately.

PRACTICE Have students complete Blackline Master 68. **Say** *Separate each word into a prefix and a base word. Then write the meaning of the word.*

> **CORRECTIVE FEEDBACK**
>
> If students have trouble identifying prefixes and base words, have them circle the prefix in each word. After they have defined the prefix, have them combine it with the base word.

Answers: 1. dis + allow, allow 2. un + done, done 3. re + sell, sell 4. dis + trust, trust 5. re + appear, appear

Prefixes

I agree with Mom about our favorite team, but I disagree with Dad.

When I write a letter, I check it for mistakes, then I recheck it for spelling errors.

PRACTICE

1. disallow = _____ + _____ = not _____

2. undone = _____ + _____ = the opposite of _____

3. resell = _____ + _____ = _____ again

4. distrust = _____ + _____ = do not _____

5. reappear = _____ + _____ = _____ again

Prefixes / C

TEACHING FRAME: BLM 69 Say *A prefix is a word part added before the beginning of a base word to change its meaning.* Ask students to repeat. **Ask** *Who can define* prefix? **Say** *Understanding the meanings of base words and prefixes helps you understand new words and increase your vocabulary.*

MODEL Read the first sentence on the teaching frame together. **Say** *This sentence has a few long words. Let me see whether they have a base word and a special beginning.* Underline *incorrect.* **Say** *I can divide this into the base word* correct *and the prefix* in-. Circle the prefix. **Say** in- *means not. So* incorrect *means not correct. I think* unbreakable *has a base word and a prefix.* Underline it and circle *un-. I know that the prefix* un- *means the opposite of or not. So* unbreakable *must mean what?* (not breakable)

Say *Let's watch for prefixes in the next sentence.* Read the sentence aloud. **Ask** *Which words have prefixes?* (disobeyed, reevaluate) Underline the words. *What's the prefix in* disobeyed? (dis) Circle it. **Say** Dis- *means not.* **Ask** *Did Mitch obey his mother?* (no) *What's the prefix in* rethink? (re). Circle it. **Say** Re- *means again. So what does Mitch have to do about his behavior?* (He needs to think about it again.)

> ### CORRECTIVE FEEDBACK
>
> If students have trouble defining words with prefixes, have them first identify the base word in each word. Then ask them to find the prefix and define it.

PRACTICE Have students complete Blackline Master 69. **Say** *Read each sentence. On the first lines provided, write the prefix and base word. Then write what the new word means.*

> ### CORRECTIVE FEEDBACK
>
> If students cannot use prefixes correctly, have them begin by identifying the base word from which each new word will be built. (excite, please, multiply, complete, discover)

Answers: 1. unexciting, not exciting 2. displeased, not pleased 3. remultiply, multiply again 4. incomplete, not complete 5. rediscovered, discovered again

Name _____ Date _____ Instructor _____

Prefixes

Chrissy is incorrect in thinking that her skateboard is unbreakable.

When Mitch disobeyed Mom, she said he should rethink his behavior.

PRACTICE

1. I was very bored because the movie was unexciting.

_____ _____ means _____

2. My dog was displeased that I wouldn't let her jump on the sofa.

_____ _____ means _____

3. Jerry had to remultiply the math problem when he got it wrong.

_____ _____ means _____

4. A visit to Grandma's is incomplete until we have homemade pie.

_____ _____ means _____

5. Dad rediscovered soccer when I joined a league.

_____ _____ means _____

Multiple-Meaning Words / A

TEACHING FRAME: BLM 70 Say *Listen to these two sentences and see if you can hear words that sound the same: The duck was swimming in the water. When people throw snowballs, I always duck.* **Ask** *Which words sound the same?* (duck and duck) *But do they mean the same thing?* (no) *In the first sentence, the word* duck *means a swimming bird. In the second sentence, the word* duck *means bend down quickly. Both words are spelled exactly alike, but they mean completely different things. Now let's look at this first pair of sentences.* Read them aloud. **Ask** *Which words sound the same?* (ship and ship) Circle those words. **Ask** *Which sentence uses the word* ship *that means boat?* (the first sentence) **Say** *Yes, and there's a clue in the sentence: the word* sailed. Underline *sailed.* **Say** *This lets you know that a ship is something that sails.* **Ask** *What is the meaning of* ship *in the second sentence?* (mail) **Say** *Good. The clue phrase is* **U.S. mail.** Underline it.

Say *Now let's look at the next pair of sentences.* Read them aloud. **Ask** *Which are the words with more than one meaning?* (type, type) Circle those words. **Ask** *Which sentence refers to entering letters on a computer screen?* (the second) **Ask** *What clue words help you know?* (e-mail and keyboard) Underline those words. **Ask** *What does* type *mean in the first sentence? How do you know?* (*kinds* is a clue word) Underline *kinds*.

CORRECTIVE FEEDBACK

If students have trouble identifying multiple-meaning words, have them ask themselves: "Which words sound and look the same?"

PRACTICE Have students complete Blackline Master 70. **Say** *Read each sentence. Circle the letter of the meaning that matches each underlined word.*

CORRECTIVE FEEDBACK

If students cannot define multiple-meaning words, help them identify and underline clues in the sentences.

Answers: 1. b 2. a 3. c

Multiple-Meaning Words

As the ship sailed away, we waved goodbye.

I will ship your birthday present by the U.S. mail.

I know many kinds of dogs, but I don't know what type that one is.

My father likes to type his e-mail holding the keyboard in his lap.

PRACTICE

1. The <u>bat</u> flew out of the cave.

    a. stick for hitting a baseball
    b. mammal with wings
    c. blink of an eye

2. The <u>band</u> played a song I really liked.

    a. group of musicians
    b. plain ring
    c. flat ribbon

3. I ate the peach and threw the <u>pit</u> away.

    a. deep hole
    b. dent in a surface
    c. stone of a fruit

Multiple-Meaning Words / B

TEACHING FRAME: BLM 71 Say *Multiple-meaning words are spelled the same but have different meanings.* Ask students to repeat. **Say** *Multiple-meaning words may be pronounced the same or differently. To know which meaning is intended, the reader must look at the sentence for clues.*

MODEL Read the first sentence pair on the teaching frame together. **Say** *I see and hear the word charge in each sentence.* Circle *charge* in both. **Say** *But clearly it doesn't mean the same thing. In the first sentence,* **charge** *is used as a noun, or thing. I know the charge is only ten cents.* Underline the clue *only ten cents.* **Say** *In the second sentence,* **charge** *is used as a verb, something a bull does that makes me run.* Underline the clues *bull* and *I ran.* **Say** *The clues that I've underlined give me enough information to make a good guess about the different meanings. In the first sentence,* **charge** *must mean something like cost. In the second sentence, it must mean something like* **rush** *or* **attack.**

Say *Let's look for multiple-meaning words in the next pair of sentences.* Read the sentences aloud. **Ask** *Which word has two meanings?* (utter) Circle *utter* in both sentences. **Ask** *What does* **utter** *mean in the first sentence?* (say) **Ask** *What does* **utter** *mean in the second sentence?* (total or complete)

> **CORRECTIVE FEEDBACK**
>
> If students have trouble defining multiple-meaning words, have them underline clues in the sentence.

PRACTICE Have students complete Blackline Master 71. **Say** *Match each underlined word with its definition. Write the letter on the line.*

> **CORRECTIVE FEEDBACK**
>
> If students have trouble defining multiple-meaning words, ask them to underline clues in each sentence. Then have them substitute each answer choice for the underlined word and discuss the meaning of the sentence.

Answers: 1. b   2. d   3. e   4. c   5. a   6. f

Name _____ Date _____ Instructor _____

Multiple-Meaning Words

The charge for the phone call was only ten cents.

The bull began to charge directly at me, so I ran.

I never utter a bad word, even when I'm angry.

The movie was an utter bore, a total dud.

PRACTICE

____ **1.** Ramon hit the <u>ball</u> into the bleachers.

____ **2.** I think that flower is very <u>pretty</u>.

____ **3.** Cinderella danced all night at the <u>ball</u>.

____ **4.** I will <u>crack</u> the code and solve the puzzle.

____ **5.** I can sing <u>pretty</u> well if I know the tune.

____ **6.** The mirror had a <u>crack</u> because it fell.

a. fairly

b. round object used in games

c. figure out

d. attractive

e. large formal party

f. break, flaw

Multiple-Meaning Words / C

TEACHING FRAME: BLM 72 **Say** *Multiple-meaning words are spelled the same but have different meanings.* Ask students to repeat. **Ask** *Who can define multiple-meaning words and give me an example?* **Say** *You can usually tell the meaning of words you don't know by looking at their context, the other words and phrases around them.*

MODEL Read the first sentence pair on the teaching frame together. **Say** *Both sentences use the word* **perch,** *but I can see that the words mean different things.* Circle *perch* in both sentences. *In the first sentence,* **perch** *is a noun or thing. It's something my parents caught when they were fishing.* Underline *fishing* and *caught*. **Say** *I can guess from the context that* **perch** *is a kind of fish. In the second sentence,* **perch** *is used as a verb or action word. It's something resting birds might do on branches and telephone poles.* Underline *resting, tree branches,* and *telephone poles*. **Say** *My guess is that* **perch** *means sit.*

Say *Now let's look for multiple-meaning words in the next pair of sentences.* Read the sentences aloud. **Ask** *What is the multiple-meaning word?* (toll) *What does* **toll** *mean in the first sentence?* (cost or fee to travel) *How do you know?* (the context says *paid* and *allowed to cross*) *What does* **toll** *mean in the second sentence?* (ring) *How do you know?* (the context says *bells* and *loudly*)

> **CORRECTIVE FEEDBACK**
>
> If students have trouble defining multiple-meaning words, ask them to identify the part of speech of the word in question, and then find context clues.

PRACTICE Have students complete Blackline Master 72. **Say** *Read each sentence. Then complete the definition of the underlined word.*

> **CORRECTIVE FEEDBACK**
>
> If students have trouble defining multiple-meaning words, have them begin by underlining the context clues in each sentence.

Possible Answers: 1. make a dog's loud sound 2. outside layer of a tree 3. intelligent 4. hurt 5. a kind of book 6. new

Name _____ Date _____ Instructor _____

Multiple-Meaning Words

My parents went fishing and caught a huge perch.

Resting birds perch on tree branches or even telephone poles.

We paid the toll and were allowed to cross the bridge.

The bells will toll loudly tonight.

PRACTICE

1. My dogs sometimes <u>bark</u> and growl at each other.
Bark means _____.

2. The <u>bark</u> of the tree was covered in sap.
Bark means _____.

3. It takes a <u>smart</u> person to do well on this test.
Smart means _____.

4. The needle may <u>smart</u>, but you'll only feel pain for a second.
Smart means _____.

5. You can't tell if the <u>novel</u> has a good story until you read it.
Novel means _____.

6. That's a <u>novel</u> idea, since nobody has thought of it before.
Novel means _____.

Root Words / A

TEACHING FRAME: BLM 73 **Say** *Listen to these words:* telephone, television, telescope. **Ask** *What do they all have in common?* (They all contain the word part *tele*.) **Say** *These words all have the same root.* **Tele** *is a Greek root that means far. A telephone is an instrument that carries voices far. A television is a device that carries pictures far. Since we know that the root* **tele** *means far, we have a good clue to the meaning of telescope.* **Ask** *If I tell you that* **scope** *means an instrument for viewing, what's a telescope?* (an instrument for viewing far) **Say** *Knowing the meanings of roots can help you figure out what longer words mean. Now read along as I read the first sentence.* Read it aloud, and underline *telegraph.* **Say** *The word* **telegraph** *comes from two roots.* Circle tele and graph. **Say graph** *is a root meaning writing.* **Ask** *So a telegraph is for what?* (writing far) **Say** *If I saw a big word like* **telegraph,** *and had trouble defining it, I could think of other words with the same root. Recognizing roots in words that I know helps me understand words I've never seen before.*

Say *Now let's look at the next sentence.* Read it aloud. **Ask** *Do you see a long word with a root we just discussed? Which word is it, and what's the root?* (biography, graph) Underline the word and circle *graphy.* **Say** *We already know that* **graph** *means writing.* **Ask** *Now what if I tell you that* **bio** *means life? What's a biography?* (life writing) **Say** *A biography is a story about a person's life.*

CORRECTIVE FEEDBACK

If students have trouble using roots to define a word, have them practice taking the words apart and defining each root separately.

PRACTICE Have students complete Blackline Master 73. **Say** *Read the root and its meaning. Then circle the letter of the word that contains that root.*

CORRECTIVE FEEDBACK

If students cannot define words using roots, help them define the roots and then discuss the meaning of the word.

Answers: 1. c 2. a 3. b

Root Words

Before the days of e-mail, people used a telegraph.

My favorite kind of book to read is a biography.

PRACTICE

1. *aqua:* "water"

 a. sailor

 b. dolphin

 c. aquarium

2. *phon:* "sound"

 a. earphones

 b. loudness

 c. music

3. *meter:* "measure"

 a. yard

 b. thermometer

 c. distance

Root Words / B

Part 2 VOCABULARY

TEACHING FRAME: BLM 74 Say *Many English words are based on Greek or Latin words. The original Greek or Latin word is called the root of the English word.* Have students repeat. **Say** *Sometimes, a number of English words share a common root. We say that those words are part of a word family.*

MODEL Read the first sentence on the teaching frame together. **Say** *I see two words that are part of a word family.* **Ask** *Can you tell me what they are?* (aquatic and aquarium) Underline them. **Say** *Aquatic and aquarium both come from the same root. When I look in the dictionary, I discover that* aqua *is a Latin word meaning* water. *Even if I didn't know that, I might be able to get an idea of what* aquatic *means if I know what* aquarium *means. So when I recognize a root from a word I already know, I'm on my way to being able to figure out the meanings of new words.*

Say *Let's look in the next sentence for words that are in the same word family.* Read the second sentence aloud. **Ask** *Which words share a common root?* (communication, community) Underline them. **Say** *These words share the Latin root* communis *which means* common *or* for all. **Communication** *is speaking in common, or to each other.* **Community** *is a place where people live in common.*

CORRECTIVE FEEDBACK

If students have trouble defining unfamiliar words by their roots, have them think of other words they know in the same word family.

PRACTICE Have students complete Blackline Master 74. **Say** *Read each pair of root words and their definitions. Then complete the definition of the underlined word.*

CORRECTIVE FEEDBACK

If students have trouble defining words with roots, have them identify other words in the same word family. Then they can use their understanding of a familiar word to find the meanings of other words.

Answers: 1. sound 2. pressure 3. life 4. half 5. move

Name _____ Date _____ Instructor _____

Root Words

I learned about interesting aquatic creatures at the aquarium.

Saying "hello" is a friendly form of communication in our community.

PRACTICE

1. *tele:* far   *phon:* sound
A <u>telephone</u> is a device for hearing _____ from far away.

2. *baro:* pressure   *meter:* measure
A <u>barometer</u> is an instrument for measuring air _____.

3. *bio:* life   *logy:* study
<u>Biology</u> is the study of _____.

4. *hemi:* half   *sphere:* a round solid, like a globe
The northern <u>hemisphere</u> is the northern _____ of the earth.

5. *auto:* self   *mobile:* move
When it was invented, the <u>automobile</u> seemed to _____ by itself.

Root Words / C

Part 2

VOCABULARY

TEACHING FRAME: BLM 75 Say *Many English words are based on Greek or Latin words. The original Greek or Latin word is called the root of the English word.* Ask students to repeat. **Say** *Sometimes English words share a common root. We say that those words are part of a word family.*

MODEL Read the first sentence on the teaching frame together. **Ask** *Which words have a root in common? What is it?* (rupt) Underline *interrupting* and *rupture*, and circle *rupt* in each. **Say** *If I checked a dictionary, I'd learn that the root* rupt *comes from the Latin word* rumpere, *which means* break. *To* interrupt *is to break in, and to* rupture *is to break apart. I never saw the word* rupture *before, but I knew what* interrupt *meant. I can guess the meaning of the word I don't know from the word I already know.*

Say *Look in the next sentence for words that belong to the same family.* Read the sentence aloud. **Ask** *Which two words share a root?* (telephone and symphony) Underline the words and circle *phon.* **Say** *The Greek root* phon *means* sound. *I already know what a telephone is. It's a device for hearing sound. But what's a symphony? I know it has to do with sound. If I looked in a dictionary, I'd find that* sym- *is a Greek root meaning* together. **Ask** *What could* together-sound *mean?* (music when sounds are played together)

CORRECTIVE FEEDBACK

If students have trouble identifying words in families, have them first look for common roots. Remind them that the spelling may not be exactly the same.

PRACTICE Have students complete Blackline Master 75. **Say** *Read each root and its definition. Then complete the definition of the underlined word.*

CORRECTIVE FEEDBACK

If students have trouble defining words with roots, have them identify other words in the same word family.

Possible Answers: 1. has one horn   2. handmade   3. two languages   4. call together 5. eats flesh   6. the study of measures

---

Name _____ Date _____ Instructor _____

Root Words

> If you keep interrupting me, you'll rupture our friendship.
>
> On the telephone, I told Pat about the beautiful symphony I heard.

PRACTICE

1. *uni:* "one"   *cornis:* "having a horn"
A <u>unicorn</u> is a mythical animal that _____.

2. *manus:* "hand"   *factus:* "made"
In olden times, a <u>manufactured</u> item was _____.

3. *bi:* "two"   *lingua:* "language"
Toshiro is <u>bilingual</u>; he speaks _____.

4. *con:* "together"   *vocare:* "to call"
To <u>convoke</u> a meeting is to _____.

5. *carni:* "flesh"   *vorare:* "to eat"
A <u>carnivore</u> is an animal that _____.

6. *metron:* "measure"   *logy:* "the study of"
<u>Metrology</u> is _____.

Figurative Language / A

TEACHING FRAME: BLM 76 **Say** *Listen to these two sentences. The tall building has a wooden door. The building is a monster whose wooden door is like its mouth.* **Ask** *Which one paints a more interesting picture in your mind?* **Say** *The second sentence uses figurative language. Figurative language paints a picture. Writers use it to make their work more interesting. Obviously, we know that the building isn't really a monster. But it's much more interesting to say the building is a monster than just a tall building. When we compare the building to a monster, we are using a metaphor. When we use like or as to compare— the wooden door is like its mouth—we are using a simile. Metaphors and similes are examples of figurative language.* **Say** *Now let's read the first pair of sentences.* Read them aloud. **Ask** *Which sentence paints a picture in your mind?* (the second one) *What is the package compared to?* (a house) Underline *package* and *house*. **Ask** *Does the comparison contain the word* like *or* as? (yes) Circle *as.* **Ask** *What is that kind of figurative language called?* (a simile)

Say *Let's read the next pair of sentences.* Read them aloud. **Ask** *Which sentence uses figurative language?* (the second one) *What is the moon compared to?* (a balloon) Underline *moon* and *balloon.* **Ask** *Is this a simile or a metaphor? (metaphor)*

CORRECTIVE FEEDBACK

If students cannot differentiate similes from metaphors, remind them that a simile includes the word *like* or *as*.

PRACTICE Have students complete Blackline Master 76. **Say** *Look for the figurative language in each sentence. Circle the letter to show which kind of figurative language is used.*

CORRECTIVE FEEDBACK

If students cannot identify the type of figurative language used, have them circle the things that are being compared and then look for *like* or *as*.

Answers: 1. a 2. a 3. b

Name _____ Date _____ Instructor _____

Figurative Language

That package is pretty big.

That package is as big as a house.

The moon is yellow and round.

The moon is a big, white balloon.

PRACTICE

1. My best friend is as slow as a turtle.

    a. simile   **b.** metaphor

2. The salad is like a garden in my plate.

    a. simile   **b.** metaphor

3. Bob's homework was a nightmare.

    a. simile   **b.** metaphor

Figurative Language / B

TEACHING FRAME: BLM 77 Say *Figurative language is used to add interest to writing. There are different kinds of figurative language. A metaphor compares one unlike thing to another.* Have students repeat. *A simile uses the word like or as to compare one unlike thing to another.* Have students repeat. *An idiom is a phrase whose meaning does not come directly from its words.* Have students repeat. **Say** *Listen to these examples: That boy's voice is a squeaky door, is a metaphor. This boy's voice is as sweet as syrup, is a simile. I have a frog in my throat, is an idiom. The sentence means that my voice is hoarse.*

MODEL Read the first sentence pair on the teaching frame together. **Say** *The second sentence paints a vivid picture of how Carmen swims. She's compared to a fish.* Underline *Carmen* and *fish.* **Say** *Notice that the word like is used.* Circle *like.* **Say** *This is an example of a simile.*

Say *Let's look for figurative language in the next pair of sentences.* Read them aloud. **Ask** *Which sentence contains figurative language?* (the second sentence) *Which phrase is figurative?* (join hands) *What kind of figurative language is this?* (idiom)

CORRECTIVE FEEDBACK

If students have trouble identifying figurative language, have them ask themselves, "Does this language compare two unlike things? Does it use *like* or *as*? Does this language mean something different than the words would normally mean?"

PRACTICE Have students complete Blackline Master 74. **Say** *Read the sentence. Look at the underlined figurative language in each sentence. Circle the letter to show which kind of figurative language is used.*

CORRECTIVE FEEDBACK

If students cannot identify the type of figurative language, ask them to test it against the definitions given above. Have students look at the underlined phrase and look for key words such as: *as, like, is,* and *are.*

Answers: 1. c 2. a 3. a 4. b 5. c

Figurative Language

Carmen swims extremely well.

Carmen swims like a fish.

Why don't we work together on this project?

Why don't we join hands on this project?

PRACTICE

1. Billy may get angry, but he never <u>loses his head</u> completely.

    a. simile   **b.** metaphor   **c.** idiom

2. The tree stood <u>like a proud giant</u> in his yard.

    a. simile   **b.** metaphor   **c.** idiom

3. Behind her glasses, my grandma's eyes are <u>as blue as the sky</u>.

    a. simile   **b.** metaphor   **c.** idiom

4. My brother runs slowly, but my sister <u>is a rocket</u>.

    a. simile   **b.** metaphor   **c.** idiom

5. I'm not sure what to do, so I'll <u>play it by ear</u>.

    a. simile   **b.** metaphor   **c.** idiom

Figurative Language / C

TEACHING FRAME: BLM 78 Say *Figurative language is used to add interest to writing. There are different kinds of figurative language. A metaphor compares one unlike thing to another.* Have students repeat. *A simile uses the word* like *or* as *to compare unlike things.* Have students repeat. *An idiom is a phrase whose meaning does not come directly from its words.* Have students repeat. *Personification gives human qualities to something that is not human.* Have students repeat.

MODEL Read the first sentence pair on the teaching frame together. **Say** *The second sentence is more interesting because it uses figurative language.* Underline *lost my heart to.* **Say** *This doesn't mean that I couldn't find my heart. It must be an idiom that means I began to love the puppy.*

Say *Let's look for figurative language in the next pair of sentences.* Read them aloud. **Ask** *Which sentence uses figurative language?* (the second one) *What is the phrase that is figurative?* (sang "Wake up, Sleepyhead!") Underline that phrase. **Ask** *What kind of figurative language is this?* (personification) **Ask** *How do you know?* (The sun doesn't sing, only a person does.)

CORRECTIVE FEEDBACK

If students have trouble explaining why this is personification, ask them to repeat the definitions above, and test which one fits the sentence.

PRACTICE Have students complete Blackline Master 75. **Say** *Read the underlined phrase. Identify it as a simile (S), metaphor (M), idiom (I), or personification (P). Then tell what the phrase means.*

CORRECTIVE FEEDBACK

If students have trouble completing the chart, have them write the definitions for the types of figurative language on a sheet of paper and use is a guide.

Possible Answers: 1. P, blew softly and put me to sleep 2. S, told many times before 3. I, quickly 4. S, refreshing 5. M, big and tall 6. I, a lot of money

Figurative Language

The puppy was so cute that I loved it immediately.

The puppy was so cute that I lost my heart to it.

The sun outside my window woke me up.

The sun outside my window sang "Wake up, Sleepyhead!"

PRACTICE

PHRASE	TYPE OF FIGURATIVE LANGUAGE (S, M, I, P)	MEANING
1. The evening breeze whispered a lullaby.		
2. The story was as old as a dinosaur.		
3. In the wink of an eye, I completed my homework.		
4. That nap was like a cool drink of water on a hot day.		
5. The man coming toward us was a mountain.		
6. My father says his new car cost an arm and a leg.		

Denotation and Connotation / A

TEACHING FRAME: BLM 79 Say *Listen as I read two sentences. Think about the difference between the two: His gift was fancy. His gift was wasteful. Which sentence puts the gift in a positive light?* (the first) *Which puts the gift in a negative light?* (the second) **Say** *Both* **fancy** *and* **wasteful** *suggest extreme expense. However, the two words have very different tones.* **Fancy** *has a positive feeling, and* **wasteful** *has a negative feeling. Now let's read the first pair of sentences.* Read the first sentence pair aloud. **Ask** *What is the meaning that the underlined words share?* (They both mean *new.*) *Which word has a positive feeling?* (fresh) *Which word has a negative feeling?* (inexperienced) **Say** *Fresh* *makes you think of students who are eager.* **Inexperienced** *makes you think of students who know very little. Understanding that some words set a tone or feeling helps you pick which synonym to use as you write.*

Say *Now try the second pair of sentences.* Read the sentence pair. **Ask** *What denotation do the underlined words share?* (They mean *asked for.*) *Which word has a positive connotation?* (requested) *Which word has a negative connotation?* (demanded)

CORRECTIVE FEEDBACK

If students have difficulty labeling words as positive or negative, ask: "What do you picture when you hear this word?"

PRACTICE Have students complete Blackline Master 79. **Say** *Read each sentence pair. Identify the underlined word as positive or negative. Circle the correct answer.*

CORRECTIVE FEEDBACK

If students cannot identify words as positive or negative, have them begin by asking themselves: "What do I picture when I hear this word?" or "How do I feel when I hear this word?"

Answers: 1. positive, negative   2. negative, positive   3. positive, negative

Denotation and Connotation

A <u>fresh</u> batch of students joined the class.

An <u>inexperienced</u> batch of students joined the class.

She <u>requested</u> some more information.

She <u>demanded</u> some more information.

PRACTICE

1. She <u>posed</u> on the diving board.   positive   negative

She <u>teetered</u> on the diving board.   positive   negative

2. Thomas <u>hissed</u> to his friend.   positive   negative

Thomas <u>whispered</u> to his friend.   positive   negative

3. She sat <u>delicately</u> on the sofa.   positive   negative

She sat <u>weakly</u> on the sofa.   positive   negative

Denotation and Connotation / B

TEACHING FRAME: BLM 80 Say *A word's denotation is its dictionary meaning.* Have students repeat. **Say** *A word's connotation is your personal response to the word.* Have students repeat. **Say** *Knowing the connotations of a word, or how a word makes a reader feel, helps you choose the correct synonym to use when you write.*

MODEL Read the first sentence pair on the teaching frame together. **Say** *The underlined words share a denotation, or meaning. They both mean* **playful.** *However, I would think a frisky dog was better behaved than a mischievous dog. I picture a frisky dog as running around happily. I picture a mischievous dog as getting into trouble. Frisky has a positive connotation, or feeling, to me.* **Mischievous** *has a negative connotation.*

Say *Now look at the second sentence pair.* Read the sentence pair aloud. **Ask** *What is the shared denotation, or meaning, of the underlined words?* (They mean *excitedly.*) **Ask** *Which word has a positive connotation?* (eagerly) *Which word has a negative connotation?* (anxiously)

CORRECTIVE FEEDBACK

If students have trouble identifying positive and negative connotations, ask them to picture in their minds the situation described by each sentence.

PRACTICE Have students complete Blackline Master 80. **Say** *Read each word pair and its shared denotation. Then identify the connotation of each word in the pair. Write* positive *or* negative *after each letter.*

CORRECTIVE FEEDBACK

If students cannot identify words as positive or negative, have them use each word in a sentence and talk about its meaning. If they do not know the word's meaning, give a definition and model using the word in a sentence.

Answers: 1. a positive b negative 2. a negative b positive 3. a positive b negative 4. a positive b negative 5. a negative b positive

Part 2 VOCABULARY

Name _____ Date _____ Instructor _____

Denotation and Connotation

My dog is unusually <u>frisky</u>.

My dog is unusually <u>mischievous</u>.

He jumps <u>eagerly</u> when I arrive home.

He jumps <u>anxiously</u> when I arrive home.

PRACTICE

WORDS	SHARED DENOTATION	CONNOTATIONS
I. a. fragrant **b.** rancid	scented	**a.** **b.**
2. a. submissive **b.** loyal	obedient	**a.** **b.**
3. a. merry **b.** hysterical	happy	**a.** **b.**
4. a. studious **b.** pondering	thoughtful	**a.** **b.**
5. a. arrogant **b.** proud	self-satisfied	**a.** **b.**

Denotation and Connotation / C

TEACHING FRAME: BLM 81 Say *A word's denotation is its dictionary definition.* Have students repeat. *A word's connotation is your personal response to the word, or the way it makes you feel.* Have students repeat. **Say** *Understanding the connotations of a different word can help you choose the correct synonym to use when writing or speaking.*

MODEL Read the first sentence pair on the teaching frame together. **Say** *The underlined words share a denotation. Both of them mean* calmed down. *However, the two sentences feel very different.* Appeased *has a connotation of* calming with soothing words or actions. *It is a fairly positive word.* Repressed *has a negative connotation. The police in these two sentences behaved differently. I might use the first sentence to describe a scene. I might use the second sentence to describe an action involving force.*

Say *Let's look at the next sentence pair.* Read the sentence pair aloud. **Ask** *What is the shared denotation of the underlined words?* (They mean *excitedly* or *emotionally*.) **Which word has a positive connotation?** (enthusiastically) **Which word has a negative connotation?** (zealously)

CORRECTIVE FEEDBACK

If students have trouble identifying positive and negative connotations, ask them to describe the image they get from reading each sentence.

PRACTICE Have students complete Blackline Master 81. **Say** *Read each word pair. Write the shared denotation. Then identify the connotation of each word in the pair. Write* positive *or* negative *after each letter.*

CORRECTIVE FEEDBACK

If students cannot identify denotation and connotation, help them use each word in a sentence.

Possible Answers: 1. inviting a positive b negative 2. slowly a negative b positive 3. flattering a positive b negative 4. constant a negative b positive 5. clever a negative b positive

Denotation and Connotation

The police quickly appeased the angry crowd.

The police quickly repressed the angry crowd.

One man spoke enthusiastically into the microphone.

One man spoke zealously into the microphone.

PRACTICE

WORDS	SHARED DENOTATION	CONNOTATIONS
1. a. appealing **b.** tempting		**a.** **b.**
2. a. lazily **b.** leisurely		**a.** **b.**
3. a. complimentary **b.** fawning		**a.** **b.**
4. a. pesky **b.** steady		**a.** **b.**
5. a. shrewd **b.** quick-witted		**a.** **b.**

Analogies / A

TEACHING FRAME: BLM 82 Ask *How are these words related:* slow, fast? (They are antonyms.) *How are these words related:* big, huge? (They are synonyms.) *How are these words related:* arm, elbow? (An elbow is part of an arm.) **Say** *Analogies are used to compare the relationships between words. Words might be antonyms, synonyms, or have some other relationship. Listen as I read the first analogy.* Read the first sentence aloud. **Ask** *What are the first two underlined words?* (go and stop) Circle those words. **Ask** *How are they related?* (They are antonyms.) Draw an arrow to connect *go* and *stop*. *What is the third underlined word?* (awake) **Say** *In order to complete this analogy, we need to find a word that has the same relationship to awake that stop has to go. In other words, we need to find a word that is the antonym for awake. What is a possible answer?* (asleep) Write *asleep* in the blank. **Say** *The completed analogy should read:* <u>Go</u> *is to* <u>stop</u> *as* <u>awake</u> *is to* <u>asleep</u>.

Say *Now try the second analogy.* Read the sentence. **Ask** *How are the first two underlined words related?* (A toe is part of a foot.) *What word might complete the analogy?* (hand) Write *hand* in the blank. **Say** *So toe is to foot as* finger *is to* hand. *A* <u>toe</u> *is part of a* <u>foot,</u> *and a* <u>finger</u> *is part of a* <u>hand</u>.

CORRECTIVE FEEDBACK

If students have trouble completing the analogy, have them circle the first two underlined words and draw an arrow to connect them.

PRACTICE Have students complete Blackline Master 82. **Say** *Complete each analogy. Circle the letters of each correct answer.*

CORRECTIVE FEEDBACK

If students cannot complete analogies, have them begin by asking: "How are the first two underlined words related?" Have them try each answer choice. For problem 1 **ask** *is pretty a synonym for hideous? Do they mean the same thing?* Continue with the other answer choices and the other problems.

Answers: 1. b 2. a 3. c

Analogies

Go is to stop as awake is to _____.

Toe is to foot as finger is to _____.

PRACTICE

1. Lovely is to beautiful as hideous is to

   a. pretty   **b.** ugly   **c.** delicious

2. Mug is to handle as purse is to

   a. strap   **b.** open   **c.** clothing

3. Fat is to skinny as wide is to

   a. whole   **b.** broad   **c.** narrow

Analogies / B

TEACHING FRAME: BLM 83 Say *An analogy compares the relationships, or connections, between two pairs of words.* Have students repeat. **Say** *A pair of words in an analogy may be related in different ways. They may be antonyms or synonyms. They may have a part-whole relationship. To decide what the connection is, you need to ask: "How are these words related?"*

MODEL Read the first analogy in the teaching frame together. **Say** *I need to figure out what the relationship between the first pair of underlined words is. I ask myself, "How is pencil related to write?" Well, you use a pencil to write. The first word names an object, and the second word names its use. This relationship should hold true for the second pair of words. You use a pencil to write, and you use a ruler to measure.* Write *measure* in the blank. **Say** *Pencil and write have the same relationship that ruler and measure do. You use a pencil to write, and you use a ruler to measure.*

Say *Now try to complete the next analogy.* Read the analogy aloud. **Ask** *What is the relationship between the first two underlined words?* (A tabby is a kind of cat.) **Ask** *What word has the same relationship to spaniel that cat has to tabby?* (dog) Write *dog* in the blank.

CORRECTIVE FEEDBACK

If students have trouble completing the analogy, have them restate it using the structure: "A tabby is a kind of cat. A spaniel is a kind of _____."

PRACTICE Have students complete Blackline Master 83. **Say** *Think of a word that will complete each analogy. Write it on the line.*

CORRECTIVE FEEDBACK

If students cannot complete analogies, help them define the underlined words. Discuss the relationship between the first two underlined words. Ask questions such as "What do noses do?" to guide students.

Possible Answers: 1. smell 2. full 3. fur 4. utensil or silverware 5. rude

Name _____ Date _____ Instructor _____

Analogies

Pencil is to write as ruler is to _____.

Tabby is to cat as spaniel is to _____.

PRACTICE

1. Mouth is to speak as nose is to _____.

2. Far is to near as empty is to _____.

3. Duck is to feather as bear is to _____.

4. Screwdriver is to tool as fork is to _____.

5. Loud is to raucous as impolite is to _____.

Analogies / C

TEACHING FRAME: BLM 84 Say *An analogy compares the relationships between two pairs of words.* Have students repeat. **Say** *A pair of words in an analogy may be connected in any of several different ways. They may be antonyms or synonyms. They may have a part-whole relationship. One word may name an object, and the other may tell how it's used or who uses it. To find the connection, ask yourself: "How are these words related?"*

MODEL Direct students' attention to the first analogy. **Say** *Analogies may be written with marks like colons. I would read this analogy this way: "Snout is to pig as trunk is to BLANK." I need to figure out the relationship between the words in the first pair. I know that the words in the next pair will have the same relationship. I can ask myself, "If a pig has a snout, what has a trunk?" The answer, is elephant.* Write *elephant* in the blank. **Say** *If an analogy is true, the word pairs will be parallel parts of speech. In this analogy, all the words are nouns.*

Say *Let's try the next analogy.* Read the analogy aloud. **Ask** *What is the relationship between the words in the first pair?* (A gymnast wears a leotard.) **Say** *Now complete the analogy.* (ballerina) Write ballerina in the blank.

> ### CORRECTIVE FEEDBACK
>
> If students have trouble completing the analogy, have them restate it: "If a gymnast wears a leotard, who wears a tutu?"

PRACTICE Have students complete Blackline Master 84. **Say** *Complete each analogy. Circle the letter of the best answer.*

> ### CORRECTIVE FEEDBACK
>
> If students cannot complete analogies, help them define each word. Then have them identify the relationship between the words in the first pair. Remind them to check that the parts of speech are parallel in each pair of words.

Answers: 1. c 2. b 3. c 4. b 5. a 6. c

Name _____ Date _____ Instructor _____

Analogies

> SNOUT : PIG : : trunk : _____
>
> LEOTARD : GYMNAST : : tutu : _____

PRACTICE

1. REMARKABLE : OUTSTANDING : : terrible : _____
   - **a.** fear
   - **b.** outgoing
   - **c.** dreadful

2. FLYSWATTER : SWAT : : spatula : _____
   - **a.** spat
   - **b.** flip
   - **c.** cling

3. EASEL : ARTIST : : steering wheel : _____
   - **a.** soldier
   - **b.** architect
   - **c.** driver

4. LION : MANE : : rooster : _____
   - **a.** crow
   - **b.** comb
   - **c.** claw

5. ORCA : WHALE : : brontosaurus : _____
   - **a.** dinosaur
   - **b.** huge
   - **c.** extinct

6. INCREDIBLE : BELIEVABLE : : dishonest : _____
   - **a.** ridiculous
   - **b.** deceitful
   - **c.** forthright

Study Skills

Book Cover and Table of Contents / A

TEACHING FRAME: BLM 85 Hold up a grade-appropriate chapter book. **Say** *All books have features that make it easy to find information. What information does the cover give?* (the title, the editor or author's and illustrator's names) Open the book, and display the table of contents. **Say** *This is the table of contents. This helps you find a chapter or page that interests you. The table of contents lists the names of chapters and their page numbers. Here's the cover and a page from the same book.* **Ask** *What information does the cover give?* (title, editor, photographers) *What information does the table of contents give?* (the names of chapters and pages where they begin)

MODEL Look at the chart together. **Say** *I'm interested in finding out about giraffes. I can run my finger down the left side of this table of contents to see if there's a chapter about* Giraffes. *Oh, here it is!* Make a checkmark by that chapter title. **Say** *Now that I know there's a chapter, I also want to know the page number it starts on. By sliding my finger across and reading the number, I can see that the chapter begins on page 137.* Circle that page number. **Say** *Now let's look again at the table of contents. Suppose you want to read about elephants. Where would you turn?* (page 61)

> ## CORRECTIVE FEEDBACK
>
> If students have trouble finding information in a table of contents, have them use their fingers to locate the correct chapter and then slide it across to find the page number.

PRACTICE Have students complete Blackline Master 85. **Say** *Use the book cover and table of contents to answer the questions.*

> ## CORRECTIVE FEEDBACK
>
> If students cannot use parts of a book correctly, have them read each question aloud, and tell what kind of answer the question requires— a name, book part, chapter number, or page number.

Answers: 1. Africa's Wonderful Wild Animals 2. took photographs 3. page 3 4. Hyenas 5. chapter 5 6. the index

Name _____ Date _____ Instructor _____

Book Cover and Table of Contents

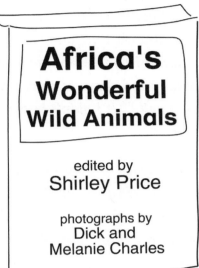

Africa's Wonderful Wild Animals

edited by
Shirley Price

photographs by
Dick and Melanie Charles

Contents

PRACTICE

1. What is the title of the book? _____

2. What did Dick and Melanie Charles do? _____

3. On what page does the introduction begin? _____

4. What would you find beginning on page 123? _____

5. What's the chapter number of the chapter about birds? _____

6. What can you find at the end of the book? _____

Glossary / B

TEACHING FRAME: BLM 86 Say *A glossary is a small dictionary in the back of a book.* Have students repeat. **Ask** *Who can tell me what a glossary is?* **Say** *A glossary tells you the pronunciation and meaning of a word or term as it is used in the book. Glossary words are listed in alphabetical order.*

MODEL Look at the G entries on the teaching chart together. Model using a glossary. **Say** *I see three words listed in alphabetical order under G. Each entry has the word, its definition, its syllable division, its pronunciation, and its part of speech.* Point to each as you mention it. **Say** *Suppose I came upon a word I didn't know: g-a-r-d-e-n-i-a. I could look it up in the glossary and discover that it is used in this book to mean "a white flower with a pleasant smell."" If I didn't know how to say the word, I could check its pronunciation.*

Say *Now, let's say you came across the word goose, which you know is a kind of bird. But in the book, a person is referred to as a goose. What could that mean? Would you find that word before or after gardenia in the glossary?* (after) *This word has two meanings listed because they're both used in the book. But which one are we looking for?* (the second) *What is that meaning of goose?* (a silly person) *What part of speech is the word?* (noun) *What's the plural?* (geese)

CORRECTIVE FEEDBACK

If students have trouble using the glossary, review each part of the entry, one by one. Have students repeat your explanation of each part until they can explain each themselves.

PRACTICE Have students complete Blackline Master 86. **Say** *Use the entries under letters G and H to answer the questions.*

CORRECTIVE FEEDBACK

If students cannot answer the questions, have them begin by identifying the information requested, and pointing to the part of the glossary entry that contains it. Make immediate corrections.

Answers: 1. to decorate 2. adjective 3. hay fever 4. hasty 5. the h 6. between "garnish" and "goose"

Part 2 — STUDY SKILLS

Name _____ Date _____ Instructor _____

Glossary

gardenia | hunch

G
gardenia A white flower with a pleasant smell.
 gar•de•nia (gär dē′nyē) *noun, plural* **gardenias**
garnish To decorate.
 garnish (gär′ nısh) *verb* **garnished, garnishing**
goose (1) A wild bird similar to the duck but larger, and with a longer neck and legs. (2) A silly person.
 goose (go͞os) *noun, plural* **geese**

H
hasty Moving or acting in a hurry.
 ha•sty (hā′ stē) *adjective* **hastier, hastiest**
hay fever Sneezing and runny eyes caused in some people by breathing pollen.
 hay fe•ver (ha′ fē′ vēr) *noun*
herb A plant used for medicine, flavoring, or scent.
 herb (ûrb) *noun, plural* **herbs**

PRACTICE

1. What does *garnish* mean? _____

2. What part of speech is the word *hasty*? _____

3. Which term is made up of more than one word? _____

4. Which word means "moving in a hurry?" _____

5. When you pronounce *herb*, which letter don't you say? _____

6. If you added the word *goldenrod* to this glossary, where would it fit?

_____

Index / C

TEACHING FRAME: BLM 77 **Say** *An index lists a book's major topics in alphabetical order, with page numbers.* Have students repeat. **Ask** *Who can tell me what an index is?* **Say** *You can use an index to locate information quickly by looking up a topic and finding its page number.*

MODEL Look at the first two entries on the Teaching Chart together. Model using an index. **Say** *Two topics found in this book are* **Canada** *and* **Cherokees.** **Cherokees** *comes after* **Canada,** *because the index is in alphabetical order.* **Canada** *is such a big topic in this book that it's divided into three subtopics. I could use this book to learn specifically about French influence in* **Canada,** *or the geography of* **Canada,** *or the history of* **Canada.** *If I wanted to learn just about the geography of* **Canada,** *I would look for that subentry. Then I would read across to find the page numbers. I can learn about the geography of* **Canada** *on page 3 and also on pages 52 through 55.* **Say** *Suppose you wanted to read about* **Frederick Douglass.** *What letter would you look under?* (D) **Why?** (because people are alphabetized by their last names) *Where would you find information in this book about* **Frederick Douglass?** (pages 177-179)

> ## CORRECTIVE FEEDBACK
>
> If students have difficulty using the index, have them first identify and name the major topics before looking for any subtopics. Give students immediate feedback.

PRACTICE Have students complete Blackline Master 87. **Say** *Use the index to answer the questions.*

> ## CORRECTIVE FEEDBACK
>
> If students cannot use the index, have them name the topic they're looking for, and spell it aloud. **Ask** *What is the first letter of the major topic you are looking for?* Then have them run down the list of entries to find the one they want.

Answers: 1. 152   2. 96, 225, 333   3. causes of the Civil War, Canada's opinion of the Civil War, and major battles of the Civil War   4. smallpox and typhoid fever   5. between "Delaware" and "diseases"

Name _____ Date _____ Instructor _____

Index

Canada | Eastern

C
Canada.
  French influence in, 56, 58
  geography of, 3, 52-55
  history of, 56-59, 197
Cherokees, 12-14, 223-224, 300
Civil War, U.S.
  causes of, 195-197
  Canada's opinion of, 197
  major battles of, 198-205

D
Dallas, George M., 152
dance.
  in Canada, 57
  in the U.S. 113, 363, 364
Delaware, 96, 225, 333
diseases.
  smallpox, 247, 250
  typhoid fever, 247-250
Douglass, Frederick, 177-179

PRACTICE

1. On which page would you find information about George M. Dallas?

_____

2. On which pages would you find information about Delaware? _____

3. What three subtopics can you learn about the Civil War from this book?

_____

4. Which diseases are discussed in this book? _____

5. If an entry on *Detroit* were added to this book, between which two entries should it appear?_____

Telephone Directory / A

TEACHING FRAME: BLM 88 Hold up a telephone directory. **Ask** *What would you use this book for?* (to find phone numbers) Show each part of the book as you **say** *This book has two sections. The white pages lists people alphabetically by last name. Next to a person's name, is that person's address and phone number. The yellow pages list businesses alphabetically under categories of business. For example,* **Book Stores** *come before* **Car Rental Agencies.** *If you were looking for your family's phone number, which color pages would you use?* (white) *How would you look it up?* (By our last name)

MODEL Look at the teaching chart together. **Say** *This shows some listings from the white pages and from the yellow pages. What is the first listing from the white pages?* (Betty Bookman) *What is the first listing from the yellow pages?* (Adventure Bookshop) **Say** *I have a friend named* Bob Borden. *I want to find his phone number. I look in the white pages under B. I search the alphabetical listings until I find this one,* Robert L. Borden. *This must be Bob. Now I run my finger across until I find his phone number. It's 555-9402. His address is also listed.*

Say *Now find the phone number of Bob's Book Nook. Which colored pages would you search?* (yellow pages) *Under what category is the store listed?* (Book Stores) *What is the store's phone number?* (555-6060)

CORRECTIVE FEEDBACK

If students have trouble finding the phone number, have them use their fingers or a ruler to read across the listing.

PRACTICE Have students complete Blackline Master 88. **Say** *Use the white and yellow pages to answer the questions.*

CORRECTIVE FEEDBACK

If students cannot answer the questions, have them begin by reading aloud the name, address, and telephone number for each listing.

Answers: 1. 555-1995 2. 3721 Chestnut Dr. 3. Robert L. Borden 4. Bob's Book Nook 5. 555-8888 6. Betty Bookman

Name _____ Date _____ Instructor _____

Telephone Directory

Bookman Betty 17 Highgate Rd. 555-9774	**Book Stores**
Bookman Steven 3721 Chestnut Dr. 555-2323	**Adventure Bookshop** 64 Highgate Rd. ...555-5500
Bopp Carmela 16A Alfred Court 555-1995	**Bob's Book Nook** 1989 Rte. 1 555-6060
Borden Robert L. 235 High St. 555-9402	**Downtown Books**
	& Records 35 Ave. D 555-8888

PRACTICE

1. What is Carmela Bopp's phone number? _____

2. What is Steven Bookman's address? _____

3. Who has this phone number: 555-9402? _____

4. Which book store is on Rte. 1? _____

5. What is the phone number of Downtown Books & Records?

_____

6. Who lives on the same street as the Adventure Bookshop?

_____

Dictionary / B

TEACHING FRAME: BLM 89 Hold up a dictionary and **say A dictionary is an alphabetical listing of words and their meanings.** Have students repeat. **Ask Who can tell me what a dictionary is? Say Dictionaries also contain other useful information about words in addition to the meanings.**

MODEL Look at the first entry on the teaching chart together. Model using a dictionary. **Say I just read a sentence that said "The man wanted to chuck his job, but he needed the money." I think I can tell from the context what chuck means, but I'm not a hundred percent sure. So I want to check the meaning in the dictionary. I will turn to the C section and find this entry. It gives three different meanings for chuck. It doesn't make any sense to say that the man wanted to toss his job or tap it lightly. So the definition I want is clearly the third one, to quit. The dictionary also tells me how to pronounce the word, what part of speech it is, and what other forms it might have. It also sometimes gives example sentences.** Point to the parts of the entry as you mention them. **Say Now what about this sentence. "When I visited my grandma, she chucked me under the chin." Which meaning of chuck is used there?** (meaning 2) **I even have an example sentence for that meaning.** Point to it. **What part of speech is chuck?** (verb) **How do you spell the past-tense form?** (c-h-u-c-k-e-d).

CORRECTIVE FEEDBACK

If students have trouble using the dictionary, review the parts of the entry one by one.

PRACTICE Have students complete Blackline Master 89. **Say Use the remaining entries to answer the questions.**

CORRECTIVE FEEDBACK

If students cannot answer the questions, ask them to read the question aloud. **Ask What part of the dictionary entry would answer this question?**

Answers: 1. shoot 2. a freshwater fish found in Europe 3. two 4. chub 5. chummiest 6. by shortening

Name _____ Date _____ Instructor _____

Dictionary

---

chub/dress

chub (chub) *noun, plural* **chub**. 1. a freshwater fish found in Europe.
  2. Any of several kinds of fishes found in America's Great Lakes.
chuck (chuk) *verb* **chucked, chucking.** 1. to toss or throw. 2. to tap lightly.
  He chucked me under the chin. 3. to quit.
chummy (chum/ ee) *adjective* **chummier, chummiest.** friendly, like a chum.
chute (shoot) *noun.* 1. a slanted gutter for water. 2. a waterfall.
  3. a water slide, as at an amusement park. 4. *(by shortening)* a parachute.

PRACTICE

1. How do you write the pronunciation of *chute?* _____

2. What's the first meaning of *chub?* _____

3. How many syllables are in the word *chummy?* _____

4. What's the plural of *chub?* _____

5. What word would you use to mean the *"most chummy"*? _____

6. How did *chute* get to mean parachute? _____

Encyclopedia / C

TEACHING FRAME: BLM 90 **Say** *An encyclopedia is a set of books with articles giving information about people, places, things, events, and ideas.* Ask students to repeat. **Ask** *Who can tell me what an encyclopedia is?* **Say** *Encyclopedias often come in many books, called volumes. Articles are listed in alphabetical order. To know which volume to use, you need to choose the key word in the topic that interests you. Then use the Index to find all the articles that relate to your key word.*

MODEL Look at the volumes in the Teaching Frame together. Model using an encyclopedia. **Say** *I'd like to find out about* **Mount Everest.** *My key word might be* **Mount,** *but the word* **Everest** *seems much more important. Volume 5 has all the articles that start with D and E. Sure enough, there's* **Mount Everest.** *As I read, I discover that* **Mount Everest** *is on the border of* **Nepal.** *I never heard of* **Nepal.** *I could learn more about* **Nepal** *by looking in the N–O volume.*

Say *Now let's imagine that you wanted some information about the president named* **Bill Clinton.** *What's the key word?* (Clinton) *Which volume would you look in?* (4 Ci–Cz) *Suppose you wanted to learn about the* White House. *Which volume would you use for that?* (20 W–Z)

CORRECTIVE FEEDBACK

If students have difficulty deciding what volume to use, have them try to explain which word is the key word.

PRACTICE Have students complete Blackline Master 90. **Say** *Use the sample set of encyclopedias to complete the chart. For some of the topics, you might want to look in more than one book.*

CORRECTIVE FEEDBACK

If students cannot complete the chart, have them first identify the most important word(s) that they would use for key words. **Ask** *What is the first letter of your key word? Which volumes have entries for this key word?*

Answers: *1. 20 W-Z 2. 19 U-V 3. 7 Fos-G 4. 17 So-Sz 5. 9 I, 2 B 6. 5 D-E, 10 J-K*

Name _____ Date _____ Instructor _____

Encyclopedia

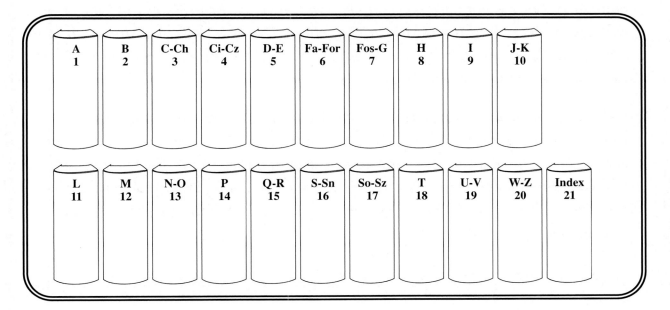

PRACTICE

TOPIC	VOLUME(S)
1. Yellowstone National Park	
2. Queen Victoria	
3. The life of Benjamin Franklin	
4. The history of softball	
5. Bridges in Italy	
6. Dinosaurs of the Jurassic period	

Chart / A

TEACHING FRAME: BLM 91 Draw a chart on the board with two columns and three rows. Write *color* and *number* above the columns. Have volunteers suggest three colors to list. Then have them count objects in the room with those colors. Write these numbers in the second column. **Ask** *What does this chart show?* (the number of objects with given colors) Above the chart, write "Colored Objects in the Room." **Say** *This is the title of the chart. The title tells you the main idea of the chart.* Have students repeat. **Say** *A chart gives information using headings, rows, and columns.* Have students repeat.

MODEL Look at the first chart together. **Say** *This chart is about the presidents whose faces are shown on coins. The row headings say* **Coin** *and* **President.** Point to each heading. *If I want to know whose face is on a nickel, I go to the row headed* **Coin** *and find* **nickel.** Demonstrate this movement. *Below, I find the name of the president, Jefferson.* **Ask** *Whose face is on a quarter?* (Washington's) *What coin has Lincoln's face on it?* (penny)

> **CORRECTIVE FEEDBACK**
>
> If students have trouble reading a chart, have them use their fingers or a straight edge to move along rows and down columns.

PRACTICE Have students complete Blackline Master 91. **Say** *Use the chart entitled "Some Skyscrapers" to answer the questions.*

> **CORRECTIVE FEEDBACK**
>
> If students cannot use the chart, have them first locate the column headings and then read aloud the information under each heading. Then have them read the information that pertains to each building in complete sentences. For example: The Sears Tower is in Chicago, Illinois.

Answers: 1. New York, NY 2. John Hancock 3. 60 4. 1,454 ft 5. Sears Tower 6. 8 stories

Chart

Presidents on Coins

Coin	penny	nickel	dime	quarter
President	Lincoln	Jefferson	Roosevelt	Washington

Some Skyscrapers

Building	Location	Height	Stories
Sears Tower	Chicago, IL	1,454 ft.	110
Empire State	New York, NY	1,250 ft.	102
John Hancock	Boston, MA	790 ft.	60

PRACTICE

1. Where is the Empire State Building? _____

2. Which skyscraper is in Boston? _____

3. How many stories are in the John Hancock Tower? _____

4. How tall in feet is the Sears Tower? _____

5. Which of these skyscrapers is tallest? _____

6. How many more stories does the Sears Tower have than the

Empire State Building? _____

Graph / B

TEACHING FRAME: BLM 92 **Say** *A graph uses a vertical axis and a horizontal axis to display information.* Have students repeat. **Ask** *Who can tell me what a graph is?* **Say** *Graphs use headings and numbers to compare information.*

MODEL Look at the first graph on the teaching chart together. Model reading a graph. **Say** *The title of this bar graph tells me that it compares the areas of some continents. Along the vertical axis are the names of those continents.* (Run your finger down that list.) *Along the horizontal axis are some numbers. These represent area in millions of square miles.* Run your finger along that list of numbers. *I've heard that Asia's the biggest continent. I want to know its area. First, I find Asia on the vertical axis.* Put your finger on Asia. *Now I'm going to run my finger to the end of the bar for Asia.* Run your finger to the end of the bar. *Last, I look below the end of the bar for the number on the horizontal axis. It's between 16 and 18, so I'll say Asia's area is about 17 million square miles.*

Say *Now use the same technique to work backward. Find the continent whose area is nearly 12 million square miles.* (Africa)

CORRECTIVE FEEDBACK

If students have trouble using the graph, have them run their fingers along the horizontal axis to 12 and then move up along the vertical axis to find the bar that comes closest.

PRACTICE Have students look at the second graph. **Say** *This is a line graph. Unlike the bar graph, it compares change over time. You still use the horizontal and vertical axes, and the dots above each heading on the horizontal axis show you that year's enrollment.* Have students complete Blackline Master 92.

CORRECTIVE FEEDBACK

If students cannot answer the questions, have them first use their fingers to locate the enrollment figure for each year shown on the horizontal axis.

Answers: 1. 1960–1970 2. 1000 3. 1970–1980 4. 500

Name _____ Date _____ Instructor _____

Graph

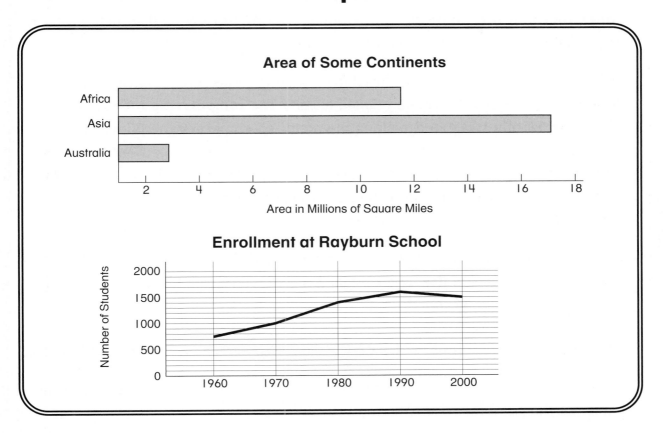

Area of Some Continents

Africa

Asia

Australia

2   4   6   8   10   12   14   16   18

Area in Millions of Square Miles

Enrollment at Rayburn School

Number of Students

2000

1500

1000

500

0

1960   1970   1980   1990   2000

PRACTICE

1. In what years was the student population below 1000? _____

2. About how many students were enrolled in 1970? _____

3. Which ten-year period saw the steepest climb in students?

_____

4. About how many more students were enrolled in 2000 than in 1970?

_____

Map / C

TEACHING FRAME: BLM 93 Say *A map shows where places in the world are located in relation to each other.* Have students repeat. **Say *A compass rose shows the direction: north, south, east, or west.*** Point to the compass rose on the map and have students repeat the definition. **Say *The scale of miles tells the true distance pictured on the map.*** Have students repeat. Review until students can say the definitions and identify the compass rose, map key, and scale.

MODEL Look at the map in the Teaching Frame together. Model using a map. **Say *This map shows the country called Iceland. The compass rose shows me directions.*** Place a straightedge along the north-south part of the compass rose to extend the arms. Then rotate it to extend the east-west arms. **Say *I need to imagine that the arrows on this compass rose extend to cover the whole map. Now I can see that the Denmark Strait is to the west of the island, and the Greenland Sea is to the north and east.*** Point to these places as you mention them.

Say *Where is Reykjavik in relation to the rest of Iceland?* (to the south and west of the island) ***Suppose you flew in a straight line from Reykjavik to Akranes. In which direction would you fly?*** (north)

> **CORRECTIVE FEEDBACK**
>
> If students have difficulty using the map, have them use a straightedge along the axes of the compass rose to extend the arrows.

PRACTICE Have students complete Blackline Master 93. **Say *Use the map to answer the questions.***

> **CORRECTIVE FEEDBACK**
>
> If students cannot use the map, have them begin by identifying the western edge and reading the names of the cities until they reach the eastern edge.

*Answers: 1. Seydisfjordur 2. Vik 3. The North-West and The West 4. About 250 km
5. east 6. northwest*

Name _____ Date _____ Instructor _____

Map

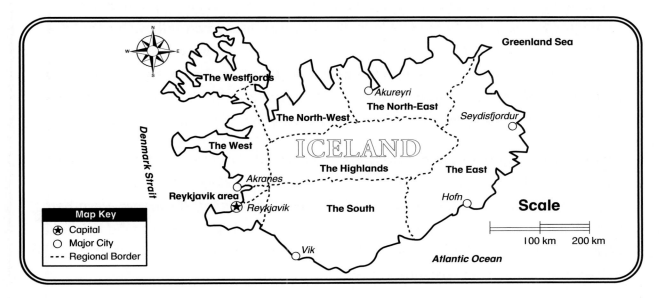

PRACTICE

1. Which of the cities shown is farthest east? _____

2. Which of the cities shown is farthest south? _____

3. Which two regions border on The Westfjords region? _____

4. About how many kilometers is it from Vik to Hofn? _____

5. In what direction would you go to fly from Reykjavik to Hofn?

   _____

6. In what direction would you go to travel from Hofn to Akureyri?

   _____

Newspaper / A

TEACHING FRAME: BLM 94 **Say** *A newspaper article gives information about a real event. It answers the questions* who, what, when, *and* where.

MODEL Read the first article with the students. **Say** *Every newspaper article has a headline that tells a bit about the main idea of the article. Here, the headline is "Students Break State Record."* Underline the headline. *I can tell by this that the main idea of the article is a record-breaking event on the part of some students. The dateline tells me when and where the article was written. According to this, it was written in Gainesville, Florida, on March 10.* Underline the dateline. *The article was written by Dan Teeter. His name is above the dateline.* Underline the author's name.

Say *Now we will read the article itself. Think about the answers to the questions* who, what, where, *and* when. Read the article aloud. **Ask** *Who was involved in this story?* (state legislators, students) *What was happening?* (Students were being congratulated for breaking the state record on a math test.) *Where did this take place? (*at Westlake Middle School) *When did the story happen?* (March 9, the day before the article was written)

CORRECTIVE FEEDBACK

If students have difficulty locating information, have them underline parts of the article that answer the questions *who, what, where,* and *when.*

PRACTICE Have students complete Blackline Master 94. **Say** *Use the second article to answer the questions.*

CORRECTIVE FEEDBACK

If students cannot answer the questions, have them return to the article and underline parts that answer the questions *who, what, where,* and *when.*

Answers: 1. The Xenia Xtra 2. outside Xenia, OH 3. took down trees, destroyed the main office of the Sunshine Trailer Park 4. Sunday 5. July 7 6. Linda Alvarez

Part 2
STUDY SKILLS

Name _____ Date _____ Instructor _____

Newspaper

The Floridian

Students Break State Record
by Dan Teeter

Gainesville, FL, March 10— Members of the state legislature were on hand yesterday at Westlake Middle School to congratulate students on their outstanding scores on the 8th grade math tests. Westlake students outscored every other school in the state, a marked improvement on last year's scores...

THE XENIA XTRA

Storm Batters Trailer Park
by Linda Alverez

Xenia, OH, July 7— A freak summer storm caused thousands of dollars of damage along a narrow path outside of Xenia Sunday. Hardest hit was the Sunshine Trailer Park, which had dozens of trees down and lost its main office to winds that reached as high as 85 mph...

PRACTICE

1. Which newspaper reported on a storm? _____

2. Where did the storm take place? _____

3. What effect did the storm have? _____

4. When did the storm take place? _____

5. When was the article published? _____

6. Who wrote the article? _____

Help-Wanted Ad / B

TEACHING FRAME: BLM 95 Say *A help-wanted ad contains the information a person needs to apply for a particular job.* Have students repeat. **Ask** *Who can tell me what a help-wanted ad is?* **Say** *Unlike other ads, help-wanted ads are factual. They may include a job description, the background needed to do the job, and salary information.*

MODEL Read the first ad on the Teaching Chart together. Model analyzing a help-wanted ad. **Say** *The heading of this ad tells me what the job is. This ad contains information about the kind of person the advertiser wants to apply for the job. The ideal applicant is an American citizen between the ages of 17 and 34 with a high school degree.* Circle these requirements as you mention them. **Say** *These requirements tell me that someone who is in high school now or who is older and retired might not be their first choice.* **Say** *Now suppose you are applying for this job. What should you do?* (call 800-555-3232) *Look at the last line before the phone number. Should someone who wants to stay in town apply for this job? Explain.* (No, the job requires relocating, or moving away.)

CORRECTIVE FEEDBACK

If students have difficulty analyzing help-wanted ads, Have them underline the information about the kind of person the advertiser wants, how to get in touch with the company, and the job description.

PRACTICE Have students complete Blackline Master 95. **Say** *Use the second help-wanted ad to answer the questions.*

CORRECTIVE FEEDBACK

If students cannot interpret help-wanted ads, **ask** *Which sentence in the ad describes the ideal applicant for this job? Which sentence in the ad tells what background the applicant needs?* Continue in this way until the student has successfully answered each question.

Answers: 1. social studies teacher 2. Washington certification in social studies 7-12, with a concentration in American History 3. Yes, if he or she had the background requirements 4. April 15 5. letter and resume 6. No, the job requires 7-12 certification

---

Name _____ Date _____ Instructor _____

Help-Wanted Ad

Computer Repair Trainees High school grads age 17-34, U.S. citizens only. Learn to repair state-of-the-art computers at our expense while receiving excellent salary and benefits package. Must relocate. Phone 800-555-3232.

Teacher of Social Studies 7-12 effective September 1, 2003. Must be WA certified in Social Studies 7-12 with a concentration in American History. Send letter and resume to Superintendent, Morton Central School, PO Box 64, Morton, WA 96358 by April 15.

PRACTICE

1. What kind of job is being advertised in the second ad?

_____

2. What kind of background does the applicant need?

_____

3. Could a new graduate apply for this job? Explain.

_____

4. What is the deadline for applications? _____

5. What does the applicant need to send? _____

6. Should an experienced first-grade teacher apply for this job? Explain.

_____

Editorial / C

TEACHING FRAME: BLM 96 Say *An editorial is an article in which a newspaper editor or owner states an opinion about important issues.* Have students repeat. **Ask** *Who can tell what an editorial is?* **Say** *To be effective, editorials must back up opinions with statements of fact.*

MODEL Read the first editorial in the teaching frame together. Model analyzing an editorial. **Say** *This editorial begins with a title that expresses the writer's opinion and hints at the main idea. The editorial is about the importance of voting in village elections. The writer begins with some facts—elections are held in March, and only a handful of voters turn out.* Underline those facts. *She follows this with an opinion: "This is disgraceful!"* Circle that opinion. *The remainder of the editorial explains why she thinks that it is disgraceful. The author's purpose in writing seems to be to get village residents to vote in local elections.*

Ask *Why, according to the writer, should we care about small-town elections?* (Village officials are our closest representatives.) *What fact does the writer use to support her opinion here?* (Village representatives deal with zoning, roads, and local services.)

> ## CORRECTIVE FEEDBACK
>
> If students have trouble analyzing an editorial, have them review the editorial line by line, underlining facts and circling opinions. Provide immediate feedback.

PRACTICE Have students complete Blackline Master 96. **Say** *Use the second editorial to answer the questions.*

> ## CORRECTIVE FEEDBACK
>
> If students cannot analyze the editorial, **ask** *Why did the author write this editorial? Which sentences express the opinion of the author? Which sentences support the opinion with facts?*

Answers: 1. There are too many broken-down vehicles in people's yards. 2. residents of Stanton 3. They're an eyesore. 4. He counted 75 broken-down vehicles on a random drive through town. 5. by mentioning the negative effect messy yards have on tourism

Name _____ Date _____ Instructor _____

Editorial

GREENVILLE GAZETTE
Please Vote in the Village
Every March, our local villages hold elections. Often, only a handful of voters turn out. This is disgraceful! Our village representatives are our neighbors and friends. Of all the people who represent us, they are the closest to us. They deal with zoning, roads, and local services. If we don't take an interest in the small-town elections that touch us most immediately, we are missing the point of grass-roots politics...

The Stanton Sentinel
A Sight for Eyesores
At a recent county board meeting, Frank Price suggested limiting the number of broken-down vehicles allowed in one person's yard to three. Mr. Price was joking but we think he's on to something. A recent, random tour through town netted a total of 75 smashed and ruined cars , trucks, and even one school bus. Do we expect tourists to take us seriously as a destination when we can't keep our own yards clean? It's time for a change...

PRACTICE

1. What is the main idea of the Stanton Sentinel editorial?

_____

2. To whom is this editorial addressed? _____

3. What is the writer's opinion of broken-down vehicles? _____

4. What fact does the writer use to support his opinion?

_____

5. How does the writer try to appeal to the readers' business sense?

_____

Almanac / A

TEACHING FRAME: BLM 97 **Say** *An almanac contains up-to-date information about people, places, and events.* Have students repeat.

MODEL Look at the teaching frame together and **say** *Information in an almanac is usually displayed in chart form or in tables. Knowing how to read a chart or table will help you to use an almanac.* Look at the first chart together. **Say** *The title of this chart tells me that I will find information on the languages of the world here. The headings tell me what that information is.* Circle the headings. **Say** *In the first column, I see names of languages. In the second column, I can learn how many people in the world speak that language. In the second row, I find the language Afrikaans. It is spoken in South Africa. By running my finger along the row, I can learn that about 9 million people speak Afrikaans.*

Ask *Which language on this chart is spoken by the most people?* (Arabic) *How many people speak Arabic?* (about 182 million) *Which language is spoken by the fewest people?* (Achinese) *Where is that language spoken?* (in Indonesia)

CORRECTIVE FEEDBACK

If students have trouble reading the chart, have them use their fingers or a ruler to read across each row. Have them read the entire chart aloud, and provide immediate feedback.

PRACTICE Have students complete Blackline Master 97. **Say** *Use the chart and the table to answer the questions.*

CORRECTIVE FEEDBACK

If students cannot answer the questions, have them begin by using titles and headings to tell what information is presented on each excerpt from the almanac.

Answers: 1. Akan 2. on the southern coast of West Africa 3. Accra 4. No, the country is mostly low plains and scrubland. 5. cocoa and coffee 6. No, rubber is one of Ghana's resources.

Name _____ Date _____ Instructor _____

Almanac

Languages of the World	
Languages	**Millions of Speakers**
Achinese (Indonesia)	2
Afrikaans (So. Africa)	9
Akan (Ghana)	6
Amharic (Ethiopia)	13
Arabic (Middle East, No. Africa)	182
Assamese (India, Bangladesh)	18

Republic of Ghana
Geography: Area: 92,098 sq. mi.
Location: southern coast of West Africa
Topography: low fertile plains and scrubland **Capital:** Accra
Economy: Industries: aluminum **Crops:** cocoa, coffee **Minerals:** gold, manganese, bauxite **Other Resources:** timber, rubber

PRACTICE

1. Which of the languages listed is spoken in Ghana? _____

2. Where is Ghana located? _____

3. What is the capital of Ghana? _____

4. Is Ghana a mountainous country? Explain.

_____

5. What are Ghana's major crops?

_____

6. Would you be surprised to find a rubber plantation in Ghana? Explain.

_____

Atlas / B

TEACHING FRAME: BLM 98 **Say** *An atlas is a collection of maps.* Have students repeat. **Ask** *Who can tell me what an atlas is?* **Say** *Maps come in all types. Road maps show highways and cities. Topographic maps show mountains, plains, and rivers. Political maps show borders and capitals. Other maps might show a country's products, population density, or interesting sites to visit.*

MODEL Look at the first map on the teaching chart together. Model using an atlas. Point to the map features as you discuss them. **Say** *This is a road map. It shows the state of Nevada and some major highways. I see four cities labeled. The scale of miles helps me judge distances, and the compass rose tells me directions. If I want to drive from Ely to Carson City, first I locate Ely, up and to the east. Then I locate Carson City, to the west. Then I see which road runs between them.* Run your finger from Ely to Carson City. *I'd take Route 50.*

Say *Now look at the other map. Is this a road map? How can you tell?* (It does not show highways.) **Say** *This kind of map shows the geography of a place. Find these places as I state their names: Boundary Peak, Black Rock Desert, Lake Mead. Which one is in the north of Nevada?* (Black Rock Desert)

> ### CORRECTIVE FEEDBACK
>
> If students have trouble using the atlas, ask them to name one site each in the north, east, south, and west of the state. Then ask again for students to locate the places with your help.

PRACTICE Have students complete Blackline Master 98. **Say** *Use the maps to answer the questions.*

> ### CORRECTIVE FEEDBACK
>
> If students cannot answer the questions, have them begin by pointing out which map they will use to answer the question. Then have them point to each mentioned place.

Answers: 1. the road map 2. the topographic map 3. Lake Tahoe 4. Las Vegas
5. Rtes. 93, and 50

Name _____ Date _____ Instructor _____

Atlas

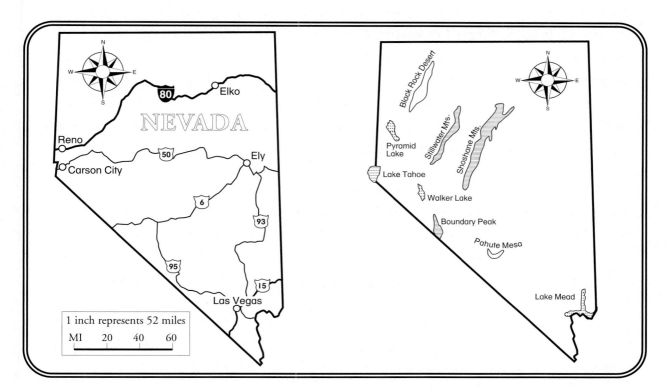

PRACTICE

1. Which map would you use to drive across Nevada? _____

2. Which map would you use to find possible ski areas? _____

3. Which lake is nearest to Carson City? _____

4. Which city is closest to Pahute Mesa? _____

5. If you drove from Las Vegas to Ely, which roads would you take?

_____

Thesaurus / C

TEACHING FRAME: BLM 99 Say *A thesaurus is a book of words and their synonyms.* Have students repeat. **Ask** *Who can tell me what a thesaurus is?* **Say** *The entry words in a thesaurus are usually listed in alphabetical order.*

MODEL Look at the first entry on the Teaching Chart together. Model using a thesaurus. **Say** *Suppose I'm writing a report on roses. I have used the word* **red** *over and over. I'd like to find another word for* **red**. *I look it up in the thesaurus. The entry tells me that it is an adjective.* Circle *adj.* in the first entry. **The entry gives me three synonyms—crimson, scarlet, and blushing. Only two of these really name colors. I could use either crimson or scarlet in my report. The entry also tells me that if I need more ideas, I can look under the word color.**

Say *Now look at the second entry. Suppose you were writing about a boat that got stuck on a reef. Which other synonym might you use in place of reef?* (shoal, sandbar) *Where else could you look for ideas?* (Under shallowness.)

CORRECTIVE FEEDBACK

If students have difficulty using the thesaurus, first make sure they understand what a thesaurus is used for. Have them use a real thesaurus to find synonyms for *eat* such as *dine* and *lunch*.

PRACTICE Have students complete Blackline Master 99. **Say** *Use the thesaurus entries to answer the questions.*

CORRECTIVE FEEDBACK

If students cannot answer the questions, have them dissect one of the entries, pointing to and identifying the entry word, the part of speech, the synonyms, and the suggested other word(s).

Possible Answers: 1. sandbar, shoal, bank, ledge 2. verb 3. receptacle 4. stagger

Name _____ Date _____ Instructor _____

Thesaurus

red | young

red, *adj.* crimson, scarlet., blushing. See COLOR.

reef, *n.* sandbar, shoal, bank, ledge. See SHALLOWNESS.

reel, *v.* sway, stagger, waver; spin, wheel, See AGITATION, ROTATION.

vase, *n.* urn, cup, chalice, jug, amphora. See RECEPTACLE.

vast, *adj.* huge, immense, infinite, boundless, immeasurable, tremendous, enormous. See SIZE, SPACE, BREADTH.

PRACTICE

1. What are three synonyms for *reef?* _____

2. What part of speech is *reel?* _____

3. If you chose not to use any of the synonyms listed for *vase*, under what

other word might you look? _____

4. Choose the synonym for *reel* that works best in this sentence:

The children _____ as they step

off the whirling ride.

Leveled Books

Dan's Time

SKILLS	High-Frequency Words	Story Vocabulary
	Synonyms and Antonyms	Problem and Solution

INTRODUCE HIGH-FREQUENCY WORDS

- Write the high-frequency words on the board. Point to and say each word. (**p. 3** *ten, year, could;* **p. 4** *were, old;* **p. 8** *watch*)
- Have students search through the story to find each high-frequency word.
- Ask volunteers to use each word in a sentence.

INTRODUCE THE STORY VOCABULARY

- Write the story vocabulary on the board.
- Tell students on which page to find each word. (**p. 2** *banner–* a flag, **p. 2** *prospered–* was successful, **p. 4** *summoned–* ordered to appear, **p. 6** *scroll–* a roll of paper, **p. 11** *conquered–* overcame by force, **p. 13** *reluctantly–* not willingly)
- Have students read the sentence with a vocabulary word and use context and picture clues to define it. If they have difficulty, read them the above definition.

INTRODUCE THE BOOK

- Have students read the title and describe the cover. **Say Old watches like the one shown were often carried in a man's pocket. Have you ever seen an old pocket watch like this?**
- Have students take a picture walk through the book. **Ask What ideas do you get about the story from the title and the illustrations?**
- Read page 2 aloud together.
- Point out the words *Mom* and *Dad* and *goofy* and *silly* on the page and **say Some word pairs, like Mom and Dad, are antonyms, or opposites. Others, like goofy and silly are synonyms, or mean the same thing. What's the opposite of stood up?** (sat down) **What word means the same as digits?** (numbers)

READ THE BOOK

- Direct students to the problem and solution chart on the BLM.
- **Say As we read, we'll look for problems and how they are solved.**
- Read together to the bottom of page 4.
- **Ask What was the problem with the dog?** (He wanted to go out.) **How was the problem solved?** (Dad took him for a walk.) **Let's write these on the chart.**
- Continue with a guided or independent reading, based on the student's abilities.

GUIDED READING

Continue reading the story together. Stop at the end of strategic pages to **ask Is there a new problem? What is the solution?** Have students add new information to the chart.

INDEPENDENT READING

Let students finish the story and fill in the graphic organizer on their own.

RESPOND/ ASSESS

After reading the story, have students retell it. If they can't, suggest they refer to the graphic organizer. For further assessment, have students answer the comprehension questions on the inside back cover. **The answers to the story questions are on page 392. For scoring guidelines and student record chart see page W5.**

Answers: Answer may vary. Problem/Solution—
2. There was a thump./ Grandfather let in the cat.
3. He wanted Dan to have the watch./ Dan took it.
4. How would he tell time?/Everyday events would tell him the time.

Dan's Time | Grade 5 — Unit 1 | Skills Intervention — Book C

Name _____ Date _____ Instructor _____

Problem and Solution

PROBLEM	SOLUTION
1.	
2.	
3.	
4.	

The Eye of the Hurricane

<table>
<tr><td>SKILLS</td><td>High-Frequency Words
Context Clues</td><td>Story Vocabulary
Story Elements</td></tr>
</table>

INTRODUCE HIGH-FREQUENCY WORDS

- Write the high-frequency words on the board. Point to and say each word. (**p. 2** *know;* **p. 5** *there;* **p. 6** *about, off;* **p. 8** *say;* **p. 12** *morning*)

- Have students search through the story to find each high-frequency word.

- Ask volunteers to use each word in a sentence.

INTRODUCE THE STORY VOCABULARY

- Write the story vocabulary on the board.

- Tell students on which page of the story to find each word. (**p. 4 offend–** *Make unhappy,* **p. 5 convenience–** *comfort,* **p. 9 presence–** *being in a certain time or place,* **p. 11 bruised–** *having a bluish mark on the skin,* **p. 12 vaguely–** *not clearly,* **p. 15 approve–** *have a favorable opinion*)

- Have students read the sentence with the vocabulary word and use context and picture clues to define it. If they have difficulty, read them the above definition.

INTRODUCE THE BOOK

- Read the title and have students describe the cover. **Ask Have you ever been in or seen a hurricane? What is the "eye" of a storm? Who is going to get caught in a hurricane?**

- Have students take a picture walk through the book to discover more about the story.

- Read page 2 aloud together, and then point out the word *gangplank* in the first sentence.

- **Say What context clues help you to understand the word gangplank?** (climbed up, ship) **What is a gangplank?** (something you go up to get on a ship)

READ THE BOOK

- Direct students to the story elements chart on the BLM.

- **Say As we read, we'll look for how the story's settings affect the characters.**

- Read the story and stop at the bottom of page 5. **Ask What is the setting? Say Let's write this on the chart under Setting.** Then **ask How does the announcement affect Susan? Say Let's write that on the chart.**

- Continue with a guided or independent reading, based on the student's abilities.

GUIDED READING

Continue reading the story together. Stop at the end of strategic pages to **ask Does this setting have an effect on the characters?** Have students add information to the chart.

INDEPENDENT READING

Let students finish the story and fill in the graphic organizer on their own.

RESPOND/ ASSESS

After reading the story, have students retell it. If they can't, suggest they refer to the graphic organizer. For further assessment, have students answer the comprehension questions on the inside back cover. **The answers to the story questions are on page 392. For scoring guidelines and student record chart see page W5.**

Answers: Answers may vary. Setting/Character: (2) p. 7 the ship's bridge/Ron jokes (3) p. 9 on the fore deck/They watch the clouds get closer. (4) p. 14 on deck/Susan feels uneasy. (5) p. 16 two days later on deck/Susan is happy her idea worked.

Part 3

LEVELED BOOK

Name _____ Date _____ Instructor _____

Story Elements

SETTING	CHARACTER
1.	
2.	
3.	
4.	
5.	

Franklin Delano Roosevelt

SKILLS	High-Frequency Words Context Clues	Story Vocabulary Cause and Effect

INTRODUCE HIGH-FREQUENCY WORDS

- Write the high-frequency words on the board. Point to and say each word. (**p. 2** *school*; **p. 3** *found, love*; **p.4** *girl*; **p. 8** *walk*; **p. 10** *again*)
- Have students search through the story to find each high-frequency word.
- Ask volunteers to use each word in a sentence.

INTRODUCE THE STORY VOCABULARY

- Write the story vocabulary on the board.
- Tell students on which page to find each word. (**p. 2** *athletic–* strong and active, **p. 3** *scholarship–* money to help pay for school, **p. 4** *luxury–* something unnecessary that gives pleasure or comfort, **p. 10** *concentrating–* keeping one's thought on something, **p. 14** *bushel–* 32 quarts, **p. 16** *astounding–* amazing)
- Have students read the sentence with a vocabulary word and use context and picture clues to define it. If they have difficulty, read them the above definition.

INTRODUCE THE BOOK

- Read the title and describe the cover. Then **ask *What do you know about FDR?***
- **Say *FDR was our 32ⁿᵈ president. He died during his fourth term.***
- Read aloud the table of contents. Then have students take a picture walk through the book to get an idea of the period in FDR's life that is presented.
- Read page 2 aloud together, then point out the word *pampered* in the fourth sentence.
- **Ask *What words help you figure out the word* pampered?** (like a prince, only child, staff of servants) Have students define *pampered.*

READ THE BOOK

- Direct students to the cause and effect chart on the BLM.
- **Say *What happened is the effect, or result. Why something happened is the cause. We'll write causes and effects on the chart.***
- Read aloud page 3 again. **Say *Franklin believed in helping others. What result came from this?*** (He tutored poor boys.) **Say *Let's write this under cause.***
- Continue with a guided or independent reading, based on the student's abilities.

GUIDED READING

Continue reading the story together. Stop at the end of strategic pages to **ask *Is a cause and effect explained on this page?*** Have students add new information to the chart.

INDEPENDENT READING

Let students finish the story and fill in the graphic organizer on their own.

RESPOND/ASSESS

After reading the story, have students retell it. If they can't, suggest they refer to the graphic organizer. For further assessment, have students answer the comprehension questions on the inside back cover. **The answers to the story questions are on page 392. For scoring guidelines and student record chart see page W5.**

Answers: Answers may vary. Cause/Effect: (2) pp. 4-5 Eleanor shared FDR's social ideals/They married. (3) pp. 6-7 Teddy set an example helping people/FDR followed Teddy (4) pp. 9-10 polio/FDR devastated (5) p. 12 baths at Warm Springs help/FDR started center for polio victims (6) pp. 13-16 Republicans questioned health/FDR won presidency.

Name _____ Date _____ Instructor _____

Cause and Effect

CAUSE	EFFECT
1.	
2.	
3.	
4.	
5.	
6.	

Diego's Sea Adventures

SKILLS	High-Frequency Words	Story Vocabulary
	Antonyms and Synonyms	Story Elements

INTRODUCE HIGH-FREQUENCY WORDS

- Write the high-frequency words on the board. Point to and say each word. (**p. 2** *fast;* **p. 4** *men, very;* **p. 6** *night, fire;* **p.8** *than*)

- Have students search through the story to find each high-frequency word.

- Ask volunteers to use each word in a sentence.

INTRODUCE THE STORY VOCABULARY

- Write the story vocabulary on the board.

- Tell students on which page to find each word. (**p. 2** *spire–* structure that becomes narrow at the top, **p. 4** *shoreline–* the outline of the land along the edge of an ocean, lake, or river, **p. 5** *ominous–* telling of trouble to come; threatening, **p. 6** *hull–* the sides and bottom of a ship, **p. 8** *treacherous–* dangerous, **p. 9** *timbers–* long, heavy pieces of wood for building)

- Have students read the sentence with the vocabulary word and use context and picture clues to define it. If they have difficulty, read them the above definition.

INTRODUCE THE BOOK

- Read the title and have students describe the cover. **Ask Do you think Diego's sea adventure takes place in modern times or long ago? How can you tell?** Read aloud the table of contents. **Say The Armada was the name given to a group of 138 ships sailing out of Lisbon harbor in Portugal in the latter part of the 1500s.**

- Have students take a picture walk through the book to discover more about the adventure.

- Read page 2 aloud together. Then write the words *ran* and *scampered* and *on* and *off* on the board. **Ask are these word pairs synonyms or antonyms?**

READ THE BOOK

- Direct students to the story elements chart on the BLM.

- **Say We'll look for ways the story's settings affect the characters.**

- Read together to the end of page 4. **Ask Where is Diego?** Write this on the chart. **How does this affect Diego?** (He feels proud) **Say Let's write this on the chart.**

- Continue with a guided or independent reading, based on the student's abilities.

GUIDED READING

Continue reading the story together. Stop at the end of strategic pages to **ask What is the setting? How does it affect the characters?** Have students add the new information.

INDEPENDENT READING

Let students finish the story and fill in the graphic organizer on their own.

RESPOND/ ASSESS

After reading the story, have students retell it. If they can't, suggest they refer to the graphic organizer. For further assessment, have students answer the comprehension questions on the inside back cover. **The answers to the story questions are on page 392. For scoring guidelines and student record chart see page W5.**

Answers: Setting/Character: (2) p. 6, 8 harbor of Calais/Diego panics when he smells smoke. (3) pp.10 rough seas/Diego gets seasick. (4) p. 13 lightning storm/Diego is lucky to get out before it broke. (5) p. 16 on deck of ship after the storm/Diego is grateful to be alive and joyful to be going home.

Name _____ Date _____ Instructor _____

Story Elements

SETTING	CHARACTER
1.	
2.	
3.	
4.	
5.	

From Dust to Hope

SKILLS	High-Frequency Words	Story Vocabulary
	Figurative Language	Make Predictions

INTRODUCE HIGH-FREQUENCY WORDS

- Write the high-frequency words on the board. Point to and say each word. (**p. 1** *cover, hope;* **p. 2** *mother;* **p. 5** *letter;* **p. 6** *mile;* **p. 8** *just;* **p. 10** *near*)

- Have students search through the story to find each high-frequency word.

- Ask volunteers to use each word in a sentence.

INTRODUCE THE STORY VOCABULARY

- Write the story vocabulary on the board.

- Explain to students on which page of the story to find each word. (**p. 2** *distressed–* having pain, **p. 2** *despair–* feeling no hope, **p. 5** *speechless–* unable to speak, **p. 5** *stifling–* stopping the breath, **p. 5** *shriveled–* withered, **p. 5** *insistent–* a strong demand)

- Have students read the sentence with a vocabulary word and use context and picture clues to define it. If they have difficulty, read them the above definition.

INTRODUCE THE BOOK

- Have students read the title and describe the cover. **Ask *What ideas do you get about the story from the title?***

- Read page 2 aloud together. **Say *Writers sometimes use figurative language called a simile to help readers form a picture in their minds.***

- Explain that a simile is a comparison using the words *like* or *as,* and point out the simile in the first 2 sentences. **Ask *To what is the dust storm compared?*** (a gigantic black buzzard).

- Point out the simile in the last 2 sentences on page 2. **Ask *What is compared in this simile?*** (the 7,000-foot-high cloud rolling in and a plague of locusts) ***What picture forms in your mind from this simile?***

READ THE BOOK

- Direct students to the make predictions chart on the BLM.

- **Say *As we read the story, we can make predictions about what will happen, write them on the chart, and then write what does happen.***

- Read the story and stop after page 5.

- **Ask *What do you think will happen?*** (Students may predict that the family will move to California.) **Say *Let's write that on the chart. Now we'll read page 6 to find out if we're right.***

- Stop at the end of page 6 and have students note what happened. (The family left Oklahoma to move to California.) **Say *Let's write this on the chart.***

- Continue with a guided or independent reading, based on the student's abilities.

GUIDED READING

Continue reading the story together. Stop at strategic places and **ask *What do you think will happen?*** Have students add new information to the chart.

INDEPENDENT READING

Let students finish the story and fill in the graphic organizer on their own.

RESPOND/ ASSESS

After reading the story, have students retell it. If they can't, suggest they refer to the graphic organizer. For further assessment, have students answer the comprehension questions on the inside back cover. **The answers to the story questions are on page 392. For scoring guidelines and student record chart see page W5.**

Answers: Answers will vary.

Name _____ Date _____ Instructor _____

Make Predictions

PREDICTION	WHAT HAPPENED
1.	
2.	
3.	
4.	
5.	

Through a Mountain and Under a Sea

SKILLS	High-Frequency Words	Story Vocabulary
	Inflectional Endings	Fact and Nonfact

INTRODUCE HIGH-FREQUENCY WORDS

- Write the high-frequency words on the board. Point to and say each word. (**p.2** *through, under, that;* **p. 4** *would, must;* **p.13** *start*)

- Have students search through the story to find each high-frequency word.

- Ask volunteers to use each word in a sentence.

INTRODUCE THE STORY VOCABULARY

- Write the story vocabulary on the board.

- Tell students on which page of the story to find each word. (**p. 3 pulverized–** *ground to dust,* **p. 3 grit–** *fine gravel,* **p. 3 acre–** *43,560 sq. ft.,* **p. 3 dynamite–** *a powerful explosive,* **p. 11 commotion–** *lots of noise,* **p. 14 rebuild–** *build again*)

- Have students read the sentence that has a given vocabulary word and use context and picture clues to form a definition. If they have difficulty, read them the above definition.

INTRODUCE THE BOOK

- Read the title and have students describe the cover. Then **ask What do you think the machines will be used to build?**

- Have students take a picture walk through the book to see what the machines are used for.

- Read page 3 aloud together.

- Point out the words *quicker* and *easier* in the first sentence of the third paragraph. Write those words on the board and underline the *–er* in each one.

- **Ask What two things are being compared?** (digging tunnels before and after the invention of dynamite)

READ THE BOOK

- Direct students to the fact and nonfact chart on the BLM.

- **Say We'll note facts and nonfacts— statements that can or cannot be proved—on the chart.**

- Tell students that most of the sentences in the book contain facts, but there is one sentence that contains a nonfact. Challenge students to find a nonfact.

- Read to page 3. **Ask what's a fact on this page?** (Nobel invented dynamite in 1867.) **How could this be proved?** (look in an encyclopedia) **Say Let's write the fact on the chart.**

- Based on the student's abilities, continue with a guided or independent reading.

GUIDED READING

Continue reading the story together. Stop after each page and write the facts in the FACT column on the chart. Have students add this information to the chart.

INDEPENDENT READING

Let students read the book and fill in the graphic organizer on their own.

RESPOND/ ASSESS

After reading the book, have students retell the important information. If they can't, suggest they refer to the graphic organizer. For further assessment, have students answer the comprehension questions on the inside back cover. **The answers to the story questions are on page 392. For scoring guidelines and student record chart see page W5.**

Answers: Nonfact: p. 13 They say you start breathing French air as soon as you enter the English side of the Channel.

Name _____ Date _____ Instructor _____

Fact and Nonfact

FACT	NONFACT

The Mills Green Team

SKILLS	High-Frequency Words	Story Vocabulary
	Inflectional Endings	Main Idea

INTRODUCE HIGH-FREQUENCY WORDS

- Write the high-frequency words on the board. Point to and say each word. (**p. 2** *didn't, said;* **p. 3** *come, window;* **p. 5** *first;* **p. 6** *green*)

- Have students search through the story to find each high-frequency word.

- Have students use the words in sentences.

INTRODUCE THE STORY VOCABULARY

- Write the story vocabulary on the board.

- Tell students the page of the story to find each word. (**p. 6** *dangled–* *hung loosely,* **p. 7** *auction–* *a kind of sale,* **p. 10** *lecture–* *to give a talk to an audience; to scold,* **p. 13** *deliveries–* *things taken to a person or place,* **p. 14** *donate–* *to give,* **p. 16** *publicity–* *information for the public*)

- Have students read the sentence with a vocabulary word and use context and picture clues to define it. If they have difficulty, read them the above definition.

INTRODUCE THE BOOK

- Read the title and have students describe the cover. **Ask What do you think the Green Team is?** Have students take a picture walk to discover more about the Green Team.

- Read page 2 aloud together.

- Point out the words *scrunched* and *carrying,* and write them on the board. **Say These words have inflectional endings. When an inflectional ending is added to a verb, it changes the way the verb is used.**

- Underline the *–ed* in **scrunched. Say Adding –ed changes the verb to past tense.**

- Underline the *–ing* in **carrying** and **say** *–ing tells the present.*

READ THE BOOK

- Direct students to the main idea chart on the BLM.

- **Say As we read, we'll look for the main idea.**

- Read together to the bottom of page 5.

- **Ask What is the story about so far? Is this the main idea of the book? Why or why not?**

- Continue with a guided or independent reading, based on the student's abilities.

GUIDED READING

Continue reading the story together. Stop at strategic places and **ask Have we found the main idea yet? What details support that idea?** Once students find the main idea— When people work together to do a good deed, everyone benefits—have them write it on the chart, then add supporting details.

INDEPENDENT READING

Let students finish the story and fill in the graphic organizer on their own.

RESPOND/ASSESS

After reading the story, have students retell it. If they can't, suggest they refer to the graphic organizer. For further assessment, have students answer the comprehension questions on the inside back cover. **The answers to the story questions are on page 392. For scoring guidelines and student record chart see page W5.**

Answers: When people work together everyone benefits. (1) The garden was planted. (2) Neighbors gave plants. (3) The place was prettier. (4) Everyone got free shirts. (5) The owner got new customers.

Name _____ Date _____ Instructor _____

Main Idea

MAIN IDEA

DETAILS

Blue-Faced Blues

INTRODUCE HIGH-FREQUENCY WORDS

- Write the high-frequency words on the board. Point to and say each word. (**p. 4** *two;* **p. 7** *blue, face, think;* **p. 8** *like;* **p. 14** *those*)

- Have students search through the story to find each high-frequency word.

- Ask volunteers to use each word in a sentence.

INTRODUCE THE STORY VOCABULARY

- Write the story vocabulary on the board.

- Explain to students on which page of the story to find each word. (**p. 4** *reserved–* set aside, **p. 6** *permission–* consent from someone, **p. 8** *snoop–* a nosy person **p. 12** *rejected–* refused, **p. 15** *afford–* have enough money, **p. 15** *submitted–* handed in)

- Have students read the sentence with a vocabulary word and use context and picture clues to define it. If they have difficulty, read them the above definition.

INTRODUCE THE BOOK

- Read the title and have students describe the cover. Then **ask What does it mean when someone has the blues?**

- Have students look at the pictures on pages 2–3 and 4–5. **Ask What else is the story about?** (art, and a painting of a man)

- Read page 2 aloud together.

- Point out the words *inside, airline,* and *whirlwind.* **Ask What two words were put together to form each compound word?** Have students tell what each compound word means.

READ THE BOOK

- Direct students to the make predictions chart on the BLM.

- **Say We can write our predictions and then find out and write what actually happened.**

- Read together through page 6.

- **Ask What do you think will happen? Say Let's write that.**

- Read page 7 and have students write what happened and compare this to their prediction.

- Continue with a guided or independent reading, based on the student's abilities.

GUIDED READING

Continue reading the story together. Stop at strategic places and **ask What do you think will happen?** Have students add new information to the chart.

INDEPENDENT READING

Let students finish the story and fill in the graphic organizer on their own.

RESPOND/ASSESS

After reading the story, have students retell it. If they can't, suggest they refer to the graphic organizer. For further assessment, have students answer the comprehension questions on the inside back cover. **The answers to the story questions are on page 392. For scoring guidelines and the student record chart see page W5.**

Answers: Answers may vary. Prediction: (1) pp. 6–7 Uncle Ted will like the portrait/Uncle Ted didn't like the portrait. (2) pp. 11–12 Frank and June liked the picture./They liked the picture. (3) pp. 14–15 Ben gets to go to art class./ Frank offers to let Ben take free classes.

Part 3
LEVELED BOOK

Name _____ Date _____ Instructor _____

Make Predictions

PREDICTION	WHAT HAPPENED
1.	
2.	
3.	

Dancers in the Spotlight

INTRODUCE HIGH-FREQUENCY WORDS

- Write the high-frequency words on the board. Point to and say each of the words. (**p. 2** *long, work, dance;* **p. 3** *today, town;* **p. 7** *turns*)

- Have students search through the story to find the high-frequency words.

- Ask volunteers to use each word in a sentence.

INTRODUCE STORY VOCABULARY

- Write the story vocabulary on the board.

- Tell students the page in the story to find each word. (**p. 3** *division– part of a group;* **p. 4** *elementary– the beginning of something;* **p. 5** *accurate– correct;* **p. 13** *glory– honor;* **p. 14** *onlookers– spectators;* **p. 16** *congratulated– gave praise*).

- Have students read the sentence with the vocabulary word and use context and picture clues to form a definition. If they have difficulty, provide them with the above definition.

INTRODUCE THE BOOK

- Read the title and have students describe the cover. **Ask What kind of dancing is taking place?** (ballet) **Where are the dancers?** (on stage)

- Have students take a picture walk through the book to learn more about the story.

- Read pages 4 and 5 aloud together. Help students pronounce and understand the French words here, and throughout the text as you read on. Point out the word *steps.* Have students define it in this context ("moves"). Then ask them for another meaning of the word *step.* ("a series of things in a process of making or doing something")

READ THE BOOK

- Direct students to the steps in a process chart on the BLM.

- **Say Knowing the steps in a process can help you understand the story.**

- Read together to the bottom of page 8.

- **Ask What is the first step to prepare students?** (tell story) **Say Let's write this step in the first box on the chart.**

- Based on the students' abilities, continue with a guided or independent reading.

GUIDED READING

Continue reading the story together and stop at the end of each page or spread. **Ask What new steps can we add?** Have students add new information to the chart.

INDEPENDENT READING

Students complete the story and graphic organizer independently.

RESPOND/ASSESS

After reading the story, have students work in small groups or with partners to review the steps that led up to the *Nutcracker* performance. Let them refer to the their graphic organizers to help them. For further assessment, students may answer the comprehension questions on the inside back cover. **The answers to the story questions are on page 393. For scoring guidelines and student record chart see page W5.**

Answers: (2) Ms. Lopez assigns parts. (3) They listen to the music. (4) They talk about the music. (5) Ms. Lopez shows them where they will stand. (6) She teaches them steps. (7) Nick and Jen learn pas de deux. (8) Costumes are made. (9) Students learn to put on makeup. (10) They perform.

Name _____ Date _____ Instructor _____

Steps in a Process

1.

2.

3.

4.

5.

6.

7.

8.

9.

10.

Human Writes!

```
┌──────────────────────────────────────────────────────────┐
│         High-Frequency Words      Story Vocabulary        │
│ SKILLS  Compound Words            Sequence of Events       │
└──────────────────────────────────────────────────────────┘
```

INTRODUCE HIGH-FREQUENCY WORDS

- Write the high-frequency words on the board. Point to and say each of the words. (**p. 3** *use;* **p. 6** *write, kind;* **p. 9** *new;* **p. 11** *help;* **p. 13** *which*)
- Have students search through the story to find the high-frequency words.
- Have students use the words in sentences.

INTRODUCE STORY VOCABULARY

- Write the story vocabulary on the board.
- Tell students the page in the story to find each word. (**p. 4** *scorched–* burnt; **p. 4** *billows–* waves about; **p. 5** *devour–* consume; **p. 9** *uprooted–* pulled up; **p. 12** *quench–* extinguish; **p. 12** *heroic–* very brave)
- Have students read the sentence with the vocabulary word and use context and picture clues to form a definition. If they have difficulty, provide them with the above definition.

INTRODUCE THE BOOK

- Read the title and have students describe the cover.
- Read the table of contents aloud. **Ask What do you think this book is about?**
- Have students take a picture walk through the book to get an idea about the different kinds of writing that are presented.
- Read the introduction on pages 2 and 3 aloud together. **Say Humankind is a compound word made up of two smaller words.** Ask students what two words form this word and what the word means.
- Help students with difficult vocabulary throughout—*Sumerians, cuneiform, hieroglyphics,* and *Phoenicians.*

READ THE BOOK

- Direct students to the sequence of events chart on the BLM.
- **Say Knowing the sequence of events helps you understand what you read.**
- Read the book to the bottom of page 5.
- **Ask What were the first forms of written communication?** (pictures)
- Based on the students' abilities, continue with a guided or independent reading.

GUIDED READING

Continue reading the book together and stop at the end of each page or spread. **Ask What was the next step in the development of written language?** Have students add new information to the chart.

INDEPENDENT READING

Students complete the story and graphic organizer independently.

RESPOND/ASSESS

After reading the story, have students work in small groups or with partners to review the steps from cave paintings to the alphabet. Let them refer to the their graphic organizers to help them. For further assessment, students may answer the comprehension questions on the inside back cover. **The answers to the story questions are on page 393. For scoring guidelines and student record chart see page W5.**

Answers: (2) pp. 6, 8 Sumerian pictograph; (3) Sumerian cuneiform; (4) p. 9 Egyptian hieroglyphics; (5) p. 10–11 Phoenician syllabic writing; (6) p. 12 Ancient Greek with individual vowels; (7) pp. 13–14 Romans changed the look of the Greek letters, Roman alphabet; (8) pp. 15–16 Cherokee alphabet

Name _____ Date _____ Instructor _____

Sequence of Events

1.

↓

2.

↓

3.

↓

4.

↓

5.

↓

6.

↓

7.

↓

8.

Dear Diary

SKILLS	High-Frequency Words	Story Vocabulary
	Figurative Language	Steps in a Process

INTRODUCE HIGH-FREQUENCY WORDS

- Write the high-frequency words on the board. Point to and say each of the words. (**p. 2** *dear, present, best;* **p. 3** *have, high;* **p. 5** *why*)

- Have students search through the story to find the high-frequency words.

- Ask volunteers to use each word in a sentence.

INTRODUCE STORY VOCABULARY

- Write the story vocabulary on the board.

- Tell students the page in the story to find each word. (**p. 5** *granite–* *a type of enameled ironware;* **p. 7** *canvas–* *strong, heavy cloth;* **p. 8** *orphanage–* *place that takes in and cares for parentless children;* **p. 12** *tornado–* *powerful storm with winds that whirl in a funnel-shaped cloud;* **p. 12** *cemetery–* *place where the dead are buried*).

- Have students read the sentence with the vocabulary word and use context and picture clues to form a definition. If they have difficulty, provide them with the above definition.

INTRODUCE THE BOOK

- Read the title and describe the cover. Then **ask** *What is a diary? Do you think this is a diary from present day or from the past? Why?* (past; because pictures and key are old-fashioned)

- Read page 2 aloud together. Then have students take a picture walk through the book. Have students note clues to the setting (dates, clothing in photographs, illustration of the old car, prices).

- Read page 3 aloud together. Write . . . *they are the cats meow,* on the board. Ask students what this metaphor suggests. **Ask** *Does Red like the flappers?*

READ THE BOOK

- Direct students to the steps in a process chart on the BLM.

- **Say** *We will list the steps of the activities in Red's life.*

- Read the story to the bottom of page 3.

- **Ask** *What is the first step in Red's day?* (wake early) *Let's write that in the first box on the chart.*

- **Say** *Take time now to fill in the other steps in a process on page 3.*

- Based on the students' abilities, continue with a guided or independent reading.

GUIDED READING

Continue reading the story together. Ask students to tell you when they notice another process with steps listed. Write the steps on the board as students list them. (p. 7 washing clothes)

INDEPENDENT READING

Students complete the story and graphic organizer independently.

RESPOND/ASSESS

After reading the story, have students work in small groups or with partners to review the steps to doing the laundry. Let them refer to the their graphic organizers to help them. For further assessment, students may answer the comprehension questions on the insde back cover. **The answers to the story questions are on page 393. For scoring guidelines and student record chart see page W5.**

Answers: Answers may vary. (1) pull on underwear; (2) black stockings; (3) elastic bands; (4) school frock; (5) tuck a handkerchief; (6) shoes

Part 3
LEVELED BOOK

Name _____ Date _____ Instructor _____

Steps in a Process

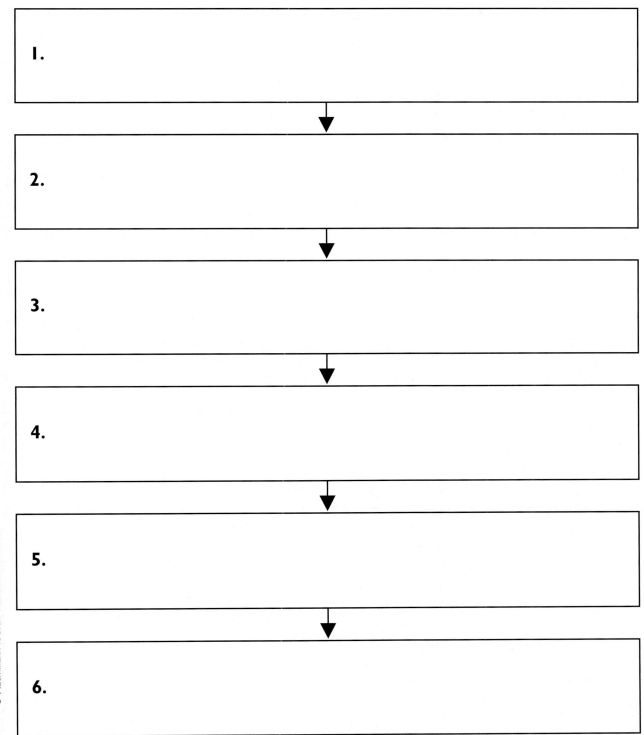

1.

2.

3.

4.

5.

6.

Maya's Mural

SKILLS	High-Frequency Words	Story Vocabulary
	Multi-meaning Words	Author's Purpose/Point of View

INTRODUCE HIGH-FREQUENCY WORDS

- Write the high-frequency words on the board. Point to and say each of the words. (**p. 2** *other, open*; **p. 5** *some, clothes*; **p. 7** *white*; **p. 9** *down*)
- Have students search through the story to find the high-frequency words.
- Have students use the words in sentences.

INTRODUCE STORY VOCABULARY

- Write the story vocabulary on the board.
- Tell students the page in the story to find each word. (**p. 4** *heritage–* traditions; **p. 5** *tiresome–* dull; **p. 6** *livestock–* animals raised for profit; **p. 10** *survival–* the act of surviving; **p. 10** *influenced–* have an effect on; **p. 14** *thrive–* to do well).
- Have students read the sentence with the vocabulary word and use context and picture clues to form a definition. If they have difficulty, provide them with the above definition.

INTRODUCE THE BOOK

- Read the title and have students describe the cover. **Ask What is a mural?**
- Read pages 2 and 3 aloud together. Ask students to identify when the story takes place (1935). Then have students tell why the title character is in a wheelchair.
- Have students take a picture walk through the book to discover what connection there is between Maya and a mural.
- Explain that Maya's heritage is Mexican. While looking through a magazine, she sees paintings by the great Mexican artist Diego Rivera. Write *Mexico, Mexican,* and *Diego Rivera* on the board. Pronounce them for students.

READ THE BOOK

- Direct students to the author's purpose/point of view chart on the BLM.
- **Say As we read the story, we will stop and see how the author informs us and provides clues as to the author's point of view.**
- Read together to the bottom of page 5.
- **Ask What new information has the author included? What do we learn about the author's purpose? Say Let's write this information on the chart.**
- Based on the students' abilities, continue with a guided or independent reading.

GUIDED READING

Continue reading the story together and stop at the end of every other page. **Ask What can we learn about the author's purpose or point of view?** Have students note new information.

INDEPENDENT READING

Students complete the story and graphic organizer independently.

RESPOND/ASSESS

After reading the story, have students retell it. If they cannot, refer them to the their graphic organizers. For further assessment, students may answer the comprehension questions on the back cover. **The answers to the story questions are on page 393. For scoring guidelines and student record chart see page W5.**

Answers: Answers may vary. Author's purpose: Inform: Polio outbreak in 1932; Entertain: Maya paints a mural; Author's POV: Maya is strong. She is creative and independent; The disabled should not be kept apart.

Part 3
LEVELED BOOK

Name _____ Date _____ Instructor _____

Author's Purpose and Point of View

AUTHOR'S PURPOSE	AUTHOR'S POINT OF VIEW

Kelley in Charge

SKILLS	High-Frequency Words	Story Vocabulary
	Suffixes	Judgments and Decisions

INTRODUCE HIGH-FREQUENCY WORDS

- Write the high-frequency words on the board. Point to and say each of the words. (**p. 2** *sister, home;* **p. 3** *look;* **p. 5** *when, idea;* **p. 16** *nothing*)
- Have students search through the story to find the high-frequency words.
- Have students use the words in sentences.

INTRODUCE STORY VOCABULARY

- Write the story vocabulary on the board.
- Tell students where to find each word. (**p. 5** *peculiar–* odd; **p. 6** *unbearable–* difficult; **p. 6** *stunned–* shocked; **p. 7** *unpleasant–* disagreeable; **p. 9** *nestled–* settled snugly; **p. 12** *tortillas–* bread made from cornmeal).
- Have students read the sentence with the vocabulary word and use context and picture clues to form a definition. If they have difficulty, provide them with the above definition.

INTRODUCE THE BOOK

- Direct attention to the book cover and read the title. **Ask How does Kelley feel about what she's doing?**
- Read the table of contents with students. Ask them what ideas they get about the story from the chapter titles.
- Read pages 2 and 3 aloud together.
- Point out the words *cooperation* and *receptionist* on page 3. Tell students that each word has a suffix, a word part added to the end. Define *–tion* as meaning "state or condition of being; *-ist* as "one who does or is." Have students use the meaning of the suffix to define the whole word.
- Have students take a picture walk to find out more about what happens.

READ THE BOOK

- Direct students to the judgments and decisions chart on the BLM.
- Read the first chapter together. **Ask What judgment did Kelley make of her dad's cooking? What decision was made based on that? Who made it? Say Let's write this on the chart.**
- Based on the students' abilities, continue with a guided or independent reading.

GUIDED READING

Stop at the end of each page or spread. **Ask Have the characters made any judgments? What happened as a result?** Have students add new information to the chart.

INDEPENDENT READING

Students complete the story and graphic organizer independently.

RESPOND/ASSESS

After reading the story, have students work in small groups or with partners to retell the story. Let them refer to the their graphic organizers to help them. For further assessment, students may answer the comprehension questions on the back cover. **The answers to the story questions are on page 393. For scoring guidelines and student record chart see page W5.**

Answers: Judgment/Decision: (2) pp. 8–11 Kelley thinks making pancakes is easy./She makes a mess. (3) pp. 13–14. Tess says they look like tortillas./Kelley gets an idea. (4) p. 16 Mom and dad think it's delicious./Dad takes them out.

Name _____ Date _____ Instructor _____

Judgments and Decisions

JUDGMENTS	DECISIONS
1.	
2.	
3.	
4.	

On Track

SKILLS	High-Frequency Words Prefixes	Story Vocabulary Important/Unimportant Information

INTRODUCE HIGH-FREQUENCY WORDS

- Write the high-frequency words on the board. Point to and say each of the words. (**p. 2** *o'clock, friends;* **p. 5** *been;* **p. 6** *back;* **p. 14** *little;* **p. 16** *took*)

- Have students search through the story to find the high-frequency words.

- Have students use the words in sentences.

INTRODUCE STORY VOCABULARY

- Write the story vocabulary on the board.

- Tell students the page in the story to find each word. (**p. 2 assignments—** *tasks;* **p. 4 automatically—** *done without a person's control;* **p. 7 normally—** *usually;* **p. 7 carelessly—** *done without close attention;* **p. 9 swerved—** *turned aside suddenly;* **p. 15 observations—** *acts of noticing*).

- Have students read the sentence with the vocabulary word and use context and picture clues to form a definition. If they have difficulty, provide them with the above definition.

INTRODUCE THE BOOK

- Direct attention to the book cover and read the title. Then **ask What tracks are kids looking at? Where are they?**

- Tell students that this is a mystery story. On the board write the characters' names and pronounce them for students.

- Read the table of contents with students. **Ask What do the titles tell you?**

- Have students take a picture walk through the book to get more of an idea of the mystery.

- Read page 5 aloud together. Write *bicycle* on the board and point out the prefix *bi-*. Tell them *bi-* can mean "two".

READ THE BOOK

- Direct students to the important/unimportant information chart on the BLM.

- Explain to students that stories contain important and unimportant information.

- Read the story to the bottom of page 5.

- **Ask What important information can we write on our charts?** Then **ask Do you think Franklin's friends rushing to his house in fifteen minutes is important or unimportant information? Say Add this detail to your charts.**

- Based on the students' abilities, continue with a guided or independent reading.

GUIDED READING

Continue reading the story together and stop at the end of each page or spread. **Ask What important information have we just read? What information may not be important?**

INDEPENDENT READING

Students complete the story and graphic organizer independently.

RESPOND/ASSESS

After reading the story, have students work in small groups or with partners to retell the story. Let them refer to the their graphic organizers to help them. For further assessment, students may answer the comprehension questions on the inside back cover. **The answers to the story questions are on page 393. For scoring guidelines and student record chart see page W5.**

Answers: p. 2 I: Franklin has initials on bike. U: They play video games; p. 5 I: Muddy tire tracks. U: Franklin shouts; p. 9 I: Phil isn't upset. U: Rupa's game is rescheduled; p. 14 I: The kitten tracks; p. 15 I: The kids explain to the police. U: They go to dinner.

Name _____ Date _____ Instructor _____

Important and Unimportant Information

IMPORTANT	UNIMPORTANT
1.	
2.	
3.	
4.	
5.	
6.	

Tourist Trap Island

```
┌─────────────────────────────────────────────────────┐
│ SKILLS    High-Frequency Words     Story Vocabulary    │
│           Suffixes                 Draw Conclusions    │
└─────────────────────────────────────────────────────┘
```

INTRODUCE HIGH-FREQUENCY WORDS

- Write the high-frequency words on the board. Point to and say each of the words. (**p. 2** *around, island, lived;* **p. 3** *specials;* **p. 4** *call;* **p. 5** *money*)

- Have students search through the story to find the high-frequency words.

- Ask volunteers to use each word in a sentence.

INTRODUCE STORY VOCABULARY

- Write the story vocabulary on the board.

- Tell students the page in the story to find each word. (**p. 8 teeming–** *swarming,* **p. 8 emerge–** *to come out,* **p. 13 barrier–** a block, **p. 13 parallel–** *being the same distance apart at all points,* **p. 16 fireball–** *a sphere of glowing light,* **p. 16 naturalist–** *someone who studies nature*).

- Have students read the sentence with the vocabulary word and use context and picture clues to form a definition. If they have difficulty, provide them with the above definition.

INTRODUCE THE BOOK

- Direct attention to the book cover and read the title. Then **ask What is a tourist trap? How do you think the girl on the cover feels about them?** (unhappy)

- Have students take a picture walk through the book to get an idea of what the island looks like as a tourist trap.

- Read page 2 and 3 aloud together. Point out the word *countless* and tell students that this word has the suffix *–less* added to the end. Tell students that *–less* can mean "without" or "that cannot be." Have students define *countless* using the meaning of *–less*.

READ THE BOOK

- Direct students to the draw conclusions chart on the BLM.

- **Say As we read the story, we will stop to draw conclusions from story details.**

- Model drawing conclusions for students. **Say From the story details on page 2, I can conclude that Lisa especially enjoys the natural beauty of Dungan Island.**

- Based on the students' abilities, continue with a guided or independent reading.

GUIDED READING

Continue reading the story together and stop at the end of pages 3, 6, 10, and 12. **Say Let's look at these details and see if we can draw a conclusion.** Have students add new information to the chart.

INDEPENDENT READING

Students complete the story and graphic organizer independently.

RESPOND/ASSESS

After reading the story, have students work in small groups or with partners to retell the story. Let them refer to the their graphic organizers to help them. For further assessment, students may answer the comprehension questions on the inside back cover. **The answers to the story questions are on page 393. For scoring guidelines and student record chart see page W5.**

Answers: Answers will vary. (1) The setting is a quiet town. The setting will be an important part of the story. (2) The characters pull together. (3) The setting has changed. (4) Lisa is not happy.

Name _____ Date _____ Instructor _____

Draw Conclusions

STORY DETAILS	CONCLUSION
1. page 3 beautiful trees, flowers and plants; the island had just one town	The setting: _____ _____ _____ _____ _____ _____
2. page 6 . . . the whole island showed up; soon everyone was shouting out ideas	The characters: _____ _____ _____ _____ _____ _____
3. page 10 "Welcome to the Dungan Island Souvenir Gift Shop Emporium"; "Welcome to Dungan Burger . . ."	The setting: _____ _____ _____ _____ _____ _____
4. page 12 "Uh, I think I'll skip it," said Lisa . . . ; Lisa . . . said, "Is everyone on Dungan Island going crazy?"	Lisa: _____ _____ _____ _____ _____

© Macmillan/McGraw-Hill School Division

Tornado!

INTRODUCE HIGH-FREQUENCY WORDS

- Write the high-frequency words on the board. Point to and say each of the words. (**p. 2** *people;* **p. 3** *let, find, day;* **p. 11** *house;* **p. 15** *cars*)

- Have students search through the story to find the high-frequency words.

- Ask volunteers to use each word in a sentence.

INTRODUCE STORY VOCABULARY

- Write the story vocabulary on the board.

- Tell students the page in the story to find each word. (**p. 4** *atmosphere–* *a layer of gases that surround Earth;* **p. 5** *uneven–* *not straight or regular;* **p. 6** *cycle–* *a series of events that happens over and over again;* **p. 15** *injured–* *harmed or damaged;* **p. 16** *collision–* *the act of crashing against each other;* **p. 16** *data–* *individual facts, figures, and other items of information*).

- Have students read the sentence with the vocabulary word and use context and picture clues to form a definition. If they have difficulty, provide them with the above definition.

INTRODUCE THE BOOK

- Direct attention to the book cover and read the title. Then have students do a picture walk through the book.

- Read the table of contents aloud with students. **Ask What kind of information do you expect to find in this book?**

- Read page 2 aloud together. Write *tornadoes, unstable* and *busiest* on the board. Have students identify the root words. (tornado, stable, busy)

READ THE BOOK

- Direct students to the judgments and decisions chart on the BLM.

- **Say As we read the book, we will stop and record the judgments and decisions the people of Jefferson County made regarding the tornado.**

- Read the story and stop after page 9.

- **Ask What decision should a driver make if he or she sees a tornado?**

- Based on the students' abilities, continue with a guided or independent reading.

GUIDED READING

Continue reading the story together and stop at the end of each page or spread. **Ask What judgments did the people of Jefferson County make? What decisions and actions saved lives?** Have students add new information to the chart.

INDEPENDENT READING

Students complete the story and graphic organizer independently.

RESPOND/ASSESS

After reading the story, have students work in small groups or with partners to retell the story. Let them refer to the their graphic organizers to help them. For further assessment, students may answer the comprehension questions on the inside back cover. **The answers to the story questions are on page 393. For scoring guidelines and student record chart see page W5.**

Answers: Judgment/Decision (1) pp. 8–9 You shouldn't try to outrun a tornado/find a safe shelter. (2) p. 11 The people of Jefferson County knew what to do./They went into basements windowless rooms hid in bathtubs or a ditch.

Name _____ Date _____ Instructor _____

Judgments and Decisions

JUDGMENTS	DECISIONS
1.	
2.	

The Riddle of the Sphinx

SKILLS	High-Frequency Words	Story Vocabulary
	Context Clues	Compare and Contrast

INTRODUCE HIGH-FREQUENCY WORDS

- Write the high-frequency words on the board. Point to and say each one. (**p. 4** *them;* **p. 5** *your, might;* **p. 6** *man, woman, leave*)

- Working with one word at a time, have students search through the story to find the high-frequency words.

- Have students use the words in sentences about their own lives.

INTRODUCE THE STORY VOCABULARY

- Write the story vocabulary on the board.

- Tell students the page in the story to find each word. (**p. 5** *apologized–* expressed regret; **p. 5** *refreshment–* food or drink; **p. 5** *inquired–* asked; **p. 5** *hasty–* quick; **p. 6** *lamented–* expressed grief; **p. 14** *debt–* something owed).

- Have students read the sentence with the vocabulary word and use contexts and picture clues to form a definition. If they have difficulty, provide them with the above definitions.

INTRODUCE THE BOOK

- Read the title and ask students to describe the cover of the book. **Say The creature is called a sphinx.**

- Write *Greece, Thebes, Demos,* and *Oedipus* on the board. Help students say each word.

- Have students take a picture walk to discover more about the story.

- Read the first paragraph on page 2 aloud. Remind students that they can figure out the meaning of new words by reading the words and sentences around it. Ask what *ferocious* means. Then ask them what clues helped them figure out the meaning.

READ THE BOOK

- Direct students to the compare and contrast chart on the BLM.

- **Say As we read the story, we will think about how two characters are alike and different. The two characters are Demos and Oedipus.**

- Read the story and stop after page 14.

- **Ask How are Demos and Oedipus similar? How are they different?**

- Based on the students' abilities, continue with a guided or independent reading.

GUIDED READING

Continue reading the story together. Stop at the end of page 16. **Ask How else are Demos and Oedipus alike and different?** Have students add new information to the chart.

INDEPENDENT READING

Students complete the story and graphic organizer independently.

RESPOND/ASSESS

After reading the story, have students retell it. If they cannot retell it, have them refer to their graphic organizers. For further assessment, students may answer the comprehension questions on the inside back cover. **The answers to the story questions are on page 394. For scoring guidelines and for the student record chart see page W5.**

Answers: Similarities: They are both in Thebes. They both try to make the Sphinx leave. They are both happy when the Sphinx leaves. Differences: Demos lives in Thebes, but Oedipus is a stranger. Demos tries to talk the Sphinx out of staying, but Oedipus tries to answer the riddle. Oedipus is the hero and becomes king of Thebes.

Name _____ Date _____ Instructor _____

Compare and Contrast

SIMILARITIES	DIFFERENCES
1.	
2.	
3.	
4.	
5.	
6.	

On the Ball

INTRODUCE HIGH-FREQUENCY WORDS

- Write the high-frequency words on the board. Point to and say each of the words. (**p. 4** *heard, something, hand;* **p. 5** *much;* **p. 6** *round;* **p. 8** *both*)

- Working with one word at a time, have students search through the story to find the high-frequency words.

- Have students work in pairs to use the words in sentences.

INTRODUCE THE STORY VOCABULARY

- Write the story vocabulary on the board.

- Tell students the page in the story to find each word. (**p. 6** *unique–* one of a kind; **p. 7** *dimensions–* measurements; **p. 9** *distinguished–* set apart; **p. 10** *landscape–* stretch of land; **p. 11** *thickness–* distance between two sides; **p. 14** *trifle–* treat carelessly).

- Have students use context and picture clues to form a definition of vocabulary words. If they have difficulty, provide them with the above definitions.

INTRODUCE THE BOOK

- Read the title and describe the cover together. **Ask Why is the boy surprised?**

- Have students look at the picture on page 4 and guess again.

- Read the table of contents with students. Have them tell what clues they get.

- Write *sphere* on the board and **say This story is about spheres. Spheres are objects in the shape of a ball.** Have students scan the pictures to find spheres

- Read aloud the last sentence on page 11. **Say Words may have different parts. The main part is called its root.** Write *disappeared* on the board and ask students to identify the root word.

READ THE BOOK

- Direct students to the author's purpose chart on the BLM.

- **Say As we read, We'll write an example of something persuasive, descriptive, informative and entertaining on the chart.**

- Read together and stop after page 4.

- **Ask Can you find a sentence that is entertaining?** (to entertain: Bobby opened his hand—the voice was coming from his baseball!)

- Based on the students' abilities, continue with a guided or independent reading.

GUIDED READING

Stop at the end of page 7. **Ask Can you find an informative sentence?** Do the same at the end of page 9 (to entertain) and page 16 (to persuade). Have students add new examples.

INDEPENDENT READING

Students complete the story and graphic organizer independently.

RESPOND/ASSESS

After reading the story, have students retell it. If they cannot retell it, have them refer to their graphic organizers. For further assessment, students may answer the comprehension questions on the back cover. **The answers to the story questions are on page 394. For scoring guidelines and student record chart see page W5.**

Answers: Answers may vary. Sample answers: to inform: "like cones and cubes, we are solid shapes and we have three dimensions."; to persuade: "Finish your math homework,"; to describe: Everywhere Bobby looked he saw balls of all sizes and colors; to entertain: the voice was coming from his baseball!

Name _____ Date _____ Instructor _____

Author's Purpose

INFORM
PERSUADE
DESCRIBE
ENTERTAIN

Teammates

SKILLS	High-Frequency Words	Story Vocabulary
	Context Clues	Problem and Solution

INTRODUCE HIGH-FREQUENCY WORDS

- Write the high-frequency words on the board. Point to and say each of the words. (**p. 2** *hard, wish, team;* **p. 4** *boy;* **p. 5** *see;* **p. 7** *brown*)

- Working with one word at a time, have students search through the story to find the high-frequency words.

- Have students use the words in sentences.

INTRODUCE THE STORY VOCABULARY

- Write the story vocabulary on the board.

- Tell students the page in the story to find each word. (**p. 5** *consented–* agreed to; **p. 7** *cleft–* crack; **p. 12** *defiantly–* in a resistant way; **p. 12** *gratitude–* thankfulness; **p. 14** *sacred–* worthy of respect; **p. 16** *tribute–* show honor).

- Have students read the sentence with the vocabulary word and use context and picture clues to form a definition. If they have difficulty, provide them with the above definitions.

INTRODUCE THE BOOK

- Ask students to describe the cover of the book. **Ask What do you call two players on the same team?**

- **Say This story is about teammates on a basketball team.** Write the words *coach, dribble, shot, pass,* and *court.* Ask volunteers to define each word.

- Read page 2. Ask students what they think *dejectedly* means. Then **ask What words gave you clues to the meaning?**

READ THE BOOK

- Direct students to the problem and solution chart on the BLM.

- **Say As we read, we will think about the problems Robert faces. We'll write them on the chart. We'll also write the solution to each problem.**

- Read the story and stop after page 4.

- **Ask What problem did Robert have? How did he solve it?** (Problem: The basketball team wasn't doing well without Ethan. Solution: Persuade Ethan to play.) Write the problem and solution on the board.

- Based on the students' abilities, continue with a guided or independent reading.

GUIDED READING

Continue reading the story together. Stop at the end of page 13. **Ask What problem does Robert have?** Have students add the new problem to the chart. Then add the solution.

INDEPENDENT READING

Students complete the story and graphic organizer independently.

RESPOND/ASSESS

After reading the story, have students retell it. If they cannot retell it, have them refer to their graphic organizers. For further assessment, students may answer the comprehension questions on the back cover. **The answers to the story questions are on page 394. For scoring guidelines and student record chart see page W5.**

Answers: Answers list problems and solutions.

Name _____ Date _____ Instructor _____

Problem and Solution

PROBLEM	SOLUTION

Unusual Bridges

SKILLS	High-Frequency Words Prefixes	Story Vocabulary Compare and Contrast

Part 3 LEVELED BOOK

INTRODUCE HIGH-FREQUENCY WORDS

- Write the high-frequency words on the board. Point to and say each of the words. (**p. 2** *build, end(s)*; **p. 7** *boat(s)*; **p. 8** *several*; **p. 12** *beautiful*; **p.13** *jump*)

- Working with one word at a time, have students search through the story to find the high-frequency words.

- Have students use the words in sentences.

INTRODUCE THE STORY VOCABULARY

- Write the story vocabulary on the board.

- Tell students the page in the story to find each word. (**p. 3** *murky–* dark and difficult to see; **p. 9** *piers–* pillars that hold up a bridge; **p. 9** *scheme–* a plan for doing something; **p. 12** *dismay–* loss of confidence; **p. 13** *gorge–* a deep valley with high sides; **p. 14** *immortals–* those lasting forever).

- Have students read the sentence with the vocabulary word and use context and picture clues to form a definition. If they have difficulty, provide them with the above definitions.

INTRODUCE THE BOOK

- Have students describe the cover. Discuss experiences with bridges.

- Read the title. **Say The word unusual is made of two parts: the base word usual and the prefix un-. Un- means "not." This article is about bridges that are not usual or ordinary.** Tell students to use the meaning of *un-* and context clues to help them understand the word *unintentionally* on page 6.

- Have students take a picture walk to discover how people travel on the bridges.

READ THE BOOK

- Direct students to the Venn diagrams on the BLM.

- **Say As we read, we will think about how two kinds of bridges are alike and different. We'll write the similarities in the middle of the chart and the differences in the outer parts of the Venn diagrams.**

- Read the story and stop after page 9.

- **Ask How are rope bridges and moving bridges alike? How are they different?** Fill in the first Venn diagram.

- Based on the students' abilities, continue with a guided or independent reading.

GUIDED READING

Continue reading the story together. Stop at the end of page 12. **Say Compare and contrast moving bridges and covered bridges. Ask How are the two kinds of bridges alike and different?** Have students fill in the second Venn diagram.

INDEPENDENT READING

Students complete the story and graphic organizer independently.

RESPOND/ASSESS

After reading the story, have students retell it. If they cannot retell it, have them refer to their graphic organizers. For further assessment, students may answer the comprehension questions on the inside back cover. **The answers to the story questions are on page 394. For scoring guidelines and student record chart see page W5.**

Answers: Answers will vary.

Name _____ Date _____ Instructor _____

Compare and Contrast

ROPE BRIDGES
Different   Alike

MOVING BRIDGES
Different

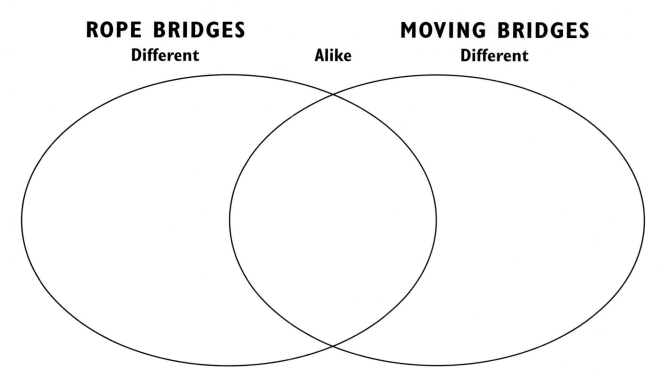

MOVING BRIDGES
Different   Alike

COVERED BRIDGES
Different

Flight of the Trumpeters

SKILLS	High-Frequency Words Context Clues	Story Vocabulary Judgments and Decisions

Part 3
LEVELED BOOK

INTRODUCE HIGH-FREQUENCY WORDS

- Write the high-frequency words on the board. Point to and say each of the words. (**p. 2** *ago, ground(s)*; **p. 5** *seven, pair*; **p. 7** *how*; **p. 8** *baby*)
- Working with one word at a time, have students search through the story to find the high-frequency words.
- Have students work in pairs to use the words in sentences.

INTRODUCE THE STORY VOCABULARY

- Write the story vocabulary on the board.
- Tell students the page in the story to find each word. (**p. 7** *perished*– died; **p. 7** *navigate*– to steer a ship; **p. 8** *coax*– to persuade gently; **p. 8** *ushered*– led to a place by another person; **p. 14** *nightfall*– the beginning of night; **p. 14** *escorted*– accompanied).
- Have students read the sentence with the vocabulary word and use context and picture clues to form a definition. If they have difficulty, provide them with the above definitions.

INTRODUCE THE BOOK

- Read the title and ask students to describe the cover. Ask students if they know what kind of bird is pictured. (swan)
- **Say** *This story is about a kind of swan called the trumpeter swan.*
- Have students take a picture walk through the book to discover more about the story.
- Read the first paragraph on page 2. Remind students that they can often figure out the meaning of a new word by reading the surrounding words. Ask them what they think *migrate* means. Then ask what words gave them clues to the meaning.

READ THE BOOK

- Direct students to the judgments and decisions chart on the BLM.
- **Say** *As we read, we will think about the decisions people make. We'll write what happened and what decision was made on the chart.*
- Read the story and stop after page 6.
- **Ask** *What happened? What did scientists and bird lovers decide to do?* Write the information on the chart.
- Based on the students' abilities, continue with a guided or independent reading.

GUIDED READING

Continue reading the story together. Stop at the end of page 15. **Ask** *What happened? What did Dr. William Sladen decide to do?* Have students add the information to the chart.

INDEPENDENT READING

Students complete the story and graphic organizer independently.

RESPOND/ASSESS

After reading the story, have students retell it. If they cannot retell it, have them refer to their graphic organizers. For further assessment, students may answer the comprehension questions on the inside back cover. **The answers to the story questions are on page 394. For scoring guidelines and student record chart see page W5.**

Answers: What Happened/Decision: (1) pp. 2-6 trumpeters were becoming extinct. /new flocks (2) pp. 7–15 no adult swans to show the baby swans how to migrate/help the cygnets follow an ultralight airplane (3) p 16 successful. Another training flight took place.

Name _____ Date _____ Instructor _____

Judgments and Decisions

WHAT HAPPENED	DECISION
1.	
2.	
3.	

A Matter of Time

INTRODUCE HIGH-FREQUENCY WORDS

- Write the high-frequency words on the board. Point to and say each of the words. (**p. 2** *piece*; **p 3** *floor*; **p. 4** *above, touch*; **p. 5** *strange(st)*; **p. 10** *straight*)

- Working with one word at a time, have students search through the story to find the high-frequency words.

- Have students use the words in sentences about their own experiences.

INTRODUCE THE STORY VOCABULARY

- Write the story vocabulary on the board.

- Tell students the page in the story to find each word. (**p. 2** *sprawled–* spread out in a disordered fashion; **p. 4** *landlord–* person who runs an inn; **p. 8** *keg–* small barrel; **p. 8** *oblige–* do a favor; **p. 12** *rascals–* mischievous people; **p. 12** *husking–* removing the outer covering from corn).

- Have students read the sentence with the vocabulary word and use context and picture clues to form a definition. If they have difficulty, provide them with the above definitions.

INTRODUCE THE BOOK

- Read the title and describe the cover of the book. **Say *Parts of this story take place in the present, future, and the past.*** Ask students to take a picture walk and guess which period of time each part illustrates.

- Read page 3 aloud together. Have students find the pair of synonyms (*stacks, piles*).

- Read page 4. Have students find two pairs of antonyms. (closed/opened; New/Old) Encourage students to look for more synonym and antonym pairs as they read.

READ THE BOOK

- Direct students to the cause and effect chart on the BLM.

- **Say *As we read the story, look for what happened and think about why it happened. What happened is the effect, or result. Why it happened is the reason, or cause. Then we'll write the causes and effects on the chart.***

- Read the story and stop after page 3.

- **Ask *What happened? Why did it happen?*** Write the cause and effect on the chart.

- Based on the students' abilities, continue with a guided or independent reading.

GUIDED READING

Continue reading the story together. Stop at the end of pages 8, 10, 12, and 16. **Ask *What happened? Why did it happen?*** Have students add new causes and effects to the chart.

INDEPENDENT READING

Students complete the story and graphic organizer independently.

RESPOND/ASSESS

After reading the story, have students retell it. If they cannot retell it, have them refer to their graphic organizers. For further assessment, students may answer the comprehension questions on the inside back cover. **The answers to the story questions are on page 394. For scoring guidelines and student record chart see page W5.**

Answers: Answers list causes and their effects.

Name _____ Date _____ Instructor _____

Cause and Effect

CAUSE	EFFECT
1.	
2.	
3.	
4.	
5.	

Making Pipes is His Bag

SKILLS	High-Frequency Words Context Clues	Story Vocabulary Sequence of Events

INTRODUCE HIGH-FREQUENCY WORDS

- Write the high-frequency words on the board. Point to and say each of the words. (**p. 2** *train;* **p. 5** *another, made, continue(d), soon, buy*)

- Working with one word at a time, have students search through the story to find the high-frequency words.

- Have students use the words in sentences.

INTRODUCE THE STORY VOCABULARY

- Write the story vocabulary on the board.

- Tell students the page in the story to find each word. (**p. 2** *cove–* a small sheltered bay; **p. 2** *driftwood–* wood that floats on water; **p. 5** *disgrace–* to cause loss of honor; **p. 6** *host–* to invite people to visit; **p. 7** *flail(s)–* to wave about wildly; **p. 10** *sizzle–* to make a hissing sound).

- Have students read the sentence with the vocabulary word and use context and picture clues to form a definition. If they have difficulty, provide them with the above definitions.

INTRODUCE THE BOOK

- Have students look at the cover of the book. Read the title. Then ask students if they know what musical instrument is pictured.

- **Say** *Let's read about bagpipes.*

- Read the table of contents with students. Ask them what kind of information they expect to find in the book.

- Have students take a picture walk through the book to discover more about the kind of information they will read.

- Read page 2 aloud. **Say** *You can figure out the meaning of a new word by reading the words around it. What does strain mean?*

READ THE BOOK

- Direct students to the sequence of events chart on the BLM.

- **Say** *As we read, we will note the sequence of events in the first chapter and write it on the chart.*

- Read the story and stop after page 3.

- **Ask** *What happened first? What happened next?* (Charley heard bagpipes when he was five. He learned to play the bagpipes in college.) **Say** *Let's write these on the chart.*

- Based on the students' abilities, continue with a guided or independent reading.

GUIDED READING

Continue reading the first chapter together. Stop at the end of each page. **Ask** *What happened?* Have students add new events to the chart, help them use transition words.

INDEPENDENT READING

Students complete the story and graphic organizer independently.

RESPOND/ASSESS

After reading the story, have students retell it. If they cannot retell it, have them refer to their graphic organizers. For further assessment, students may answer the comprehension questions on the inside back cover. **The answers to the story questions are on page 394. For scoring guidelines and student record chart see page W5.**

Answers: Answers may vary. (1) Charley heard bagpipes when he was five. (2) He learned to play the bagpipes in college. (3) Charley watched George make pipes. (4) They started a bagpipe business in 1987.

Name _____ Date _____ Instructor _____

Sequence of Events

1.

↓

2.

↓

3.

↓

4.

The Day My Grandpa Voted

SKILLS	High-Frequency Words Synonyms and Antonyms	Story Vocabulary Judgments and Decisions

INTRODUCE HIGH-FREQUENCY WORDS

- Write the high-frequency words on the board. Point to and say each of the words. (**p. 2** *important*; **p. 5** *stop*(ped); **p. 6** *while, only*; **p. 12** *seem*(s); **p. 14** *shoulder*)

- Working with one word at a time, have students search through the story to find the high-frequency words.

- Have students work in pairs to use the words in sentences.

INTRODUCE THE STORY VOCABULARY

- Write the story vocabulary on the board.

- Tell students the page in the story to find each word. (**p. 3** *interpret*– to explain the meaning of; **p. 3** *persuade*– to cause to do or believe something by pleading or giving reasons; convince; **p. 7** *shabby*– worn-out and faded; **p. 13** *soothing*– quiet or calming; **p. 16** *pelted*– struck over and over with small hard things; **p. 16** *register*– to have one's name placed on a list or record).

- Have students read the sentence with the vocabulary word and use context and picture clues to form a definition. If they have difficulty, provide them with the above definitions.

INTRODUCE THE BOOK

- Have students look at the cover of the book and read the title. Ask them to explain what voting is.

- Have students preview the illustrations. **Say** *This story is about an African American man who tried to vote at a time when that was difficult.* Ask students to scan page 2 to find the year when the story takes place.

- Read the first two paragraphs on page 13 aloud. Ask students to find two words that have opposite meanings (*open, close*).

READ THE BOOK

- Direct students to the judgments and decisions chart on the BLM.

- **Say** *As we read, we will think about the decisions people make. We'll write the judgments and what decision was made on the chart.*

- Read the story and stop after page 5.

- **Ask** *What decision does Grandpa have to make? What does he decide?* (Judgments: White men may not let him vote. Voting is his right. Decision: Grandpa decides to vote.)

- Based on the students' abilities, continue with a guided or independent reading.

GUIDED READING

Continue reading the story together. Stop at the end of page 7. **Ask** *What decision does Grandpa have to make? What does he decide?* Have students add the information to the chart. Ask similar questions after page 14.

INDEPENDENT READING

Students complete the story and graphic organizer independently.

RESPOND/ASSESS

After reading the story, have students retell it. If they cannot retell it, have them refer to their graphic organizers. For further assessment, students may answer the comprehension questions on the inside back cover. **The answers to the story questions are on page 394. For scoring guidelines and student record chart see page W5.**

Answers: Answers may vary.

Name _____ Date _____ Instructor _____

Judgments and Decisions

JUDGMENTS	DECISIONS
1.	
2.	
3.	

Knitting Circle

SKILLS	High-Frequency Words	Story Vocabulary
	Synonyms and Antonyms	Make Predictions

INTRODUCE HIGH-FREQUENCY WORDS

- Write the high-frequency words on the board. Point to and say each of the words. (**p.2** *dead, wouldn't;* **p.5** *dragon;* **p. 6** *green;* **p. 7** *everyone*)

- Working with one word at a time, have students search through the story to find the high-frequency words.

- Have students use the words in sentences.

INTRODUCE THE STORY VOCABULARY

- Write the story vocabulary on the board.

- Tell students the page in the story to find each word. (**p. 4 attitude–** *a way of thinking, acting, or feeling;* **p. 7 cringing–** *shrinking, flinching;* **p.7 pep–** *a lively, vital spirit; energy;* **p. 9 bribe–** *money or a gift offered to persuade a person to do something wrong;* **p. 12 treason–** *betraying one's group by helping the enemy;* **p. 14 defect–** *to leave one group for another*)

- Have students read the sentence with the vocabulary word and use context and picture clues to form a definition. If they have difficulty, provide them with the above definition.

INTRODUCE THE BOOK

- Read the title and discuss the cover of the book. **Ask** *What might a knitting circle be?* Have students take a picture walk through the book to find pictures of the knitting circle.

- Read pages 2 and 3 aloud together. Call students' attention to the description of the knitting circle at the end of page 3.

- **Say** *On page 2 we learn the knitting circle is a "troublesome situation" for Nora. What are some synonyms for troublesome?* (annoying, difficult, hard) *What are antonyms for troublesome?* (easy, simple, pleasant)

READ THE BOOK

- Direct students to the Make Predictions chart on the BLM.

- **Say** *As we read the story, we will stop from time to time and make predictions about how Nora will solve her problem.*

- Read the story and stop at the bottom of page 5.

- **Ask** *How do Nora's mother and Jeff feel about the circle?* (They think it will be fun.) **Say** *Write that in the clue column, then predict whether Nora will join the circle.*

- Based on students' abilities, continue with a guided or independent reading.

GUIDED READING

Continue reading the story together. After each spread, **ask** *What clues do these pages give you about how Nora feels about the knitting circle? What do you predict Nora will do?* Have students add information to the chart.

INDEPENDENT READING

Students complete the story and graphic organizer independently.

RESPOND/ASSESS

After reading the story, have students retell it. If they cannot retell it, have them refer to their graphic organizers. For further assessment, students may answer the comprehension questions on the inside back cover. **The answers to the story questions are on page 395. For scoring guidelines and student record chart see page W5.**

Answers: Clues: (2) pp. 6-7 Nora is not a good knitter and feels humiliated at the club. Prediction: Nora might quit. Clues: (3) pp. 8-9 Trina tells Nora that if she had it to do over she would have chosen a different club. Prediction: Nora will join a different club.

Name _____ Date _____ Instructor _____

Make Predictions

CLUES	PREDICTIONS
1.	
2.	
3.	

Letters from Lila

INTRODUCE HIGH-FREQUENCY WORDS

- Write the high-frequency words on the board. Point to and say each of the words. (**p. 3** *probably, guess;* **p 5.** *flowers, speak;* **p. 10.** *world;* **p.16** *almost*)

- Working with one word at a time, have students search through the story to find the high-frequency words.

- Have students use the words in sentences.

INTRODUCE THE STORY VOCABULARY

- Write the story vocabulary on the board.

- Tell students the page in the story to find each word. (**p. 4** **inflections–** *change in tense, gender, and so on;* **p. 5** **residence–** *place where you live;* **p.9** **acquainted–** *known to one, or each other;* **p. 11** **buffet–** *self-serve meal;* **p. 14** **relish–** *a mixture of spices, dip and chopped vegetables;* **p. 15** **rummage–** *used clothing and other sale items*)

- Have students read the sentence with the vocabulary word and use context and picture clues to form a definition. If they have difficulty, provide them with the above definition.

INTRODUCE THE BOOK

- Read the title and discuss the cover of the book. **Ask** *Do you recognize any countries on the map? Where might Lila be sending letters from?* Have students take a picture walk through the book to see where Lila goes.

- Read pages 4 and 5 aloud. Point out the word *inflections* in the second paragraph of page 4 and the word *elaborate* in the second paragraph of page 5. Ask students to point out context clues that suggest the meanings of these words. Remind them to use context clues to figure out new words in the story.

READ THE BOOK

- Direct students to the Sequence of Events chart on the BLM.

- **Say** *As we read, we will note the places Lila writes about in each city on the chart.*

- Read the story and stop at the bottom of page 7.

- **Ask** *What is the first city that Lila and her aunt visit? What do they see there?* (London/Buckingham Palace) **Say** *Let's write them in the chart.*

- Based on students' abilities, continue with a guided or independent reading.

GUIDED READING

Continue reading the story together. After each page or spread, **ask** *What city does Lila visit next? What does she see there?* Have students add this information to their charts.

INDEPENDENT READING

Students complete the story and graphic organizer independently.

RESPOND/ASSESS

After reading the story, have students retell it. If they cannot retell it, have them refer to their graphic organizers. For further assessment, students may answer the comprehension questions on the inside back cover. **The answers to the story questions are on page 395. For scoring guidelines and student record chart see page W5.**

Answers: (2) Paris/ art museums; (3) Nice/beaches; (4) Florence/Renaissance buildings; (5) Rome/Roman coliseum; (6) Venice/Plaza San Marco; (7) Athens/ Parthenon; (8) Santorini/ beaches and restaurants

Part 3 LEVELED BOOK

Name _____ Date _____ Instructor _____

Sequence of Events

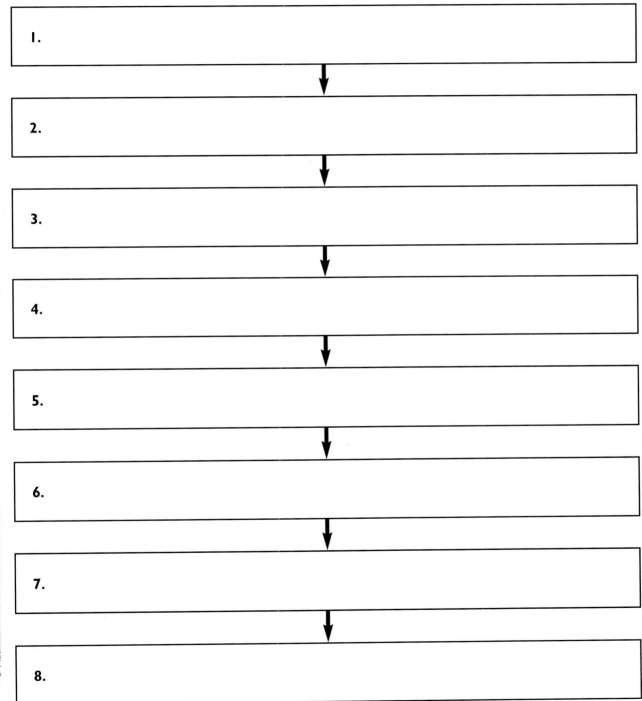

1.

2.

3.

4.

5.

6.

7.

8.

Crossings

| **SKILLS** | High-Frequency Words | Story Vocabulary |
| | Synonyms and Antonyms | Story Elements |

INTRODUCE HIGH-FREQUENCY WORDS

- Write the high-frequency words on the board. Point to and say each of the words. (**p.2** *discover;* **p. 5** *city;* **p. 6** *family;* **p. 10** *light;* **p. 15** *change*)

- Working with one word at a time, have students search through the story to find the high-frequency words.

- Have students use the words in sentences.

INTRODUCE THE STORY VOCABULARY

- Write the story vocabulary on the board.

- Tell students the page in the story to find each word. (**p. 2** *majestic–* very grand or dignified; *protruding–* sticking out; **p. 3** *mongrel–* a dog of mixed breed; *makeshift–* used temporarily in place of the usual thing; **p.7** *destination–* the place where someone is going; **p. 9** *silhouetted–* outlined against a brighter background)

- Have students read the sentence with the vocabulary word and use context and picture clues to form a definition. If they have difficulty, provide them with the above definition.

INTRODUCE THE BOOK

- Read the title and describe the cover of the book. **Say** *It looks like part of this book takes place in the country and part in the city.* Have students take a picture walk through the book to see if this is true.

- Turn to page 4. Read it together. **Say** *Mary Ellen lives in the country but wants to live in the city. The words city and country are antonyms.*

- **Say** *The words* **crowded** *and* **noisy** *might describe the city. The antonyms of these words,* **empty** *and* **quiet,** *describe the country.* Ask children to name other pairs of antonyms.

READ THE BOOK

- Direct students to the Plot and Character chart on the BLM.

- **Say** *As we read the story, we will stop and note how the plot events affect the characters.*

- *Let's start by reading pages 2 and 3 and list how having a hog get into her room affects Mary Ellen Melonseed.* (Mary Ellen decides she hates the country.) *Let's write this in the Plot and Character chart.*

- Based on students' abilities, continue with a guided or independent reading.

GUIDED READING

Continue reading the story together. After each page or spread **ask** *What new plot event has happened on these pages. How does this event affect the characters?* Have students add this information to their charts.

INDEPENDENT READING

Students complete the story and graphic organizer independently.

RESPOND/ASSESS

After reading the story, have students retell it. If they cannot retell it, have them refer to their graphic organizers. For further assessment, students may answer the comprehension questions on the inside back cover. **The answers to the story questions are on page 395. For scoring guidelines and student record chart see page W5.**

Answers: (2) Plot: Mary Ellen tells her parents she is unhappy. Character: The Melonseeds decide they need a city vacation. (3) Plot: Mary Ellen and her family visit their relatives in the city. Character: Mary Ellen is shocked that her relatives would like to live in the country.

Part 3

LEVELED BOOK

Name _____ Date _____ Instructor _____

Story Elements

PLOT	CHARACTER
1.	
2.	
3.	

Tornado Alley

| SKILLS | High-Frequency Words | Story Vocabulary |
| | Context Clues | Make Predictions |

INTRODUCE HIGH-FREQUENCY WORDS

- Write the high-frequency words on the board. Point to and say each of the words. (**p.2** *afternoon;* **p. 8** *remember;* **p 9** *wind;* **p. 11** *against;* **p.16** *afraid, laughed*)

- Working with one word at a time, have students search through the story to find the high-frequency words.

- Have students use the words in sentences.

INTRODUCE THE STORY VOCABULARY

- Write the story vocabulary on the board.

- Tell students the page in the story to find each word. (**p. 2** *contrast–* comparison between light and dark; **p. 3** *psychology–* study of the mind and behavior; **p. 4** *existence–* the fact of being alive or real; **p. 7** *subdued–* controlled or overcome; reduced in force; **p. 11** *pedestals–* bases or supports; **p. 15** *jubilantly–* happily)

- Have students read the sentence with the vocabulary word and use context and picture clues to form a definition. If they have difficulty, provide them with the above definition.

INTRODUCE THE BOOK

- Read the title and describe the cover of the book. **Ask** *What is a tornado? Do you see a tornado on the cover?* Have students take a picture walk through the book to find out more about what happens.

- Read pages 2 and 3 together. **Say** *As you read, look for context clues that tell you what Tornado Alley is.*

- Point out the definition of "Tornado Alley" in context in the first paragraph of page 3. **Say** *You can often use the context—words and sentences around a new word—as clues to find the meaning of a new word or term.*

READ THE BOOK

- Direct students to the Make Predictions chart on the BLM.

- **Say** *As we read this story, we will stop to note clues and make predictions about what is happening in Tornado Alley.*

- Reread page 2. **Ask** *What clue do we get at the bottom of page 2? What might happen?* (three days of tornado warnings; There might be a tornado in Mary's community.) **Say** *Let's write the clue and the prediction in the predictions chart.*

- Based on students' abilities, continue with a guided or independent reading.

GUIDED READING

Continue reading the story together. After each spread, **ask** *What clues help you guess what will happen? What is your prediction now?* Have students add these to their charts.

INDEPENDENT READING

Students complete the story and graphic organizer independently.

RESPOND/ASSESS

After reading the story, have students retell it. If they cannot retell it, have them refer to their graphic organizers. For further assessment, students may answer the comprehension questions on the inside back cover. **The answers to the story questions are on page 395. For scoring guidelines and student record chart see page W5.**

Answers: Clues: (2) pps 4-5: The winds are accelerating; there is another warning. Prediction: A tornado will soon hit. Clues: (3) pps 6-7: Tornadoes hit at Humboldt, a few miles away. Prediction: A tornado will touch down near Mary's house. Clues: (4) pps 8-9: Mary hears crashing sound and hears rocks hitting the house. Prediction: The tornado is very close.

Part 3

LEVELED BOOK

Name _____ Date _____ Instructor _____

Make Predictions

CLUES	PREDICTIONS
1.	
2.	
3.	
4.	

A Summer Day

SKILLS	High-Frequency Words Multi-meaning Words	Story Vocabulary Compare and Contrast

INTRODUCE HIGH-FREQUENCY WORDS

- Write the high-frequency words on the board. Point to and say each of the words. (**p. 2** *fine;* **p. 3** *pretty;* **p. 6** *never;* **p. 11** *read;* **p. 13** *hurt*)

- Working with one word at a time, have students search through the story to find the high-frequency words.

- Have students use the words in sentences.

INTRODUCE THE STORY VOCABULARY

- Write the story vocabulary on the board.

- Tell students the page in the story to find each word. (**p. 4 desolate–** *deserted;* **p. 8 tokens–** *things given as expressions of affection;* **p. 13 fidgeted–** *acted nervously or restlessly;* **p.15 exaggerated–** *made to seem larger, greater, or more*)

- Have students read the sentence with the vocabulary word and use context and picture clues to form a definition. If they have difficulty, provide them with the above definition.

INTRODUCE THE BOOK

- Read the title and describe the cover of the book. **Ask** *Where does this story seem to take place? Who might two of the characters be?* Invite students to take a picture walk through the book to learn more about the story.

- Read page 3 together. **Say** *Many words sound the same but mean different things. Chris is enjoying the first long fine day of summer vacation. Does the word* fine *here mean "wonderful" or "a tax you pay for doing something wrong"?*(wonderful)

- Read page 4 aloud. Point out the words *pretty* and *dwell* in the second paragraphs. **Ask** *What different meanings do these words have?*

READ THE BOOK

- Direct students to the Compare and Contrast Venn diagram on the BLM.

- Read page 4 aloud. **Say** *As we read the story, we will stop to compare and contrast Chris with Naomi. We will use the diagram to show how they are alike and different. What contrast do you note about how the two characters feel about school?* (Chris doesn't like school that much; Naomi is the "class brain" and a straight-A student)

- Based on students' abilities, continue with a guided or independent reading.

GUIDED READING

Continue reading the story together. After each spread, **ask** *What do you learn about Chris on these pages? What did you learn about Naomi? How are they alike? How are they different?* Have students add this information to their Venn diagrams.

INDEPENDENT READING

Students complete the story and graphic organizer independently.

RESPOND/ASSESS

After reading the story, have students retell it. If they cannot retell it, have them refer to their graphic organizers. For further assessment, students may answer the comprehension questions on the inside back cover. **The answers to the story questions are on page 395. For scoring guidelines and student record chart see page W5.**

Answers: Chris: does not live up to his potential; likes to hang out with his friends; is popular. Naomi: is a straight-A student; likes to spend her time reading; is not that popular; Both: live on the same street; enjoy the ocean; want to take scuba lessons.

Part 3

LEVELED BOOK

Name _____ Date _____ Instructor _____

Compare and Contrast

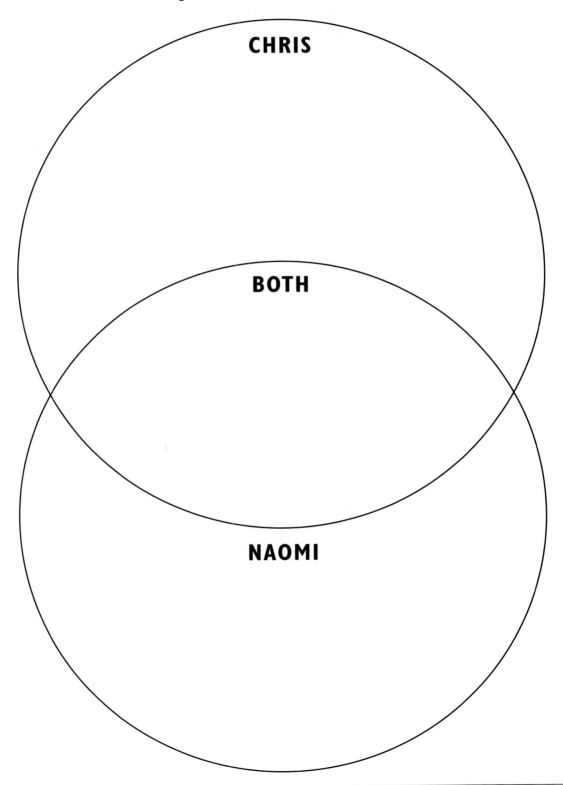

CHRIS

BOTH

NAOMI

Laurie in Charge

SKILLS	High-Frequency Words	Story Vocabulary
	Compound Words	Problem and Solution

INTRODUCE HIGH-FREQUENCY WORDS

- Write the high-frequency words on the board. Point to and say each of the words. (**p. 3** *book;* **p. 11** *water, explained;* **p. 13** *minute;* **p. 14** *came;* **p.16** *information*)

- Working with one word at a time, have students search through the story to find the high-frequency words.

- Have students use the words in sentences.

INTRODUCE THE STORY VOCABULARY

- Write the story vocabulary on the board.

- Tell students the page in the story to find each word. (**p. 3** *grimaced–* expressed pain or disgust; **ordeal–** difficult test; **p. 5** *participated–* to take part in an activity; **p.9** *spat–* forced out from the mouth; **p. 16** *victorious–* being the winner; **encounter–** a meeting)

- Have students read the sentence with the vocabulary word and use context and picture clues to form a definition. If they have difficulty, provide them with the above definition.

INTRODUCE THE BOOK

- Read the title and describe the cover of the book. **Say** *Look through the pictures in the book to find out who Laurie might be and how she is in charge.*

- Read page 2 together. **Say** *Laurie is happy because she is going to babysit for the first time.* Write the word babysit on the board. **Say** *Babysit is a compound word. It is made up of two smaller words baby and sit.*

- Read the pages 4 and 5 aloud. Point out the word *four-year-olds* in the last paragraph of page 5. Ask students to name the smaller words that form this compound word. Tell them to look for other compound words as they read.

READ THE BOOK

- Direct students to the Problem and Solutions chart on the BLM.

- **Say** *As we read the story, we will stop and note the different problems that Laurie has while babysitting, and how she solves them.*

- *Let's start by listing a problem Laurie has on page 5. Her mother thinks she is too young to babysit. How does Laurie solve this problem.* (She goes to Mrs. Martin and tells her she took babysitting classes.) **Add this solution to the chart.**

- Based on students' abilities, continue with a guided or independent reading.

GUIDED READING

Continue reading the story together. After each spread, **ask** *What problem did Laurie face on these pages? What was her solution?* Have students add to their charts.

INDEPENDENT READING

Students complete the story and graphic organizer independently.

RESPOND/ASSESS

After reading the story, have students retell it. If they cannot retell it, have them refer to their graphic organizers. For further assessment, students may answer the comprehension questions on the inside back cover. **The answers to the story questions are on page 395. For scoring guidelines and student record chart see page W5.**

Answers: Problem: (3) p 7: Jimmy falls and bangs his knee. Solution: Laurie puts ice on it. Problem: (4) p 9: Jimmy angers Laurie by breaking the bead and chewing one. Solution: Laurie keeps her temper and remains patient with Jimmy. Problem: (5) p 11: Jimmy gets his hand caught in the drain. Solution: Laurie pours soap and cold water on Jimmy's hand to free it.

Name _____ Date _____ Instructor _____

Problem and Solution

PROBLEM	SOLUTION
1.	
2.	
3.	
4.	
5.	

To the Rescue!

INTRODUCE HIGH-FREQUENCY WORDS

- Write the high-frequency words on the board. Point to and say each of the words. (**p.2** *always;* **p. 4** *sea; save;* **p. 6** *climb;* **p. 12** *snow;* **p. 16** *pushed*)

- Working with one word at a time, have students search through the story to find the high-frequency words.

- Have students use the words in sentences.

INTRODUCE THE STORY VOCABULARY

- Write the story vocabulary on the board.

- Tell students the page in the story to find each word. (**p. 2** *dramatic–* exciting action or emotion; **p. 5** *sophisticated–* showing much knowledge of the world; *improvement–* something that has been made better; **p. 8** *pouted–* thrust out the lips to show displeasure; **p. 13** *ration–* give out in small amounts; **p. 14** *exasperated–* annoyed or angry)

- Have students read the sentence with the vocabulary word and use context and picture clues to form a definition. If they have difficulty, provide them with the definition.

INTRODUCE THE BOOK

- Read the title and describe the cover of the book. **Say** *It looks like this book might describe a rescue at sea.* Have students take a picture walk through the book to see other rescues the book describes.

- Turn to page 2. Read the first paragraph together. **Say** *The word dramatic in the first sentence is a multi-meaning word. It can mean "having to do with plays in a theater" or "full of action and excitement." Which meaning do you think the word has here?* (full of action and excitement)

- **Say** *Look for other multi-meaning words as you read this story. Think about which meaning of the word makes sense.*

READ THE BOOK

- Direct students to the Compare and Contrast chart on the BLM.

- **Say** *As we read, we will stop after each rescue and write one way it was the same as, and one way it was different from the last rescue.*

- Read pages 3 through 5 together. **Ask** *How was the rescue of the Parks 15 different from the rescue of the Titanic?* (everyone on *Parks 15* lived; most on the *Titanic* were lost.) Have students add this to their charts.

GUIDED READING

Continue reading the story together. After each account, **ask** *How was this rescue similar to the last one? How was it different?* Have students add this information to their charts.

INDEPENDENT READING

Students complete the story and graphic organizer independently.

RESPOND/ASSESS

After reading the book, have students retell it. If they cannot retell it, have them refer to their graphic organizers. For further assessment, students may answer the comprehension questions on the inside back cover. **The answers to the story questions are on page 395. For scoring guidelines and student record chart see page W5.**

Answers: Compare: Andrea Doria and Josh Mitchell were both water rescues. Josh and Anna were both found by dogs. Anna and the astronauts showed great courage. Contrast: The Andrea Doria was a sea rescue. Josh was rescued from a lake. Anna was rescued from a mountain, but the astronauts were lost in space.

Part 3 LEVELED BOOK

Name _____ Date _____ Instructor _____

Compare and Contrast

COMPARE	CONTRAST

The History of Karate

INTRODUCE HIGH-FREQUENCY WORDS

- Write the high-frequency words on the board. Point to and say each of the words. (**p. 4** *sure;* **p. 8** *over;* **p. 9** *upon;* **p. 12** *name;* **p. 14** *interest;* **p. 15** *character*)
- Working with one word at a time, have students search through the story to find the high-frequency words.
- Have students use the words in sentences.

INTRODUCE THE STORY VOCABULARY

- Write the story vocabulary on the board.
- Tell students the page in the story to find each word. (**p. 5 devised–** *made up, created;* **mythology–** *legendary stories;* **p. 8 retrieved–** *brought back or recovered;* **p. 10 diminished–** *decreased or lessened;* **p. 11 edible–** *can be eaten as food;* **p. 14 cultivate–** *promote growth*)
- Have students read the sentence with the vocabulary word and use context and picture clues to form a definition. If they have difficulty, provide them with the definition.

INTRODUCE THE BOOK

- Read the title and describe the cover of the book. **Ask** *What is karate? Do you see people doing karate on the cover?* Have students take a picture walk through the book to find out more about karate.
- Read pages 3 and 4 together. **Say** *Karate is a form of self-defense and one of the martial arts.*
- Point out the word *teenage* in the first paragraph of page 4. **Say** *Teenage is a compound word too. It is made up of teen and age. Look for other compound words as you read this history of karate.*

READ THE BOOK

- Direct students to the Main Ideas and Details chart on the BLM.
- **Say** *As we read, we will stop and note the main ideas. We will also list details that tell about the main ideas.*
- Reread page 3. **Ask** *What is the main idea?* (Karate is popular in the U. S.) *What details tell about this?* (TV and movies show it; all ages study it.) Let's write this in our charts.
- Based on students' abilities, continue with a guided or independent reading.

GUIDED READING

Continue reading the story together. After each page or spread, **ask** *What main idea did you read? What details tell about this idea?* Have students add this to their charts.

INDEPENDENT READING

Students complete the story and graphic organizer independently.

RESPOND/ASSESS

After reading the story, have students retell it. If they cannot, have them refer to their graphic organizers. For further assessment, students may answer the comprehension questions on the inside back cover. **The answers to the story questions are on page 395. For scoring guidelines and student record chart see page W5.**

Answers: p 4: Main Idea/Details: Uncertain when Martial Arts began/5,000-year-old drawing may show martial arts; book from 700 B.C. shows ritual fighting. p 5: Martial arts may be based on animal movements/Monks watched and imitated how animals attack; p 6: Martial arts disciplines the body/Karate players stand for long periods in one position.

Name _____ Date _____ Instructor _____

Main Idea

MAIN IDEA	DETAILS
1.	
2.	
3.	
4.	

Ron's Story: Talking Baseball

INTRODUCE HIGH-FREQUENCY WORDS

- Write the high-frequency words on the board. Point to and say each of the words. (**p.2** *each;* **p. 8** *noticed;* **p 10** *played;* **p. 12** *run;* **p.13** *outside;* **p. 14** *fans*)

- Working with one word at a time, have students search through the story to find the high-frequency words.

- Have students use the words in sentences.

INTRODUCE THE STORY VOCABULARY

- Write the story vocabulary on the board.

- Tell students the page in the story to find each word. (**p. 3** *inquisitive–* *eager for knowledge; curious;* **p. 7** *diagonal–* *a slanted line or path;* ***visual–*** *relating to sight;* **p. 9** ***storage–*** *where objects or information are kept for later use;* **p.15** ***painstakingly–*** *very carefully and slowly;* ***unconsciously–*** *without being aware; unknowingly*)

- Have students read the sentence with the vocabulary word and use contexts and picture clues to form a definition. If they have difficulty, provide them with the definition.

INTRODUCE THE BOOK

- Read the title and describe the cover of the book. **Say** *Look through the book to see what Ron's story is about.*

- Read page 2 together. **Say** *What does the word* atrocious *in the first sentence mean? What details in the context help you with the meaning?*

- **Say** *What does* agitated *in the first sentence of paragraph 2 mean? What context clue helps you know?* **Say** *When you come to a new word, use clues in the surrounding sentences to figure out the meaning.*

READ THE BOOK

- Direct students to the Author's Purpose chart on the BLM.

- **Say** *As we read, we will stop from time to time to note how Ron overcame a speech problem—stammering.*

- Reread page 3. **Ask** *What facts do we learn about Ron's problem?* (Ron stumbles over words, especially when he is nervous.) **Say** *Let's add that to the chart.*

- Based on students' abilities, continue with a guided or independent reading.

GUIDED READING

Continue reading the story together. After each spread, **ask** *What facts help achieve the author's purpose—to tell the story of how Ron overcame stammering?* Have students add information to their charts.

INDEPENDENT READING

Students complete the story and graphic organizer independently.

RESPOND/ASSESS

After reading the story, have students retell it. If they cannot, have them refer to their graphic organizers. For further assessment, students may answer the comprehension questions on the inside back cover. **The answers to the story questions are on page 395. For scoring guidelines and student record chart see page W5.**

Answers: (2) p. 4 Ron went to class; (3) p. 7 Ron and specialist Zed loved baseball; (4) p. 8 Dr. Zed tells Ron that everyone stumbles over words; (5) p. 9 Ron practices speaking slowly and debating aloud. (6) p. 11 Ron pretends to announce the World Series. (7) p. 13 The less Ron worried, the less he stammered. (8) p. 15 Ron learned to simply try to share information. (9) p. 16 Ron became a lawyer.

Name _____ Date _____ Instructor _____

Author's Purpose/Point of View

AUTHOR'S PURPOSE: Tell how Ron overcame a speech problem.

▼

FACTS

1.

2.

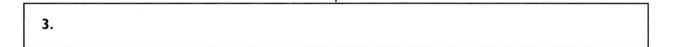
3.

4.

5.

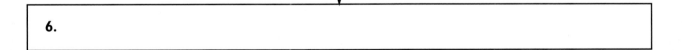
6.

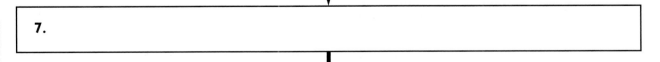
7.

8.

9.

George Balanchine: A Life of Dance

SKILLS	High-Frequency Words Context Clues	Story Vocabulary Steps in a Process

INTRODUCE HIGH-FREQUENCY WORDS

- Write the high-frequency words on the board. Point to and say each of the words. (**p. 4** *dreamed, brother;* **p. 5** *painted;* **p. 11** *traveled;* **p. 14** *hundreds* **p.15** *instead*)

- Working with one word at a time, have students search through the story to find the high-frequency words.

- Have students use the words in sentences.

INTRODUCE THE STORY VOCABULARY

- Write the story vocabulary on the board.

- Tell students the page in the story to find each word. (**p. 3 cut-outs–** *figures or designs cut out of paper or other material;* **p. 10 flurries–** *light, brief snowfall, often with wind; sudden movement* **p. 12 narrative–** *an account, tale, or story;* **p. 13 dented–** *having a small hollow caused by a blow or pressure;* **p. 14 frothy–** *like foam*)

- Have students read the sentence with the vocabulary word and use context and picture clues to form a definition. If they have difficulty, provide them with the definition.

INTRODUCE THE BOOK

- Read the title and describe the cover of the book. **Say** *Look through the book to see what George Balanchine's life was like*.

- Read page 3 together. **Say** *What does* choreographer *in the second paragraph mean? What context clues give you the meaning?*

- Read page 4 together **Say** *What does* essential *in the first sentence of paragraph 2 mean? How do the examples in the context help you figure it out?* **Say** *When you come to a new word, use clues in the surrounding sentences to figure out the meaning.*

READ THE BOOK

- Direct students to the Steps in a Process flowchart on the BLM.

- **Say** *As we read, we will stop to note the steps in the process by which George Balanchine became a great choreographer.*

- Reread page 4 and 5. **Ask** *What were the first steps in George's career as a choreographer?* (George liked to play the piano and stage shows at home.) **Say** *Let's make that step 1 on the chart.*

- Based on students' abilities, continue with a guided or independent reading.

GUIDED READING

Continue reading the story together. After each spread, **ask** *What is the next step in George Balanchine's development as a choreographer?* Have students add the step to their charts.

INDEPENDENT READING

Students complete the story and graphic organizer independently.

RESPOND/ASSESS

After reading the story, have students retell it. If they cannot, have them refer to their graphic organizers. For further assessment, students may answer the comprehension questions on the inside back cover. **The answers to the story questions are on page 396. For scoring guidelines and student record chart see page W5.**

Answers: (2) p. 7 Imperial Ballet School; (3) p. 9 George Balanchine fell in love with ballet; (4) p. 11 George Balanchine left Russia for Europe; (5) p. 12 Balanchine became very successful choreographing dances for Serge Diaghilev. (6) p. 13 In America, George worked to popularize ballet. (7) p. 15 In New York for 50 years, George choreographed dances and trained dancers.

Name _____ Date _____ Instructor _____

Steps in a Process

1.

↓

2.

↓

3.

↓

4.

↓

5.

↓

6.

↓

7.

Meet the Band

INTRODUCE HIGH-FREQUENCY WORDS

- Write the high-frequency words on the board. Point to and say each of the words. (**p. 3** *decide, wave;* **p. 4** *sound;* **p. 5** *uncle; moment;* **p. 14** *language*)

- Working with one word at a time, have students search through the story to find the high-frequency words.

- Have students use the words in sentences.

INTRODUCE THE STORY VOCABULARY

- Write the story vocabulary on the board.

- Tell students the page in the story to find each word. (**p. 2** *abide–* *support or follow along with;* *acceptable–* *what is approved;* **p. 3** *boyhood–* *for a male, the period of time between infancy and adulthood;* **p. 4** *trills–* *rapid quivering musical sound;* **p. 6** *wares–* *goods or objects for sale;* *famine–* *extreme shortage of food*)

- Have students read the sentence with the vocabulary word and use contexts and picture clues to form a definition. If they have difficulty, provide them with the definition.

INTRODUCE THE BOOK

- Read the title and describe the cover of the book. **Say** *Look through the book to see what "Meet the Band" is about.*

- Read page 2 together. **Say** *Look at the word* acceptable *in the third paragraph? What suffix does this word have?* (able) *What is the base word?* (accept)

- Read page 3 together **Say** *Look at the word* boyhood *in the fourth paragraph. What is the base word and what is the suffix?* **Say** *When you come to a new word, look to see if it is formed from a base word and a suffix. If so, you may be able to figure it out.*

READ THE BOOK

- Direct students to the Cause and Effect chart on the BLM.

- **Say** *As we read, we will stop from time to time to note cause-and-effect relationships.*

- Reread page 4. **Ask** *Why did the band start playing music in the Moreno garage?* (because Mr. Moreno left his instruments there) **Say** *Let's list that cause and effect on the chart.*

- Based on students' abilities, continue with a guided or independent reading.

GUIDED READING

Continue reading the story together. After each spread, **ask** *Did you read an important cause and effect relationship in these pages?* If so, have students add it to their charts.

INDEPENDENT READING

Students complete the story and graphic organizer independently.

RESPOND/ASSESS

After reading the story, have students retell it. If they cannot, have them refer to their graphic organizers. For further assessment, students may answer the comprehension questions on the inside back cover. **The answers to the story questions are on page 396. For scoring guidelines and student record chart see page W5.**

Answers: Answers will vary. (2) p. 3 C: The band had a gig playing at a party. E: The band had to choose a name. (3) p. 5 C: Daniel Rossi liked the band. (4) E: He asked them if he could record some of their songs. (5) p. 9 C: Daniel Rossi liked Brain Wave's recordings. (6) E: He decided to include them on a CD of new bands.

Name _____ Date _____ Instructor _____

Cause and Effect

CAUSE: WHY SOMETHING HAPPENS	EFFECT: WHAT HAPPENS
1.	
2.	
3.	
4.	
5.	
6.	

Through Alexandra's Eyes

SKILLS	High-Frequency Words Context Clues	Story Vocabulary Summarize

INTRODUCE HIGH-FREQUENCY WORDS

- Write the high-frequency words on the board. Point to and say each of the words. (**p.6** *shop;* **p. 8** *smiled;* **p. 10** *returned;* **p. 12** *finished;* **p. 14** *couldn't;* **p. 16** *whispered*)

- Working with one word at a time, have students search through the story to find the high-frequency words.

- Have students use the words in sentences.

INTRODUCE THE STORY VOCABULARY

- Write the story vocabulary on the board.

- Tell students the page in the story to find each word. (**p. 3** *scaffold–* a temporary platform; **p. 8** *sculpting–* carving or shaping; **p. 16** *hibernating–* spending the winter sleeping; **p. 16** *honeycomb–* a wax structure filled with holes in which bees store honey; **p. 16** *badge–* something worn to show a person belongs to a certain group; **p. 16** *engraved–* cut or carved into a surface)

- Have students read the sentence with the vocabulary word and use context and picture clues to form a definition. If they have difficulty, provide them with the definition.

INTRODUCE THE BOOK

- Read the title and describe the cover of the book. **Say** *Look through the book to find out who Alexandra is.*

- Read page 3 together. **Say** *Look at the word* brownstone *in paragraphs 1 and 2. What context clues help you guess that this is a type of city house?*

- **Say** *Now look at the word* intention *in the second paragraph. What context clues help you guess its meaning?* **Say** *When you come to a new word, look to see if the surrounding words and sentences help you figure it out.*

READ THE BOOK

- Direct students to the BLM chart.

- **Say** *As we read, we will list key points. Then we will sum up the points.*

- Read to page 3. **Ask** *What are the key points?* (Alexandra lives in the city. She loves to paint.) **Say** *List this on the chart.*

- Based on students' abilities, continue with a guided or independent reading.

GUIDED READING

Continue reading the story together. After each spread, **ask** *Are there any key points on these pages?* Have students add to their charts.

INDEPENDENT READING

Students complete the story and graphic organizer independently.

RESPOND/ASSESS

After reading the story, have students retell it. If they cannot, have them refer to their graphic organizers. For further assessment, students may answer the comprehension questions on the inside back cover. **The answers to the story questions are on page 396. For scoring guidelines and student record chart see page W5.**

Answers: (Answers will vary.) (2) pp. 4-5 KP: Rachel thinks Alex is lonely and should take dance lessons (3) pp. 6-7 KP: Alex wonders about Robin's Pottery shop; she looks in the shop (4) pp. 8-9 KP: shop has pottery and art supplies; Alex likes Robin's Shop (5) pp. 10-11 KP: They talk about art; Alex goes back daily S: Alex, a painter, and Robin, a gallery owner, become friends when Alez visits her shop. (6) pp. 12-13 KP: Alex gives a picture of a river to Robin (7) pp. 14-15 KP: Robin loves painting; suggests Alex sell greeting cards (8) p. 16 KP: Alex gets art prize at school S: Alex's talent is recognized by her new friend Robin.

Name _____ Date _____ Instructor _____

Summarize

KEY POINTS	SUMMARY

Nate, Steffi, and the Great Pyramid

<table>
<tr><td>**SKILLS**</td><td>High-Frequency Words
Suffixes</td><td>Story Vocabulary
Fact and Nonfact</td></tr>
</table>

INTRODUCE HIGH-FREQUENCY WORDS

- Write the high-frequency words on the board. Point to and say each of the words. (**p. 2** *because*; **p. 4** *crowded, colorful*; **p. 5** *thousand*; **p. 11** *should, next*)
- Working with one word at a time, have students search through the story to find the high-frequency words.
- Have students use the words in sentences.

INTRODUCE THE STORY VOCABULARY

- Write the story vocabulary on the board.
- Tell students the page in the story to find each word. (**p. 4** *bazaar– marketplace with shops or stalls*; **p. 5** *dramatically– strikingly*; *pharaoh– a king or queen of ancient Egypt*; **p. 6** *tomb– vault or chamber in which a dead body is placed*; **p. 6** *coffin– box in which the body of a dead person is buried*; **p. 7** *looted– stolen*)
- Have students read the sentence with the vocabulary word and use context and picture clues to form a definition. If they have difficulty, provide them with the definition.

INTRODUCE THE BOOK

- Read the title and describe the cover of the book. **Say** *Look through the book to see what Nate and Steffi are doing at the Great Pyramid.*
- Read page 2 together. **Say** *Look at the word* **excavation** *in the second paragraph. What suffix does this word have?* (ion) *What is the base word?* (excavate)
- **Say** *Look at the word* **archaeologist** *in the second paragraph. What is the base word and what is the suffix?* (archaeology; ist) **Say** *When you come to a new word, look to see if is formed from a base word and a suffix. If so, you may be able to figure it out.*

READ THE BOOK

- Direct students to the Fact and Nonfact chart on the BLM.
- **Say** *As we read, we will stop from time to time to list facts and nonfacts on the chart.*
- Read page 5 aloud. **Say What important fact do you learn about the Great Pyramid.** (It was built for King Khufu to be buried in.) **Say** *Let's list that fact on the chart.*
- Based on students' abilities, continue with a guided or independent reading.

GUIDED READING

Continue reading the story together. After every few pages, **ask** *Did you come across any important facts or nonfacts about the pyramid in these pages?* If so, have students add to their charts.

INDEPENDENT READING

Students complete the story and graphic organizer independently.

RESPOND/ASSESS

After reading the story, have students retell it. If they cannot, have them refer to their graphic organizers. For further assessment, students may answer the comprehension questions on the inside back cover. **The answers to the story questions are on page 396. For scoring guidelines and student record chart see page W5.**

Answers: p. 5 Fact: (2) p 5 King Khufu lived over 4000 years ago; (3) p.6 A man named al-Mamun once blasted through the pyramid looking for treasure. (4) p. 7 Nonfact: Many believe the tomb was looted by thieves. Some think treasures are still in the pyramid. (5) p. 9 Fact: Archaeologists use remote sensors to explore the pyramids. (6) p. 15 The scarab was sacred to the Egyptians.

Name _____ Date _____ Instructor _____

Fact and Nonfact

FACT	NONFACT

Mining the Moon

SKILLS	High-Frequency Words Root Words	Story Vocabulary Important and Unimportant Information

INTRODUCE HIGH-FREQUENCY WORDS

- Write the high-frequency words on the board. Point to and say each of the words. (**p. 3** *kitchen;* **p. 4** *ice;* **p. 14** *bottom; edge; rope; heavy*)

- Working with one word at a time, have students search through the story to find the high-frequency words.

- Have students use the words in sentences.

INTRODUCE THE STORY VOCABULARY

- Write the story vocabulary on the board.

- Tell students the page in the story to find each word. (**p. 2** *remote– far from civilization; far away;* **p. 4** *industrial– relating to manufacturing;* **p. 6** *submerged– below the surface;* **p. 7** *accumulating– increasing in size;* **p. 10** *environmental– of or relating to the environment;* **p. 13** *formations– things formed or made in nature*)

- Have students read the sentence with the vocabulary word and use context and picture clues to form a definition. If they have difficulty, provide them with the definition.

INTRODUCE THE BOOK

- Read the title and describe the cover of the book. **Say** *Look through the book to see who is mining the moon.*

- Read page 2 together. **Say** *The root word of* lunar *is* luna, *meaning "moon."* **Ask** *What do you think* lunar *means?* (having to do with the moon.)

- Read page 3 together **Say** *The root of* prospecting *in paragraph 3 is* spect, *meaning "look" as in* spectator *or* spectacle. *What do you think* prospecting *means?* (looking for something) **Say** *When you come to a new word, see if its root looks familiar. If so, you might be able to figure out the meaning of the word.*

READ THE BOOK

- Direct students to the Important/Unimportant Information chart on the BLM.

- **Say** *As we read, we will stop from time to time to add important and unimportant information to the chart.*

- Reread pages 2 and 3. **Ask** *What information on these pages is probably most important for us to know?* (Jillian lives in a lunar habitat on the moon.) *What is unimportant?* (Answers may vary.) **Say** *Let's add our answers to the chart.*

- Based on students' abilities, continue with a guided or independent reading.

GUIDED READING

Continue reading the story together. After each spread, **ask** *What information on this spread seems most important and less important?* Have students add their responses to the chart.

INDEPENDENT READING

Students complete the story and graphic organizer independently.

RESPOND/ASSESS

After reading the story, have students retell it. If they cannot, have them refer to their graphic organizers. For further assessment, students may answer the comprehension questions on the inside back cover. **The answers to the story questions are on page 396. For scoring guidelines and student record chart see page W5.**

Answers: Unimportant information will vary. (2) p. 4 Thomases prospecting for ice. (3) pp. 6–7 Jillian is lonely. (4) p. 8 Jillian's parents agree to let her explore for ice with them. (5) pp. 14-15 Jillian falls into a deep crater and discovers ice. (6) p. 16 The lunar colony will grow and Jillian will have friends there.

Name _____ Date _____ Instructor _____

Important/Unimportant Information

IMPORTANT	UNIMPORTANT

Across the Country

| **SKILLS** | High-Frequency Words | Story Vocabulary |
| | Figurative Language | Story Elements |

INTRODUCE HIGH-FREQUENCY WORDS

- Write the high-frequency words on the board. Point to and say each of the words. (**p. 2** *singing;* **p. 3** *six;* **p. 5** *full;* **p. 7** *black;* **p. 9** *left;* **p. 11** *eyes*)

- Working with one word at a time, have students search through the story to find the high-frequency words.

- Have students use the words in sentences.

INTRODUCE THE STORY VOCABULARY

- Write the story vocabulary on the board.

- Tell students the page in the story to find each word. (**p. 4 cellophane–** *a thin clear material used to wrap food;* **p. 5 triangle–** *a figure or object with three sides and three angles;* **p. 7 explosions–** *sudden outbursts of noise;* **p. 7 tollbooth–** *a small building where a fee is collected for road use;* **p. 11 hardboiled–** *boiled in water until solid;* **p. 15 appreciation–** *a feeling of being thankful*)

- Have students read the sentence with the vocabulary word and use context and picture clues to form a definition. If they have difficulty, provide them with the definition.

INTRODUCE THE BOOK

- Read the title and describe the cover of the book. **Say** *Look through the book to find out who goes across the country.*

- Read page 2 together. **Say** *Look at the word* zillion *in the last paragraph? How does this colorful exaggeration help you understand how the narrator feels?*

- Read page 4 together **Ask** *What does the narrator compare the road to in the first sentence?* (an endless treadmill) **Ask** *What does this simile tell you about the narrator's feelings?* **Say** *As you read, look for examples of figurative language to better understand the characters and events.*

READ THE BOOK

- Direct students to the BLM Plot chart.

- **Say** *Let's use this chart as we read to record the main events of this story.*

- Reread page 2. **Ask** *What did the family do on June 16th?* (They left New York for the Grand Canyon.) **Say** *Let's list that first on the Plot chart.*

- Based on students' abilities, continue with a guided or independent reading.

GUIDED READING

Continue reading the story together. After each spread, **ask** *What main event or events happened on these pages?* Have students add the information to their Plot charts.

INDEPENDENT READING

Students complete the story and graphic organizer independently.

RESPOND/ASSESS

After reading the story, have students retell it. If they cannot, have them refer to their graphic organizers. For further assessment, students may answer the comprehension questions on the inside back cover. **The answers to the story questions are on page 396. For scoring guidelines and student record chart see page W5.**

Answers: (2) p. 3 June 17th: visited Gettysburg battlefield; (3) pp. 4-5 June 18th: The narrator is bored and is annoyed with his brother; (4) pp. 6-7 June 20th: The narrator has fun riding in front with his father. (5) pp. 8-9 The narrator is awed by a visit to Mesa Verde National Park. (6) pp. 10–11 June 23rd: Jim tries driving, but is scared (7) pp. 14–15 At the Petrified Forest and the Painted Desert, the narrator tries to be nice to his brother. (8) p. 16 June 25th: The family is amazed by the Grand Canyon.

Part 3
LEVELED BOOK

Name _____ Date _____ Instructor _____

Story Elements: Plot

1.

2.

3.

4.

5.

6.

7.

8.

Sea of Treasures

INTRODUCE HIGH-FREQUENCY WORDS

- Write the high-frequency words on the board. Point to and say each of the words. (**p. 2** *shouted;* **p. 5** *questioned, safe;* **p. 9** *young;* **p. 10** *children;* **p. 11** *maps*)

- Working with one word at a time, have students search through the story to find the high-frequency words.

- Have students use the words in sentences.

INTRODUCE THE STORY VOCABULARY

- Write the story vocabulary on the board.

- Tell students the page in the story to find each word. (**p. 11** *interior–* *inside part;* **p. 11** *lifeboats–* *boats for saving lives at sea;* **p. 12** *capsule–* *a small case or covering;* **p. 12** *maiden–* *earliest or first;* **p. 13** *portholes–* *small window like openings in the side of a ship;* **p. 15** *severed–* *cut off*)

- Have students read the sentence with the vocabulary word and use context and picture clues to form a definition. If they have difficulty, provide them with the definition.

INTRODUCE THE BOOK

- Read the title and describe the cover of the book. **Say** *Look through the book to see what treasures the author writes about.*

- Read page 2 together. **Say** *Find the word* equipment *in the second paragraph.* **Ask** *What suffix does this word have?* (ment) *What is the base word?* (equip)

- Read page 3 together **Say** *Find the word* disappointment *in paragraph 4. What suffix does this word have?*(ment) *What is its base word* (disappoint) **Say** *When you come to a new word, see if it has a suffix. If so, you might be able to figure out its meaning from the base word and suffix.*

READ THE BOOK

- Direct students to the Main Idea/Supporting Details chart on the BLM.

- **Say** *As we read each chapter, we will stop to write the details, then at the end we will state the main idea.*

- Read pages 2–4. **Ask** *What are the supporting details of "No Swimming Today!"?* (Sample answer: High winds have made the sea rough.) **Say** *Use this information to start the chart.*

- Based on students' abilities, continue with a guided or independent reading.

GUIDED READING

Continue reading the story together. After each chapter, **ask** *What are the supporting details?* Have students add them to the chart. Finally, ask students to state the main idea.

INDEPENDENT READING

Students complete the story and graphic organizer independently.

RESPOND/ASSESS

After reading the story, have students retell it. If they cannot, have them refer to their graphic organizers. For further assessment, students may answer the comprehension questions on the inside back cover. **The answers to the story questions are on page 396. For scoring guidelines and student record chart see page W5.**

Answers: (Answers will vary.) Chapter 2: Annie and Andrew climb to a lighthouse; they explore the grounds. Chapter 3: Annie, Andrew, and their father meet Fisherman Jim. Chapter 4: Jim is an oceanographer. He needs help to get his underwater capsule ready. Chapter 5: Annie and Andrew help Jim. They watch his voyage; They see amazing things. Main Idea: The children realize that the sea is filled with living treasures.

Name _____ Date _____ Instructor _____

Main Idea and Supporting Details

DETAILS

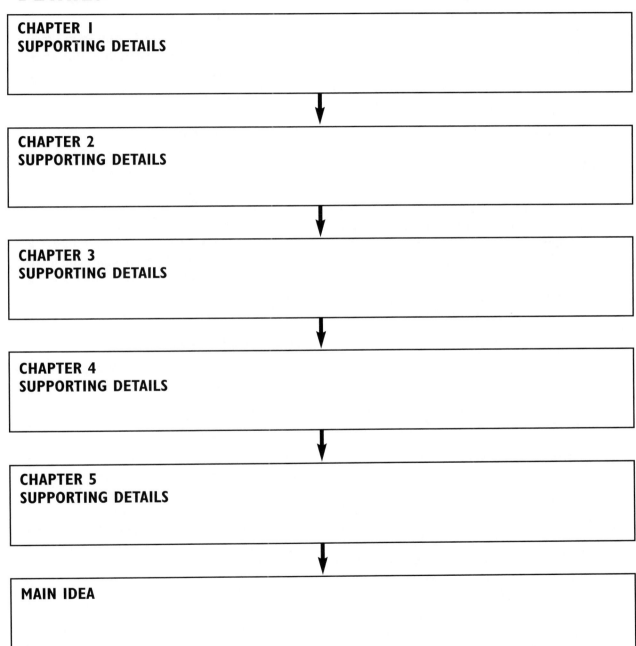

CHAPTER 1
SUPPORTING DETAILS

CHAPTER 2
SUPPORTING DETAILS

CHAPTER 3
SUPPORTING DETAILS

CHAPTER 4
SUPPORTING DETAILS

CHAPTER 5
SUPPORTING DETAILS

MAIN IDEA

© Macmillan/McGraw-Hill School Division

A Tune for Lucy

| **SKILLS** | High-Frequency Words Denotation/Connotation | Story Vocabulary Story Elements |

INTRODUCE HIGH-FREQUENCY WORDS

- Write the high-frequency words on the board. Point to and say each of the words. (**p. 3** *different, chance;* **p. 5** *arm;* **p. 6** *suppose;* **p. 11** *finger;* **p. 14** *class*)

- Working with one word at a time, have students search through the story to find the high-frequency words.

- Have students use the words in sentences.

INTRODUCE THE STORY VOCABULARY

- Write the story vocabulary on the board.

- Tell students the page in the story to find each word. (**p. 6** *troublemaking*– *causing a problem or difficulty;* **p. 8** *porcelain*– *a type of ceramic material that is hard and white;* **p. 10** *truce*– *a short stop in fighting, agreed to by both sides;* **p. 10** *grudge*– *unwillingly give or allow;* **p. 11** *banister*– *a railing along a staircase;* **p. 11** *rhythmically*– *regularly repeating sounds or movements*)

- Have students read the sentence with the vocabulary word and use context and picture clues to form a definition. If they have difficulty, provide them with the definition.

INTRODUCE THE BOOK

- Read the title and describe the cover of the book. **Say** *Look through the book to see who Lucy is.*

- Read page 2 together. **Say** *Look at the word* **beloved** *in the last paragraph. The denotation or dictionary meaning of* **beloved** *is "well loved" but it also has a connotation. The word* **beloved** *appeals to your feelings by suggesting something that is highly valued and almost worshipped. This shows us how Sarah feels about her old home.*

READ THE BOOK

- Direct students to the Character Chart on the BLM.

- **Say** *As we read, we will stop from time to time to list character details on the chart.*

- Read page 3 aloud. **Ask** *What character details seem important?* (Sarah's mother gives Sarah a big hug but Sarah does not respond.) **Say** *Add that to the chart.*

- Based on students' abilities, continue with a guided or independent reading.

GUIDED READING

Continue reading the story together. After every few pages, **ask** *What details here help tell you more about the main characters?* Urge students to add information to their charts. Finally, ask them to use their details to write descriptions of the characters.

INDEPENDENT READING

Students complete the story and graphic organizer independently.

RESPOND/ASSESS

After reading the story, have students retell it. If they cannot, have them refer to their graphic organizers. For further assessment, students may answer the comprehension questions on the inside back cover. **The answers to the story questions are on page 396. For scoring guidelines and student record chart see page W5.**

Answers: (2) p. 5 Lucy cautiously makes her way down the steps; (3) p. 6 Lucy thinks Sebastian misses music and kids; (4) p. 9 Lucy lends her piano to Sarah; (5) pp. 10-12 Sarah loves to take lessons and practices a lot; (6) pp. 14–15 shows her statue and makes a friend. Mom: warm and encouraging; Lucy: generous, thoughtful and an animal lover; Sarah: motivated, musical, open and friendly.

Name _____ Date _____ Instructor _____

Story Elements: Character

ANALYZE CHARACTER	
DETAIL	**CHARACTER**
1.	**Mom:**
2.	
3.	**Lucy:**
4.	
5.	**Sarah:**
6.	

Hercules

INTRODUCE HIGH-FREQUENCY WORDS

- Write the high-frequency words on the board. Point to and say each of the words. (**p. 2** *head; sleep;* **p. 6** *anything;* **p. 8** *garden;* **p. 10** *giant;* **p. 12** *strong*)
- Working with one word at a time, have students search through the story to find the high-frequency words.
- Have students use the words in sentences.

INTRODUCE THE STORY VOCABULARY

- Write the story vocabulary on the board.
- Tell students the page in the story to find each word. (**p. 4** *ferocious–* *fierce, dangerous;* **p. 4** *thunderous–* *extremely loud like thunder;* **p. 13** *reassure–* *to sooth or calm;* **p. 13** *waving–* *gesturing by moving arms up and down;* **p. 15** *rash–* *very quick;* **p. 16** *lavishly–* *given in great amounts*)
- Have students read the sentence with the vocabulary word and use context and picture clues to form a definition. If they have difficulty, provide them with the definition.

INTRODUCE THE BOOK

- Read the title and describe the cover of the book. **Say** *What do you know about the hero Hercules? Look through the book to find out more about him.*
- Read page 2 together. **Say** *Look at the word* phenomenal *in the second paragraph. How do the context clues—the infant Hercules killing the giant snakes—help you figure out the meaning of* phenomenal?
- **Say** *Now look at the words* mangled *and* jaded *in the same paragraph?* **Ask** *What context clues help you guess the meanings of these words?* **Say** *When you read, use the surrounding words and sentences to figure out the meanings of new words.*

READ THE BOOK

- Direct students to the Sequence of Events chart on the BLM.
- **Say** *As we read, we will stop from time to time to add events to the chart.*
- Reread page 2 aloud. **Ask** *What amazing feat did Hercules perform as an infant?* (He strangled two giant snakes.) **Say** *Write that as the first event on your chart.*
- Based on students' abilities, continue with a guided or independent reading.

GUIDED READING

Continue reading the story together. After every few pages, **ask** *What major event from Hercules' life do these pages tell about?* Have students add the information to their charts.

INDEPENDENT READING

Students complete the story and graphic organizer independently.

RESPOND/ASSESS

After reading the story, have students retell it. If they cannot, have them refer to their graphic organizers. For further assessment, students may answer the comprehension questions on the inside back cover. **The answers to the story questions are on page 397. For scoring guidelines and student record chart see page W5.**

Answers: (2) As a young man, he kills a lion bare-handed. (3) A jealous cousin imprisons Hercules. (4) Hercules works for King Argos. (5) Hercules must steal the golden apples of Hesperides. (6) Hercules kills the dragon who guards the apples. (7) Hercules holds the world while Atlas gets the apples. (8) Hercules gains his freedom.

Name _____ Date _____ Instructor _____

Sequence of Events

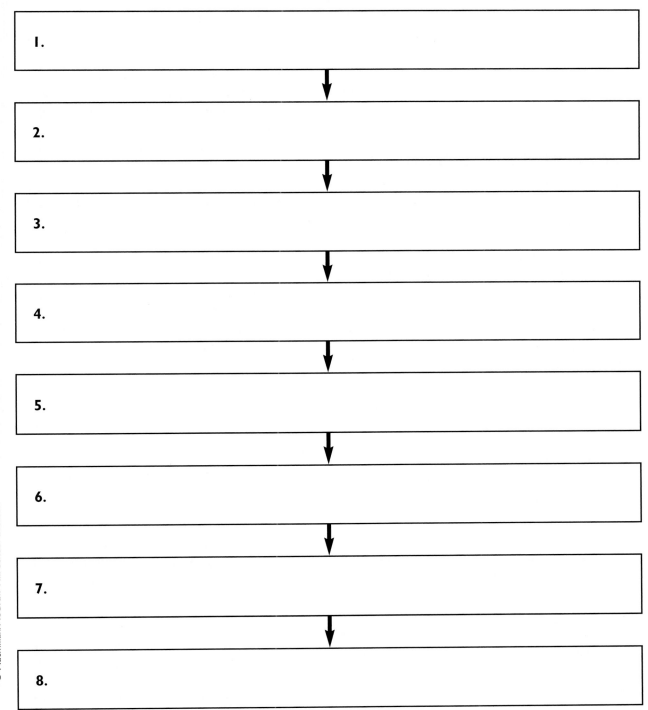

1.

2.

3.

4.

5.

6.

7.

8.

John Glenn: Space Pioneer

INTRODUCE HIGH-FREQUENCY WORDS

- Write the high-frequency words on the board. Point to and say each of the words. (**p. 2** *space;* **p. 3** *Earth;* **p. 7** *right;* **p. 9** *surprised, ride, order*)

- Working with one word at a time, have students search through the story to find the high-frequency words.

- Have students use the words in sentences.

INTRODUCE THE STORY VOCABULARY

- Write the story vocabulary on the board.

- Tell students the page in the story to find each word. (**p. 2** *void–* an empty space; **p. 7** *maneuvering–* a skillful or clever move or action; **p. 8** *deliberately–* done or said with careful thought; **p. 14** *bloodstream–* the blood flowing through the body; **p. 15** *compartment–* a separate section; **p. 16** *handshake–* an act in which two people grip and shake each other's hands*)

- Have students read the sentence with the vocabulary word and use context and picture clues to form a definition. If they have difficulty, provide them with the definition.

INTRODUCE THE BOOK

- Read the title and describe the cover of the book. **Say** *Look through the book to find out how John Glenn was a space pioneer.*

- Read page 2 together. **Say** *Look at the word* perched *in line 5. What context clues help you figure out the meaning of* perched?

- Read pages 3 and 4 together. **Say** *Now look at the word* data *in the second paragraph of page 4. What clues in the context suggest its meaning?* **Say** *When you read, use surrounding words and sentences to figure out new words.*

READ THE BOOK

- Direct students to the BLM chart.

- **Say** *Let's use this chart to record decisions that NASA and John Glenn make and the judgments and facts that lead to them.*

- Reread page 2 aloud. **Say** *Why did NASA decide to name John Glenn's first space capsule Friendship 7?* (judgment: the trip should symbolize peace and friendship; fact: there were 7 astronauts in all.) **Say** *Write this decision and the reasons on the chart.*

- Based on students' abilities, continue with a guided or independent reading.

GUIDED READING

Continue reading the story together. After every few pages, **ask** *What important decisions were made? What were the judgments and facts which lead to them?* Have students add the information to their charts.

INDEPENDENT READING

Students complete the story and graphic organizer independently.

RESPOND/ASSESS

After reading the story, have students retell it. If they cannot, have them refer to their graphic organizers. For further assessment, students may answer the comprehension questions on the inside back cover. **The answers to the story questions are on page 397. For scoring guidelines and student record chart see page W5.**

Sample Answers: Decision/Judgment: (4) p. 7 Glenn decides to maneuver his capsule through space himself./The automatic control system was using too much fuel. (5) p. 8 NASA told Glenn not to activate the retro package./That way, the heat shield would stay in place and protect Glenn.

Name _____ Date _____ Instructor _____

Judgments and Decisions

DECISIONS	JUDGMENTS/FACTS
1.	
2.	
3.	
4.	
5.	

Rosa Parks

SKILLS	High-Frequency Words	Story Vocabulary
	Denotation/Connotation	Story Elements

INTRODUCE HIGH-FREQUENCY WORDS

- Write the high-frequency words on the board. Point to and say each word. (**p. 4** *grandfather;* **p. 6** *problems;* **p. 8** *stand;* **p. 9** *most;* **p. 12** *buy;* **p. 15** *continued*)
- Working with one word at a time, have students search through the story to find the high-frequency words.
- Have students use the words in sentences.

INTRODUCE THE STORY VOCABULARY

- Write the story vocabulary on the board.
- Tell students the page in the story to find each word. (**p. 2** *barley*– *a type of grain;* **p. 5** *knickers*– *short pants that come just below the knee;* **p. 5** *mufflers*– *warm scarves that are wrapped around the neck and face in cold weather;* **p. 7** *sheepishly*– *meekly or with embarrassment for having done something wrong;* **p.13** *sweeten*– *to make sweet by adding sugar or honey;* **p. 16** *coincidences*– *happenings of two events at the same time*)
- Have students read the sentence with the vocabulary word and use context and picture clues to form a definition. If they have difficulty, provide them with the definition.

INTRODUCE THE BOOK

- Read the title and describe the cover of the book. **Say** *Take a picture walk to learn more about Rosa Parks.*
- Read page 2 together. **Say** *Look at the word* Mother *in the phrase "Mother of the Civil Rights Movement." The denotation or dictionary meaning of* mother *is "someone who gives birth," but* mother *also has a connotation. The word* mother *appeals to our feelings by suggesting someone who is deeply loved and respected. This shows us how people feel about Rosa Parks.*

READ THE BOOK

- Direct students to the Story Elements chart on the BLM.
- **Say** *Let's use this chart to record details about the story characters. Based on these details, we will infer the characters' traits.*
- Read page 4 aloud. **Say** *What details do you learn about Rosa's grandfather?* (He guarded the family home from the KKK with a shotgun.) **Ask** *What traits can you infer about him from this?* (brave and determined.) **Say** *Add this to the chart.*
- Based on students' abilities, continue with a guided or independent reading.

GUIDED READING

Continue reading the story together. After every few pages, **ask** *What details here help you make inferences about the characters?* Have students add information to their charts.

INDEPENDENT READING

Students complete the story and graphic organizer independently.

RESPOND/ASSESS

After reading the story, have students retell it. If they cannot, have them refer to their graphic organizers. For further assessment, students may answer the comprehension questions on the inside back cover. **The answers to the story questions are on page 397. For scoring guidelines and student record chart see page W5.**

Answers: (2) p. 4–5 Character: Rosa: kind, caring, hardworking; p. 6 Character: Rosa: community-minded; (3) p. 7 Character: Rosa: forward thinking; revolutionary; (4) p. 8 Rosa: brave; purposeful; (5) p. 10–11 Character: Dr. King and other black leaders: Traits: organized; determined; firm; (6) p. 12-13 Rosa: Traits: proud, successful

Name _____ Date _____ Instructor _____

Story Elements: Character

DETAILS	CHARACTER TRAITS
1.	
2.	
3.	
4.	
5.	
6.	

Last Summer at Camp Woodside

> **SKILLS** High-Frequency Words   Story Vocabulary
> Prefixes   Techniques of Persuasion

INTRODUCE HIGH-FREQUENCY WORDS

- Write the high-frequency words on the board. Point to and say each of the words. (**p. 2** *believed; summer;* **p. 6** *hold;* **p. 9** *cold;* **p. 12** *close;* **p. 16** *thank*)
- Working with one word at a time, have students search through the story to find the high-frequency words.
- Have students use the words in sentences.

INTRODUCE THE STORY VOCABULARY

- Write the story vocabulary on the board.
- Tell students the page in the story to find each word. (**p. 2 counselors–** *people who help or give advice;* **p. 2 capable–** *having skill or power;* **p. 6 stubbornness–** *the quality of not giving in or yielding;* **p. 9 equator–** *an imaginary line encircling Earth halfway between the North and South Poles;* **p. 11 nimbly–** *moving lightly or quickly;* **p. 12 foremost–** *first in importance*)
- Have students read the sentence with the vocabulary word and use context and picture clues to form a definition. If they have difficulty, provide them with the definition.

INTRODUCE THE BOOK

- Read the title and describe the cover of the book. **Say** *Look through the book to see what happened at Camp Woodside.*
- Read page 4 together. **Say** *Look at the word* **reappeared** *in the fourth paragraph. What is the base word of* **reappeared**? *What prefix does it have?* (appear; re) **Say** *If you know that the prefix* re- *means "again," you can figure out that* **reappeared** *means, that "appeared again."*

READ THE BOOK

- Direct students to the Techniques of Persuasion chart on the BLM.
- **Say** *First let's list the change Jenny desires: Overcome fear and climb the wall. As we read, we will stop to list ways in which Jenny is persuaded to make this change.*
- Read page 6 aloud. **Ask** *How does Counselor Matt in the third paragraph persuade Jenny?* (he suggests she try again and reassures her that many don't make it on the first try.) **Say** *Add that information to the chart.*
- Based on students' abilities, continue with a guided or independent reading.

GUIDED READING

Continue reading the story together. After every few pages, **ask** *What new development is bringing about the change that Jenny wants?* Ask students to add this to their charts.

INDEPENDENT READING

Students complete the story and graphic organizer independently.

RESPOND/ASSESS

After reading the story, have students retell it. If they cannot, have them refer to their graphic organizers. For further assessment, students may answer the comprehension questions on the inside back cover. **The answers to the story questions are on page 397. For scoring guidelines and student record chart see page W5.**

Answers: Persuasion: (2) p. 6 Jenny vows to do it no matter what. (3) p 10 Diane shows that the plastic holds and equipment are safe; (4) p. 11 Diane shouts "Congratulations." (5) p. 12 Jenny sets a new goal, the best climber in camp.

Name _____ Date _____ Instructor _____

Techniques of Persuasion

CHANGE/GOAL	PERSUASION
1.	**1.**
	2.
	3.
2.	**4.**
	5.

Symphony Weekend

INTRODUCE HIGH-FREQUENCY WORDS

- Write the high-frequency words on the board. Point to and say each of the words. (**p. 2** *month; every;* **p. 3** *music;* **p. 9** *set;* **p. 11** *warm;* **p. 15** *dresses*)

- Working with one word at a time, have students search through the story to find the high-frequency words.

- Have students use the words in sentences.

INTRODUCE THE STORY VOCABULARY

- Write the story vocabulary on the board.

- Tell students the page in the story to find each word. (**p. 3 poring–** *reading deeply, quickly, intently;* **p. 3 darning–** *mending with woven stitches;* **p. 12 sauntered–** *strolled; walked casually and with confidence;* **p. 13 concealed–** *hid, disguised;* **p. 14 rebellious –** *defiant; resistant to authority*)

- Have students read the sentence with the vocabulary word and use context and picture clues to form a definition. If they have difficulty, provide them with the definition.

INTRODUCE THE BOOK

- Read the title and describe the cover of the book. **Say** *Take a picture walk to find out what happens on Symphony Weekend.*

- Read page 6 together. **Say** *Look at the word* reunion *in the last line of the page. What is the base word of* reunion? *What prefix does it have?* (union; re)

- Read page 9 together. **Ask** *What word with the prefix* over- *do you see in the third paragraph?* (overseeing) *What do you think it means?* (looking after or seeing about) **Say** *Checking for prefixes and base words will help you figure out new words when you read.*

READ THE BOOK

- Direct students to the Problem and Solution chart on the BLM.

- **Say** *As we read, we will stop to list problems that arise and their solutions.*

- Read page 6 aloud. **Ask** *What does David Wiley do when the players don't have that much time to rehearse together?* (He sends them their scores to practice at home.) **Say** *Add this to the chart.*

- Based on students' abilities, continue with a guided or independent reading.

GUIDED READING

Continue reading the story together. After every few pages, **ask** *What problem did you read about? How did the people in Roanoke solve it?* Have students add to their charts.

INDEPENDENT READING

Students complete the story and graphic organizer independently.

RESPOND/ASSESS

After reading the story, have students retell it. If they cannot, have them refer to their graphic organizers. For further assessment, students may answer the comprehension questions on the inside back cover. **The answers to the story questions are on page 397. For scoring guidelines and student record chart see page W5.**

Answers: Problem/Solution: (2) p. 4 violinists must move bows together/bowing instructions on scores (3) p. 6 cannot play some weekends/substitutes when necessary (4) p. 7 no audiences/advertise and promote (5) p. 9 equipment in place on time/operations manager brings in equipment (6) p. 12 instruments in tune/player plays a tuning note (7) p. 13 rough spots/extra rehearsals

Name _____ Date _____ Instructor _____

Problem and Solution

PROBLEM	SOLUTION
1.	
2.	
3.	
4.	
5.	
6.	
7.	

The Reluctant Princess

SKILLS	High-Frequency Words	Story Vocabulary
	Compound Words	Evaluate Evidence and Sources

INTRODUCE HIGH-FREQUENCY WORDS

- Write the high-frequency words on the board. Point to and say each of the words. (**p. 2** *grandmother*; **p. 3** *same*; **p. 5** *early*; **p. 6** *took*; **p. 8** *please*; **p. 14** *herself*)

- Working with one word at a time, have students search through the story to find the high-frequency words.

- Have students use the words in sentences.

INTRODUCE THE STORY VOCABULARY

- Write the story vocabulary on the board.

- Tell students the page in the story to find each word. (**p. 2** *tutors–* teachers who give private lessons; **p. 4** *cavalry–* a group of soldiers fighting on horseback; **p. 7** *surveyors–* people who study and measure land; **p. 12** *plundered–* stolen or robbed; **p. 13** *botanist–* person who studies plants; **p. 16** *worthwhile–* good enough or important enough to spend time, effort, or money on)

- Have students read the sentence with the vocabulary word and use context and picture clues to form a definition. If they have difficulty, provide them with the definition.

INTRODUCE THE BOOK

- Read the title and describe the cover of the book. **Say** *Look through the book to find out about the reluctant princess.*

- Read page 2 together. **Say** *Look at the word* **sunlit** *in line 3. What two smaller words form this word?* (sun and lit) *What does the word mean?* (lit by the sun)

- Read page 3 together. **Ask** *What compound word do you see in the second paragraph* (downright) *What two smaller words form it?* (down and right) **Say** *Some unfamiliar words may be compound words. Looking at the smaller words that form them will help you figure out these compounds.*

READ THE BOOK

- Direct students to the Evaluate Evidence and Sources chart on the BLM.

- **Say** *Let's use this chart to decide whether Princess Ella was indeed a reluctant princess. We will list evidence from the story that supports this idea.*

- Read pages 2 and 3 aloud. **Ask** *What does the princess say on these pages to show she is a "reluctant princess?"* (She occasionally sighs, "Why do I have to be a princess.") **Say** *Add that information to the chart.*

- Based on students' abilities, continue with a guided or independent reading.

GUIDED READING

Continue reading the story together. After every few pages, **ask** *What new evidence do we have that shows whether Ella is reluctant to be princess?* Have students add to their charts.

INDEPENDENT READING

Students complete the story and graphic organizer independently.

RESPOND/ASSESS

After reading the story, have students retell it. If they cannot, have them refer to their graphic organizers. For further assessment, students may answer the comprehension questions on the inside back cover. **The answers to the story questions are on page 397. For scoring guidelines and student record chart see page W5.**

Answers: Evidence: (2) pp. 3–5 : dislikes rules; tries to break walking backwards rule; (3) pp. 8–10: questions clapping at sleeping babies rule; (4) pp. 12–13: changes rule about wild animals; likes having power to change rules; (5) p. 14: likes giving a party (6) p. 16: likes being princess, and a wise ruler. Conclusion: In the end Ella was not a reluctant princess.

Name _____ Date _____ Instructor _____

Evaluate Evidence

QUESTION: IS PRINCESS ELLA A RELUCTANT PRINCESS?

EVIDENCE
1.
2.
3.
4.
5.
6.
CONCLUSION:

Lake Joy, at Last

INTRODUCE HIGH-FREQUENCY WORDS

- Write the high-frequency words on the board. Point to and say each of the words. (**p. 2** *asked;* **p. 4** *dear;* **p. 10** *once, wondrous; mountain;* **p. 15** *circle*)

- Working with one word at a time, have students search through the story to find the high-frequency words.

- Have students use the words in sentences.

INTRODUCE THE STORY VOCABULARY

- Write the story vocabulary on the board.

- Tell students the page in the story to find each word. (**p. 2** *husky*– big and strong; brawny; **p. 6** *acquire*– gain as one's own; **p. 8** *drone*– a low steady, humming sound; **p. 10** *enthusiastically*– eagerly or excitedly; **p. 13** *instinctively*– showing a natural tendency to act in a certain way; **p. 14** *hesitantly*– in an unsure way)

- Have students read the sentence with the vocabulary word and use context and picture clues to form a definition. If they have difficulty, provide them with the definition.

INTRODUCE THE BOOK

- Read the title and describe the cover of the book. **Say** *Take a picture walk to find out where this story takes place.*

- Read page 4 together. **Ask** *What does Chip's mother say her children look like in paragraph 4?* (aliens) *How does this figurative language help you see the children?*

- Read page 5 together. **Ask** *What simile does Mom use in the first paragraph to describe the children?* (they dress like astronauts) **Say** *Be on the lookout for other examples of figurative language when you read. Figures of speech will help you see what the author intends.*

READ THE BOOK

- Direct students to the problems and solutions chart on the BLM.

- **Say** *Let's use this chart to keep track of the problems that the Nolans face and how they solve their problems.*

- Read the top of page 4 aloud. **Ask** *What problem do the Nolans have?* (Hibbing castle is too cold.) *What solutions does Mr. Nolan use to try to solve the problem?* (covers the walls with leaves and aluminum foil; designs special outfits for the children.) **Say** *Add this to the chart.*

- Based on students' abilities, continue with a guided or independent reading.

GUIDED READING

Continue reading the story together. After every few pages, **ask** *What problems do the Nolans face? How do they solve these problems?* Have students add to their charts.

INDEPENDENT READING

Students complete the story and graphic organizer independently.

RESPOND/ASSESS

After reading the story, have students retell it. If they cannot, have them refer to their graphic organizers. For further assessment, students may answer the comprehension questions on the inside back cover. **The answers to the story questions are on page 397. For scoring guidelines and student record chart see page W5.**

Answers: Problem/Solution: (2) p. 6 The roof of Summit House is unsafe/ties a helium balloon to it. (3) pp. 8–10 river rose and flooded the home/family moves to Summit House. (4) pp. 12–16 rock slide cuts off electricity/Mr. Nolan rigs up batteries using lemons and pennies.

Name _____ Date _____ Instructor _____

Problem and Solution

PROBLEM	SOLUTION
1.	
2.	
3.	
4.	

Fluency

Introduction

Fluency is defined as the rate (words per minute) and the accuracy (number of correct words) with which students perform reading tasks. At the earliest stage of reading development, students' oral reading is usually slow and labored. This is to be expected in late kindergarten through early first grade. However, when students have learned to decode and automatically recognize many words by sight, they begin to read simple text aloud in a way that sounds like natural speech.

Oral Reading Fluency norms are highly indicative of reading comprehension ability. Teachers can use the norms to rank student performance and tailor instruction to students' individual needs. In addition to providing a way to assess a student's current reading level, Oral Reading Fluency norms can be used to monitor student progress over time. This is especially important for students whose fluency is in the at-risk range of the 25th percentile or below. Any student who falls significantly below the 50th percentile needs systematic instruction to increase reading fluency.

Using the Lesson Plans

Based on the student's result from the Diagnostic Tests, choose the passage that is appropriate for the student's reading level (see page 40). The passages are written to increase in both vocabulary difficulty and complexity of sentence structure. In this book the passages begin at an end-year grade 2 reading level and build to an end-year grade 6 reading level.

It is important to use each lesson plan in sequence.

- **Week 1 — Week 2** Lesson 1: Repeated Reading / Echo Reading

- **Week 3 — Week 4** Lesson 2: Repeated Reading / Choral Reading

- **Week 5**   Lesson 3: Phrasing and Lesson 1

- **Week 6**   Lesson 4: Phrasing / Readers' Theater and Lesson 2

After week 6, repeat the lessons that you feel will most benefit the student.

Reading Fluency Norms

The curriculum-based norms chart below shows the results from a one-minute timed sampling of students who read aloud at least two passages from their basal readers. Because the data was carefully gathered and interpreted, you may rely on these norms to interpret your students' oral reading fluency performance and to tailor instruction to their individual needs.

Curriculum-Based Norms in Oral Reading Fluency for Grades 2–5 (Medians)								
Grade	Percentile	Fall		Winter		Spring		SD*** of raw scores
		n*	WCPM**	n	WCPM	n	WCPM	
2	75	4	82	5	106	4	124	39
	50	6	53	8	78	6	94	
	25	4	23	5	46	4	65	
3	75	4	107	5	123	4	142	39
	50	6	79	8	93	6	114	
	25	4	65	5	70	4	87	
4	75	4	125	5	133	4	143	37
	50	6	99	8	112	6	118	
	25	4	72	5	89	4	92	
5	75	4	126	5	143	4	151	35
	50	6	105	8	118	6	128	
	25	4	77	5	93	4	100	

*n = number of median scores from percentile tables of districts (maximum possible = 8)
**WCPM = words correct per minute
***SD = the average standard deviation of scores from fall, winter, and spring for each grade level

SOURCE
From "Curriculum-Based Oral Reading Fluency Norms for Students in grades 2 Through 5" (1992) by Jan E. Hasbrouck and Gerald Tindal. *Teaching Exceptional Children*, Vol. 24 (Spring).

Timed Reading Chart

110					
108					
106					
104					
102					
100					
98					
96					
94					
92					
90					
88					
86					
84					
82					
80					
78					
76					
74					
72					
70					
68					
66					
64					
62					
60					
58					
56					
54					
52					
50					
48					
46					
44					
42					
40					

182					
180					
178					
176					
174					
172					
170					
168					
166					
164					
162					
160					
158					
156					
154					
152					
150					
148					
146					
144					
142					
140					
138					
136					
134					
132					
130					
128					
126					
124					
122					
120					
118					
116					
114					
112					

Part 4

FLUENCY

Name _____

Lesson 1
Repeated Reading / Echo Reading

MATERIALS Fluency Passages Blackline Masters; Fluency Graphs; Timer

INTRODUCTION First Timed Reading Based on your earlier assessment of fluency levels, provide a copy of fluency passages to each student. Tell students to read the assigned passage orally for one minute and underline unknown words. At the end of one minute, tell them to draw a vertical line after the last word read. By counting the total number of words read and subtracting the number of underlined words, they should be able to arrive at a WCPM [words correct per minute] fluency score.

PRETEST Use the Fluency Graph Model how to fill in the box for the BLM number. Have students color the first bar with a red marker to show their initial scores on their fluency graphs.

MODEL **Echo Reading** Read aloud the fluency passage one word or phrase at a time. Have the student repeat each phrase after you and track his or her progress in the text. Guide the student to blend long or difficult words smoothly by repeating problematic words a second or third time. Have students do an independent read of the entire passage.

PRACTICE Repeated Readings with a Partner Have students work with a partner and take turns reading aloud the assigned passage. Remind students not to rush, and to allow for natural pauses due to punctuation. Each student should listen closely as the other reads and assist as needed with difficult words or phrases. Encourage students to read the passage a number of times until each partner is able to read at the level of fluency shown in the norms chart on page 345. Have the listener time and score his or her partner's reading.

ASSESS/CLOSE Final Timed Reading Invite each student to read aloud from the assigned passage for one minute. If students don't know a word, they should try it once or skip over it. They should not spend a long time (more than 3 seconds) on problematic words or phrases as this will lead to an inaccurate score. Subtract the errors from the total number of words read. Provide students with their scores and have them record their final WCPM with a green marker on their fluency graphs.

Lesson 2
Repeated Reading/Choral Reading

MATERIALS Fluency Passages Blackline Masters; Fluency Graphs; Timer

INTRODUCTION First Timed Reading Based on your assessment of fluency levels, provide a copy of the fluency passage to each student. Have students read the assigned passage orally for one minute and underline unknown words as they go. For each student, count the total number of words read and subtract the number of underlined words. This will provide the student's initial WCPM [words correct per minute] fluency score.

PRETEST Use the Fluency Graph Tell students to write the number of the blackline master in the correct box on their fluency graphs. Then have them color the first bar with a red marker to record their initial fluency scores.

MODEL **Choral Reading** Read aloud the assigned passage and have students follow along by tracking the text. Point out how you use punctuation as a cue to adjust your pace and pitch—for example, raising the pitch when reading a question or stressing the last word in an exclamation. Next, invite a group of students to read the passage aloud with you simultaneously. You might even consider using your hands to "conduct" the group, gesturing when you raise your pitch or pause for punctuation.

PRACTICE Repeated Readings in a Small Group Have students break into small groups of three or four. Begin with a group choral reading, perhaps selecting one student to act as the "conductor." Students should then take individual turns reading aloud the assigned passage. As each student reads, the others should listen attentively and provide word identification help and feedback. Ask students to time and score each other's fluency rate. Continue until each student has noticeably improved his or her fluency level.

ASSESS/CLOSE Final Timed Reading Invite each student to read aloud from the assigned passage for one minute. If students hesitate on a word, they should try it once or skip over it. They should not spend a long time on difficult words or phrases as this will lead to an inaccurate rate. Subtract the errors from the total number of words read in the time allowed. Provide students with their final WCPM and have them record it with a green marker on their fluency graphs.

Lesson 3

Phrasing

MATERIALS Fluency Passage Blackline Masters; Pencils

INTRODUCTION Phrase-Cued Text Distribute copies of the level-appropriate Fluency Blackline Master. Explain to students that good readers learn to read groups of words together in phrases. They use these phrases along with punctuation to guide how they read a passage.

MODEL **Choral Reading** Write the first few sentences of the passage on the board. Read them aloud with expression. **Ask When did I pause as I read the sentences?** As students respond, put a slash (/) after words on the board to indicate a pause, and two slashes (//) to denote a full stop at the end of a sentence. Tell students to follow along as you reread the passage aloud in an expressive voice, pausing at the slash marks. Point out how your pitch rises when reading a question and how you stress a word or phrase to indicate an exclamation. Repeat reading the passage chorally with students at least two more times.

PRACTICE Using Phrase-Cued Text Have students work in pairs to read the remainder of the fluency passage. Invite them to discuss where the natural pauses occur between phrases and ask them to mark their text accordingly. Once they have penciled in the slashes, have them check their work by reading the passage aloud. Students should move or modify their markings until they agree that the phrasing is correct. Then invite partners to read their phrase-cued passage aloud to the whole group. Discuss why students marked their passages the way they did, and why some pairs may have marked theirs differently.

ASSESS/CLOSE Provide students with an unmarked copy of the fluency passage. Have them test their skill by reading the passage aloud with the appropriate phrasing and expression. You may also invite students to read aloud a different, self-selected passage to the class. Invite them to discuss how working with phrase cues has improved their fluency.

Lesson 4
Readers' Theater

MATERIALS Fluency Passage Blackline Masters; Highlighting pens

INTRODUCTION Distribute copies of the Fluency Passage Blackline Master. Discuss the format of the passage together with students, noting how character names, stage directions, and dialogue are presented. Tell students that the passage will be used to create a performance in the classroom and that their fluent, expressive reading of the script will increase everyone's enjoyment of the play.

MODEL **Choral Reading** Have students listen carefully as you read all parts in the play aloud. Point out how you use your voice to show the characters' feelings, how your pace changes, and how you use punctuation as a clue to convey meaning. Tell students to count off so that each one has a number that corresponds to a part in the play. Students will then read aloud their respective parts with you in a choral reading. Repeat until they can read their parts confidently. If time allows, reassign the parts.

PRACTICE Readers' Theater Divide the students into as many small groups as there are parts in the passage. Assign roles and have students highlight the lines for their parts on their scripts. Then have them practice reading the play aloud from beginning to end. Coach them to focus on fluency and expression as they read. When groups have read through the play once, have them pass their scripts to other students and have everyone repeat the reading with new parts. Repeat as time allows. At the end of the process, have group members choose the part they wish to read in the final presentation. (If disputes arise, have them vote as a group on who should play which part.) The students should discuss as a group where each character will stand in the final performance. They may also wish to create simple props or costumes for their performance. Tell them to read and reread their parts until they feel comfortable that they are ready to present the play to the whole class.

ASSESS/CLOSE Present Have students perform before a live audience—their classmates, another class, or a group of family members and friends. Observe how effortlessly and expressively they read their lines. Encourage the audience to applaud the performers' efforts. Have students discuss how they felt about their own performance after each presentation.

Name _____ Date _____ Instructor _____

How Dad Scared Marcia

	My dad sings in the shower. He's not a very good singer!
12	The other day, my friend Marcia was visiting. We were in my room,
25	just minding our own business and playing a game —
34	when suddenly Dad started shrieking as if the place were on fire.
46	Marcia looked afraid. I could tell that she thought something
56	was very wrong.
59	I explained that the noise was only Dad making music.
69	Marcia wouldn't believe me. She was sure something
77	scary was happening. **80**

First Timed Reading	**Final Timed Reading**
Words Read in one minute _____	*Words Read in one minute* _____
Number of Errors − _____	*Number of Errors* − _____
Words Correct per Minute **Score** _____	*Words Correct per Minute* **Score** _____

Name _____ Date _____ Instructor _____

The Double

	"Daniel, put that book down," said his mother. "Come on
11	into the kitchen and have your supper."
17	"I'm reading, Ma," said Daniel. "Please let me just finish this
28	page. Okay?"
30	Daniel's mother was very glad that her son was reading. But
41	she couldn't understand what had happened to him. He had
51	never, ever read that much before.
57	When Daniel finally came in to have his dinner, he was
68	smiling brightly.
70	"Well, what's so funny?" his mother asked.
77	"I'm reading a story about the old days," Daniel said.
87	"There's a young knight in it. He could be my exact double!" 99

First Timed Reading		Final Timed Reading	
Words Read in one minute	_____	Words Read in one minute	_____
Number of Errors	– _____	Number of Errors	– _____
Words Correct per Minute **Score**	_____	Words Correct per Minute **Score**	_____

Name _____ Date _____ Instructor _____

Windows

9	Ali and his friend Cathy were neighbors. Sometimes Ali
21	would sit near the window in his room and Cathy would sit
32	near the window in her room. They would whisper to each
42	other through the windows. They thought this was terrific fun.
53	When the winter came, it was too cold to keep the
64	windows open. Ali and Cathy were sad that they couldn't speak
75	with each other through the windows any more. Cathy came up
87	with a great idea, though. They could write signs, and hold them
90	against the windows.
102	The children sat in their rooms. They each had a huge stack
116	of paper. Cathy had a box of colorful crayons. Ali had only a plain
	pencil. But the messages they sent delighted them both. **125**

First Timed Reading		**Final Timed Reading**	
Words Read in one minute	_____	*Words Read in one minute*	_____
Number of Errors	**–** _____	*Number of Errors*	**–** _____
Words Correct per Minute **Score**	_____	*Words Correct per Minute* **Score**	_____

Name _____ Date _____ Instructor _____

The Mouse and the Robin

	A mouse and a robin were talking one day.
9	"I wish I were a mouse," said the robin. "I could skitter
21	wherever I wanted to go. It looks like fun."
30	"I wish I were a robin," said the mouse. "Flying is cool."
42	"Let's change places," said the robin. "I'll skitter, and you fly."
53	While they were both trying to move, a hungry fox came by.
65	The fox saw that the small animals were not getting very far.
77	"Well," he said to himself, "it looks like I'll have a big dinner."
90	Just then the mouse and the robin saw the fox. The mouse
102	ran away. The robin flew off.
108	"I'm glad I can skitter," called the mouse.
116	"I'm glad I can fly," called the robin. 124

First Timed Reading	**Final Timed Reading**
Words Read in one minute _____	Words Read in one minute _____
Number of Errors – _____	Number of Errors – _____
Words Correct per Minute **Score** _____	Words Correct per Minute **Score** _____

Name _____ Date _____ Instructor _____

King Bob's Plan

	King Bob was worried. His daughter never smiled. She wasn't
10	really sad about anything. She just didn't feel like using her face
22	except to frown.
25	The king had read stories about princesses who never
34	smiled. In the stories, kings always sent for the wisest people
45	in the kingdom. But nobody could make the girl smile. Finally, some
57	silly boy came to the castle. He got the king's daughter to laugh.
70	Then the king's daughter and the silly boy lived happily ever after.
82	King Bob didn't want his daughter living happily ever after
92	with some dunce. He thought long and hard. What could he do?
104	Finally, he decided. He'd turn the stories upside down!
113	He'd *begin* by trying to get the silliest boys to help his daughter.
	126

First Timed Reading		**Final Timed Reading**	
Words Read in one minute	_____	*Words Read in one minute*	_____
Number of Errors	– _____	*Number of Errors*	– _____
Words Correct per Minute **Score**	_____	*Words Correct per Minute* **Score**	_____

Name _____ Date _____ Instructor _____

Adding at the Theme Park

	Pablo had never been to a theme park before. So when his
12	aunt and uncle took him to Funworld, he was very excited.
23	When they got to the park, they paid their admission. Then
34	they entered. His uncle handed him a map that showed all
45	the rides. Pablo was thrilled. "I want to go on that ride,
57	and that one, and also that one, and let's not miss that one!"
70	"Hey," said his uncle. "Take a breath, please. There are only
81	so many hours in a day!"
87	Pablo reached into his pocket. He took out a small
97	calculator that he liked to carry around. Quickly, he began pushing
108	some of its buttons. "Look, Uncle," Pablo said. "I added up
119	the times for each ride. We can go on everything!" 129

First Timed Reading		**Final Timed Reading**	
Words Read in one minute	_____	Words Read in one minute	_____
Number of Errors	– _____	Number of Errors	– _____
Words Correct per Minute **Score**	_____	Words Correct per Minute **Score**	_____

Name _____ Date _____ Instructor _____

Carmen Lopez and Her Brothers

	Carmen Lopez had eight older brothers. When she was
9	born, her mother was very happy, because the family finally had
20	enough children to make a baseball team.
27	Carmen's father was not positive that a girl would want to
38	play baseball with eight older brothers. But Mrs. Lopez
47	promised him that Carmen would turn out to be the
57	best player of all.
61	And she was right. As Carmen grew, her family noticed
71	how strong and quick she was becoming. By the time Carmen
82	was nine, she was the best ballplayer in the playground. She could
94	hit, she could catch, and she could run. Her brothers couldn't
105	believe their good fortune in having her on their team.
115	But the Lopez boys got worried when Carmen started
124	taking an interest in chess. Suddenly, there were some days
134	when she just didn't feel like playing baseball. 142

First Timed Reading	**Final Timed Reading**
Words Read in one minute _____	Words Read in one minute _____
Number of Errors − _____	Number of Errors − _____
Words Correct per Minute **Score** _____	Words Correct per Minute **Score** _____

Name _____ Date _____ Instructor _____

The Boy Who Loved Spaghetti

	Louis was devoted to spaghetti. He would eat it for
10	breakfast, lunch, and supper — if his mother allowed him!
19	Every day, he'd arrive happily at the breakfast table, and say,
30	"Mom, let's have spaghetti."
34	"Louis!" she would reply. "I'm not going to cook you spaghetti
45	in the morning. Eat your oatmeal. It's good for you."
55	Louis even dreamed about spaghetti. Sometimes he would
63	dream that he was a big human meatball, living in a bowl
75	of noodles. At other times, he would dream that he lived
86	in a house made of spaghetti.
92	"Guess what I dreamed last night?" he would ask his mother.
103	"You dreamed of spaghetti," she would guess. She was rarely
113	wrong.
114	"Right," he would say. "Let's have some now!"
122	"I've told you a hundred times," his mother would say with a
134	sigh. "Not for breakfast!" 138

First Timed Reading		Final Timed Reading	
Words Read in one minute	_____	*Words Read in one minute*	_____
Number of Errors	− _____	*Number of Errors*	− _____
Words Correct per Minute **Score**	_____	*Words Correct per Minute* **Score**	_____

Name _____ Date _____ Instructor _____

A Movie Critic

11	Maybe you've read something in a newspaper written by a movie
25	critic. That's a person who goes to a movie and then writes an opinion.
37	Sometimes the critic really likes a movie, but sometimes he or she
39	hates it.
51	The critic can't just say, "this movie is great" or "this movie
64	stinks." A good critic always tries to give a reason for an opinion.
76	You may not agree, but you will always know why the critic
88	thinks a certain way. Try this: Think of a movie that you
100	saw. Then ask yourself some questions about it. Did you like it
111	or not? Why? Really explain your ideas and feelings to yourself.
	In no time at all, you'll become a movie critic, too! **122**

First Timed Reading	**Final Timed Reading**
Words Read in one minute _____	*Words Read in one minute* _____
Number of Errors **–** _____	*Number of Errors* **–** _____
Words Correct per *Minute* **Score** _____	*Words Correct per* *Minute* **Score** _____

Name _____   Date _____   Instructor _____

Saturday for a Turtle

	Betsy enjoyed talking to her pet turtle, and she sometimes
10	imagined that the turtle responded.
15	"Good morning," she said in a cheery voice to the turtle
26	one day.
28	"What's so good about it?" the turtle asked.
36	"Just look around," Betsy said. "The sun is shining, and the
47	weather is warm, and it's Saturday! I'm free to play all
58	day, because there's no school."
63	"Well, that sounds just terrific for you," grumped the turtle.
73	"But I'm still stuck in this bulky glass bowl. To me, there's
85	no difference between Saturday and any other day. I can't
95	see the sun or feel the warmth. All I see is bowl and more
109	bowl. All I feel is glass and more glass." **118**

First Timed Reading		Final Timed Reading	
Words Read in one minute	_____	*Words Read in one minute*	_____
Number of Errors	– _____	*Number of Errors*	– _____
Words Correct per Minute **Score**	_____	*Words Correct per Minute* **Score**	_____

Name _____ Date _____ Instructor _____

A Smart Saying

11	A man named Samuel Johnson once said, "To a poet nothing can be useless."
14	What the saying really means is this: If you're a person who
26	likes to write about life, everything that happens gives you food
37	for thought. If something makes you happy, it's worth writing about.
48	But if something makes you sad, it's also worth writing about.
59	Things that make you worry, or laugh, or get angry are
70	all worth writing about, too.
75	To a poet, everything has a use. It all goes into the big pot in
90	the writer's mind. The poet cooks up a beautiful poem by
101	mixing together the things in that pot. **108**

First Timed Reading	**Final Timed Reading**
Words Read in one minute _____	*Words Read in one minute* _____
Number of Errors – _____	*Number of Errors* – _____
Words Correct per Minute **Score** _____	*Words Correct per Minute* **Score** _____

Name _____ Date _____ Instructor _____

Sir Kay and the Sword

14	In the center of a small town sat a big stone with a sword stuck in it. A note in the stone said, "He who lifts this sword
28	shall be king!"
31	All the strong young men came from miles around. One
41	young man was named Kay.
46	"Surely," he said, "I will be able to lift the sword, and become king."
60	Kay had a page named Arthur, who was just a youth. "I'd like
73	it if you were king," Arthur said to Kay.
82	Kay chuckled and said, "I think you'd prefer it, if you were
94	king yourself. Too bad you're just a tiny boy!"
103	Sir Kay took his turn at the stone, and tried to lift the sword
117	with all his might — but he couldn't! 124

First Timed Reading	**Final Timed Reading**
Words Read in one minute _____	Words Read in one minute _____
Number of Errors − _____	Number of Errors − _____
Words Correct per Minute **Score** _____	Words Correct per Minute **Score** _____

Name _____ Date _____ Instructor _____

San Marino

11	San Marino is one of the world's smallest countries. See if
26	you can find it on a map. It's just a slight speck. Look for Italy,
31	which is all around it.
42	San Marino sits on the slope of a mountain. The country
54	takes up only 24 square miles. That's much smaller than the size
65	of many parks in America. Its population is only about 25,000.
76	Just think! Fewer people live in the whole country than live
88	in most of the small towns in the United States. The capital
97	city of San Marino is also called San Marino.
108	San Marino's main industry is tourism. Lots of people visit it
118	every year. San Marino is also known for its ceramics.
125	Ceramics are items made out of clay.
137	San Marino has a very high literacy rate, even higher than ours.
	Almost everyone in the country can read. **144**

First Timed Reading	**Final Timed Reading**
Words Read in one minute _____	*Words Read in one minute* _____
Number of Errors – _____	*Number of Errors* – _____
Words Correct per Minute **Score** _____	*Words Correct per* Minute **Score** _____

Name _____ Date _____ Instructor _____

Edward's Code

	"I have a code," Edward said to the teacher.
9	"Is it something you'd like the class to help you figure out?"
21	asked the teacher.
24	"It's code. Dot code!"
28	"Yes, yes," said the teacher. He was getting impatient. "I
38	know it's a code. Are you saying that it's a code with dots?"
51	"Dough!" said Edward.
54	"It's a code using dough?" asked the teacher. "Can we read
65	the code by looking at bread?"
71	Edward tried to explain. "It's a doze code."
79	The teacher couldn't understand him. "Am I supposed to
88	believe that it's a code you can solve only when you're
99	taking a nap?"
102	"Dough, it's dot!"
105	Edward sneezed. Suddenly, the teacher got it. "Oh," he said,
115	"your nose is stuffed because you have a *cold*. You're having
126	trouble pronouncing words." **129**

First Timed Reading		**Final Timed Reading**	
Words Read in one minute	_____	*Words Read in one minute*	_____
Number of Errors	– _____	*Number of Errors*	– _____
Words Correct per Minute **Score**	_____	*Words Correct per Minute* **Score**	_____

Name _____ Date _____ Instructor _____

Chewing Gum for the Eyes

	The TV was on, but Benjy wasn't actually watching or listening.
11	He was thinking about something his teacher mentioned that day. The
22	teacher told the class a funny thing that a famous man named
34	Frank Lloyd Wright once said. Wright was a renowned
43	architect, so the teacher showed them some pictures of his
53	most beautiful buildings.
56	Here's what Wright said: "Television is chewing gum for the
66	eyes."
67	The teacher asked the class to go home and spend a few hours
80	watching TV. That wouldn't be difficult! While they watched, she
90	asked them to try to figure out what Frank Lloyd Wright meant. The
103	teacher suggested a question they could toss around in their
113	imagination. What's the difference between sitting idly in front of the
124	TV and going out to build a house? Tomorrow, they would discuss it.
137	Benjy tried to think about what it would feel like to chew
149	with his eyes. Ouch! That didn't make any sense. 158

First Timed Reading		**Final Timed Reading**	
Words Read in one minute	_____	*Words Read in one minute*	_____
Number of Errors	– _____	*Number of Errors*	– _____
Words Correct per Minute **Score**	_____	*Words Correct per Minute* **Score**	_____

Name _____ Date _____ Instructor _____

The Talking Homework

8	Lauren yawned. She had been doing her arithmetic
18	assignment for a half hour, and the numbers were all
29	starting to look alike to her. Seven times six, eight divided
36	by two, three plus one plus five.
47	Suddenly, one of the numbers on the page began talking to her.
48	"Hello," it said. "I'm Four. Do you recognize me?"
57	Lauren shook her head in disbelief. "I must be dreaming,"
67	she assured herself.
70	"No, you're not dreaming," said Four. "I'm addressing you
79	from this multiplication problem."
83	"What do you want?" asked Lauren.
89	"I want to know if you like me as much as you like my
103	buddy Nine."
105	"Well," said Lauren, "I suppose I like you both the same.
116	Nine is more, though."
120	"I knew you preferred Nine," cried Four.
127	"Not necessarily," said Lauren. "I like Nine better if we're
137	talking about toys. Nine is more fun than Four. But
147	if we're referring to arithmetic problems, I definitely
155	like Four better than Nine!" **160**

First Timed Reading	**Final Timed Reading**
Words Read in one minute _____	*Words Read in one minute* _____
Number of Errors – _____	*Number of Errors* – _____
Words Correct per Minute **Score** _____	*Words Correct per Minute* **Score** _____

Name _____   Date _____   Instructor _____

The First World Almanac

	The World Almanac is an important reference book. It has
10	all kinds of interesting facts. Most people think the World
20	Almanac got its name because it tells us things about the
31	world. But it really got its name because it was first put
43	out by a newspaper called *The New York World.* That happened
54	back in 1868.
57	The first World Almanac was supposed to be used mainly by
68	writers who worked on the newspaper. The book gave its
78	information in lists and short articles. Writers could look up things
89	they might want to mention in their stories.
97	That first World Almanac told the prices of cotton at
107	different times of the year. Cotton was very important then.
117	The book had many short articles about what had happened in 1867.
129	It also told about the best times to see the moon and the
142	stars. It still does that today!
148	The 1868 World Almanac cost only 20 cents. **156**

First Timed Reading		**Final Timed Reading**	
Words Read in one minute	_____	*Words Read in one minute*	_____
Number of Errors	− _____	*Number of Errors*	− _____
Words Correct per Minute **Score**	_____	*Words Correct per Minute* **Score**	_____

Name _____ Date _____ Instructor _____

Sasha's Order

11	Sasha always got excited when his parents took him to a restaurant, but he could never decide what to order. Here's
21	what happened the last time they went out to eat.
31	"What would you like?" the server asked.
38	"I'll have chicken," said Sasha's mother.
44	"Make mine fish," said Sasha's father.
50	Sasha couldn't make a decision. "I'm positive that I don't
60	want chicken or fish," he said.
66	"May I suggest the vegetable platter?" asked the server.
75	"No," said Sasha. "That doesn't sound very fascinating."
83	"How about a hamburger?" tried Sasha's mother.
90	"Nope," said Sasha. "A hamburger is boring!"
97	"Why don't you get the stew?" Sasha's father prompted.
106	"You like stew."
109	"Not today," said Sasha. "I want to sample something entirely
119	different for a change."
123	Sasha's mother and father were losing their patience.
131	"Come on," pleaded Sasha's father. "We're starving."
138	"I've got it!" said Sasha. "Can you make me a stew with
150	chicken, fish, vegetables, and hamburger?" **155**

First Timed Reading	**Final Timed Reading**
Words Read in one minute _____	*Words Read in one minute* _____
Number of Errors − _____	*Number of Errors* − _____
Words Correct per Minute **Score** _____	*Words Correct per Minute* **Score** _____

Name _____   Date _____   Instructor _____

The Worst Kind of Hurting

	The old man trudged slowly down the street. A crowd
10	of children was playing with a ball. They chucked it to
21	each other and ran after it if they failed to catch it.
31	One of the boys wasn't paying attention to where he was
44	going, and he accidentally bumped into the old man.
53	Fortunately, the old man didn't fall, although he lost his
63	balance a little.
66	The boy apologized immediately. The old man shrugged his
75	shoulders and chuckled. He had been young once, too, he
85	told the boy, and he understood what it was like to be
97	careless. It was fortunate that he hadn't fallen, though. He
107	might have been hurt physically, somewhere on his body. But the
118	boy would have been hurt, too. He would have been hurt
129	in his conscience. "And that's the worst kind of hurting,"
139	the old man said. **143**

First Timed Reading		**Final Timed Reading**	
Words Read in one minute	_____	*Words Read in one minute*	_____
Number of Errors	− _____	*Number of Errors*	− _____
Words Correct per Minute **Score**	_____	*Words Correct per Minute* **Score**	_____

Name _____ Date _____ Instructor _____

Lunch

	Simon examined Mary's lunch. "I'll trade you my pickle for
10	your carrot," he suggested.
14	Mary pondered for a while and then she replied, "Okay. But
25	only if I can swap you my peanut butter and jelly sandwich
37	for your baloney."
40	Simon didn't hesitate. "All right," he said. "But then how about
51	if I give you my apple, and you let me have your grapes?"
64	"That sounds reasonable to me," said Mary. "Would you
73	mind switching my cookie for your brownie?"
80	"Well," said Simon, with a big smile, "that's acceptable. But
90	can I also throw in my juice for your chocolate drink?"
101	Mary had an idea. "Why don't we just trade our paper bags
113	and everything that's in them?"
118	"Oh, no," said Simon. "That wouldn't be right. My mother
128	prepared this lunch especially for me." **134**

First Timed Reading	**Final Timed Reading**
Words Read in one minute _____	Words Read in one minute _____
Number of Errors — _____	Number of Errors — _____
Words Correct per Minute **Score** _____	Words Correct per Minute **Score** _____

Name _____   Date _____   Instructor _____

The Story of Raji

12	Once upon a time there was a young man named Raji, who lived all by himself in an immense cave. He had to
23	labor very hard to gain nourishment every day. He spent
33	many hours fishing in the nearby river and picking fruit from
44	the nearby trees.
47	One day, an old, old man came to the cave. The old man told
61	Raji that he was very hungry. He asked for a small morsel of food.
75	Raji offered the man a big piece of fish and a handful of tasty berries.
90	While the man ate, Raji went to the river to fetch some
102	water for the old man to drink.
109	After the man was done eating, he asked Raji if the young
121	man had any particular wish. **126**

First Timed Reading	**Final Timed Reading**
Words Read in one minute _____	Words Read in one minute _____
Number of Errors – _____	Number of Errors – _____
Words Correct per Minute **Score** _____	Words Correct per Minute **Score** _____

Name _____ Date _____ Instructor _____

Now Pitching for the Littletown Lions

10	Henry Lee had leaned against his father's shoulder at the baseball game, and had fallen fast asleep. He was startled
20	awake by the sound of the loudspeaker.
27	"Now pitching for the Littletown Lions," woofed the
35	loudspeaker, "is Henry Lee!"
39	Henry's dad nudged him. "Wake up, lazybones" he said.
48	"You're pitching!"
50	"What do you mean?" asked Henry. "I'm just a little kid. I'm
62	not good enough to play with these immense professionals."
71	"Well," said Henry's dad, "that might be your opinion. But
81	according to the loudspeaker, you'd better scurry down there on
91	the field and take the mound."
97	"Henry Lee!" the loudspeaker repeated. "Now pitching for
105	the Littletown Lions."
108	Henry heard what sounded like a million hurrahs. The man
118	sitting behind him in the stands tapped him on the shoulder.
129	"You'd better get going, sonny," said the man. "And make
139	sure you throw strikeouts." **143**

First Timed Reading	**Final Timed Reading**
Words Read in one minute _____	*Words Read in one minute* _____
Number of Errors − _____	*Number of Errors* − _____
Words Correct per Minute **Score** _____	*Words Correct per Minute* **Score** _____

Name _____ Date _____ Instructor _____

Buck Rogers

10	None of us knows exactly what will occur tomorrow. It's awfully hard to picture what the world will be like
20	hundreds of years from now. But people have always had
30	fun trying to envision the future.
36	In 1929, the head of a big newspaper had an idea. He
48	thought it would be interesting to create a new kind
58	of comic strip for children. He asked a writer and an artist
70	to use their imaginations on something that would make
79	readers love science.
82	The two men decided to set their stories in the future. It
94	wasn't long before they thought up Buck Rogers. Buck Rogers was
105	a man who had many adventures in a future century. He
116	wandered all over the universe in a spaceship. He attempted to
127	combat evil wherever he found it.
133	Buck Rogers was popular. Soon, there were Buck Rogers
142	radio shows and movies. Of course, there were Buck Rogers
152	toys, too. **154**

First Timed Reading	**Final Timed Reading**
Words Read in one minute _____	*Words Read in one minute* _____
Number of Errors **–** _____	*Number of Errors* **–** _____
Words Correct per Minute **Score** _____	*Words Correct per Minute* **Score** _____

Name _____ Date _____ Instructor _____

On the Trail

11	The girl and her mother were hiking on the trail. They
19	weren't going anywhere in particular. They weren't concerned
30	about what time it was. All they cared about were the
40	gorgeous flowers they saw all around them, and the chirping
	birds they heard.
43	"I just adore it out here in the fresh air," said the girl.
56	"Me, too," said the woman. "I really love being able to amble
68	along without having a definite destination. I love being able to
79	feel like I'm part of nature. And I mostly love
89	being able to share these things with my daughter."
98	The girl smiled. Back at home, occasionally she and her
108	mother argued a trifle. That's typical for most families. But
118	in the park, it was as if the same mind was in two
131	different bodies. "You know, Mom," she said, "the silly things we
142	disagree about in our house seem so unimportant here." 151

First Timed Reading		**Final Timed Reading**	
Words Read in one minute	_____	Words Read in one minute	_____
Number of Errors	− _____	Number of Errors	− _____
Words Correct per Minute **Score**	_____	Words Correct per Minute **Score**	_____

Name _____ Date _____ Instructor _____

Free Speech

10	The United States Constitution guarantees all of us the right to free speech. The government isn't allowed to tell you that you
22	can't say something just because some people may disagree with it.
33	There are other countries, however, that don't give people
42	the same right. In those countries, an individual might even get
53	put in jail if he or she voices an opinion.
63	Here in America, we all have the right to speak out about
75	what we think. Some ideas may be unpopular. It doesn't matter,
86	though. The Constitution says that we can have free discussions
96	about our ideas, whether everyone agrees with us or not. We can
108	voice our opinions even if nobody else shares them.
117	The people who wrote the Constitution imagined that the
126	world of ideas was like a huge marketplace. We are all free to
139	pick the ideas we believe in, the same way we are free
151	to pick the kind of food we want to eat. 161

First Timed Reading		**Final Timed Reading**	
Words Read in one minute	_____	*Words Read in one minute*	_____
Number of Errors	– _____	*Number of Errors*	– _____
Words Correct per Minute **Score**	_____	*Words Correct per Minute* **Score**	_____

Name _____ Date _____ Instructor _____

The Play

	"Hey," said Tina, "why don't we put on a play?"
10	"What would it be about?" asked Carlos.
17	Tina had a terrific idea for a production. "Why don't we put
29	on a play about putting on a play? I volunteer to write it
42	and direct it."
45	"Yeah, and I could make believe I'm sewing the costumes
55	and organizing the makeup," said Marie.
61	"That doesn't sound any good," said Carlos.
68	"Of course it does," said Tina. "You're just jealous that you
79	didn't think of it."
83	"I could pretend that I'm constructing scenery," suggested
91	Tammy.
92	"Who wants to watch somebody pretending to make stuff?"
101	asked Carlos.
103	"You're just being a sourpuss," said Tina.
110	"Who would come to this ridiculous performance?" asked
118	Carlos. "Who would be our audience?"
124	"We could invite our parents and friends," said Tina.
133	"And what would I do?" asked Carlos.
140	"You could be the star," said Tina. "You could be the grouch
152	who thinks the entire idea is silly!" 159

First Timed Reading		Final Timed Reading	
Words Read in one minute	_____	*Words Read in one minute*	_____
Number of Errors	– _____	*Number of Errors*	– _____
Words Correct per Minute **Score**	_____	*Words Correct per* Minute **Score**	_____

Name _____ Date _____ Instructor _____

James Thurber

10	One of the funniest writers who ever lived was named
19	James Thurber. Some of his most entertaining stories, collected
30	in a short autobiography called *My Life and Hard Times*, are
34	about his own boyhood.
42	The eccentric people in Thurber's tales are always
50	somewhat bewildered. They perceive things happening that really
61	aren't. The reader guffaws at their confusion. The titles of Thurber's
73	stories often reflect this. In "The Night the Bed Fell on Father,"
86	the bed doesn't fall. In "The Day the Dam Broke," the dam doesn't
87	break.
97	These stories are hilarious. But Thurber was also known for
107	his wonderful cartoons, even though he was nearly blind. That
118	didn't stop him from putting his strange squiggly people on paper.
128	He frequently drew weird animals, too. Thurber liked to make
140	fun of his drawings. He said they were nothing but doodles. Still,
153	the great sense of humor we find in his stories is also quite
	evident in the pictures that came from his pencil. **162**

First Timed Reading		**Final Timed Reading**	
Words Read in one minute	_____	*Words Read in one minute*	_____
Number of Errors	– _____	*Number of Errors*	– _____
Words Correct per Minute **Score**	_____	*Words Correct per Minute* **Score**	_____

Name _____ Date _____ Instructor _____

The Missing Emerald

9	The emerald was missing. Detective Potts was sure that someone in the house had pilfered it.
16	But who? Who could have stolen the thing? The thief would
27	have needed ample opportunity to go upstairs and enter
36	Mrs. Smith's bedroom. None of the guests had ever left the
47	party on the first floor, though. And besides, the bedroom
57	door had been locked by Mrs. Smith herself, long before the party
69	had started.
71	"I can't comprehend it," said Mrs. Smith. "If nobody went up
82	there, how did the emerald disappear?"
88	"Perhaps someone came in via the window," suggested the
97	detective.
98	"Preposterous!" said Mrs. Smith. That window was closed
106	and latched from the inside. I secured it myself, right before the
118	reception."
119	Detective Potts stopped and listened for a moment. "What's
128	that racket upstairs?" he asked.
133	"Why that's just Fluffball, probably batting a toy around," said
143	Mrs. Smith.
145	"I locked her in my bedroom, because she can be such
156	a nuisance at parties." **160**

First Timed Reading		Final Timed Reading	
Words Read in one minute	_____	Words Read in one minute	_____
Number of Errors	**–** _____	Number of Errors	**–** _____
Words Correct per Minute **Score**	_____	Words Correct per Minute **Score**	_____

Name _____ Date _____ Instructor _____

Puzzles

12	An interesting way to exercise your mind is to do a puzzle.
22	Puzzles come in many varieties. The difficulty level of each kind can run from extremely easy to outrageously hard.
31	You probably already know about jigsaw puzzles. Pieces of
40	varied shapes interlock to form a picture. Some jigsaw
49	puzzles have very few pieces, and they are oversized ones
59	at that. Those puzzles are a cinch to assemble. Some other
70	puzzles may have hundreds of small pieces, and many of those
81	pieces may look similar! Those puzzles can take days or
91	even weeks to finish.
95	Crosswords are another type of popular puzzle. In a
104	crossword, the solver sees a grid of black and white squares.
115	The white squares are to be filled in with letters to make
127	words. Clues help the solver. 132

First Timed Reading	**Final Timed Reading**
Words Read in one minute _____	*Words Read in one minute* _____
Number of Errors − _____	*Number of Errors* − _____
Words Correct per Minute **Score** _____	*Words Correct per Minute* **Score** _____

Name _____ Date _____ Instructor _____

Wet Waiting

12	"Why is it that the bus always takes much longer to arrive
23	when it's pouring out?" I asked my friend Danny. We were
32	anxiously standing at the stop and getting drenched because
	neither one of us had remembered to bring an umbrella.
42	Danny sighed and said, "Hey, that's just your imagination. It
52	just seems to take longer when the weather conditions are
62	unpleasant. Actually, it takes about the same amount of time,
72	no matter what the sky is doing. It's 10 minutes, regardless of
84	whether it's raining or not."
89	I glanced at my watch. "We've been anticipating the bus's
99	arrival for nearly 15 minutes already," I whined, "so your
109	brilliant theory doesn't hold water!"
114	"Oh, but you're mistaken," he replied, and laughed.
122	"Everything holds water today!" To prove it, he patted his
132	sopping sleeve as hard as he could and a fine spray flew
144	up from his arm. **148**

First Timed Reading			**Final Timed Reading**		
Words Read in one minute		_____	Words Read in one minute		_____
Number of Errors	**–**	_____	Number of Errors	**–**	_____
Words Correct per Minute **Score**		_____	Words Correct per Minute **Score**		_____

Name _____   Date _____   Instructor _____

The Mystery of Mrs. Sanchez

	Yes, Jennifer loved a mystery, but that didn't necessarily
9	mean that she wanted to be caught smack in the middle
20	of one. However, she couldn't help wondering, "Why did
29	Mrs. Sanchez hustle out of here at lunchtime and leave us with a
42	substitute for the remainder of the afternoon? And why'd
51	she wink at me as if I had some clue about where she was going?"
66	Mrs. Sanchez was one of those teachers with a perfect
76	attendance record. She never took a day off. Jennifer's older
86	sister and brother had both been in Mrs. Sanchez's class.
96	They never complained about her missing even a milli-second
105	of school. Someone nicknamed her "Wonder Woman," because
113	no one could recall her ever having been sick. But today,
124	she had skittered out in a huge hurry, and she acted as if
137	Jennifer knew why! 140

First Timed Reading		Final Timed Reading	
Words Read in one minute	_____	Words Read in one minute	_____
Number of Errors	− _____	Number of Errors	− _____
Words Correct per Minute **Score**	_____	Words Correct per Minute **Score**	_____

Name _____ Date _____ Instructor _____

Fresh Fish Sold Here

	Here's an old joke.
4	A man opens a store, and purchases a decorative sign that
15	says, "Fresh Fish Sold Here." He displays the sign, admires it,
26	and proudly exclaims, "Stunning!"
30	"Hey," a passing woman hollers, "isn't it pointless to say
40	'Fresh'? If you're offering fish, it's supposed to be Fresh."
50	"Precisely," says the man, and paints out the word "Fresh."
60	"And why bother to say 'Sold'?" asks the woman. "Would
70	anyone presume that you were giving fish away entirely
79	free?"
80	"Yeah, you're correct," says the man, and obliterates the
89	word "Sold."
91	"What about 'Here'?" the woman continues. "Where else
99	could you conceivably be referring to?"
105	"I agree," says the merchant, and he removes that word, too.
116	Now the sign merely says "Fish".
122	"Gosh," says the woman, "you don't have to tell me that —
133	because I can smell your stinky fish from a mile away!" **144**

First Timed Reading		**Final Timed Reading**	
Words Read in one minute	_____	Words Read in one minute	_____
Number of Errors	– _____	Number of Errors	– _____
Words Correct per Minute **Score**	_____	Words Correct per Minute **Score**	_____

Name _____   Date _____   Instructor _____

Tigers

12	The lion is often referred to as the king of beasts. Actually, though, the tiger is the biggest member of the feline family.
23	Unlike lions, who live in groups called prides, tigers live
33	alone. Baby tigers may stay with their mothers for a short
44	while. But after they get to be two or three years old, tiger
57	children have to go out on their own.
65	Each tiger marks its territory. It uses scent, and it also
76	occasionally scratches trees. All other tigers acknowledge,
83	by their absence, that it's a good idea to stay away. Neighbor
95	tigers get to recognize each others' signs, and are
104	careful not to cross the boundary line into the other's home.
115	That's how they stay good neighbors. A tiger depends on its good
127	physical condition to find food, so tigers try to avoid fights
138	with each other if they can. Even another tiger doesn't
148	want to get in trouble with a tiger! 156

First Timed Reading	**Final Timed Reading**
Words Read in one minute _____	Words Read in one minute _____
Number of Errors − _____	Number of Errors − _____
Words Correct per Minute **Score** _____	Words Correct per Minute **Score** _____

Name _____ Date _____ Instructor _____

Storks

11	Gwen was overjoyed to see the wood storks come back to the small stream near her house. Her father had informed her
22	that wood storks were an endangered species, and they might
32	not survive for many more years. But as Gwen peered out
43	her window, she was able to count five storks, all digging in the
56	water with their beaks, seeking nourishment.
62	"Dad," she called. "Bring the binoculars and come quick."
71	Her father came hustling into the room. Gwen indicated the
81	big birds feeding nearby. Her father lifted the binoculars to
91	his eyes, and said, "They're certainly stunning."
98	The storks ate for a long while, but eventually they flew off.
110	"Aren't they glorious?" exclaimed Gwen's father. "Look at
118	those wings, white with black borders. They're breathtaking."
126	Gwen watched as the creatures seemed to evaporate into
135	the far horizon.
138	Then she turned to her father. "I'm so glad we have storks,"
150	she said.
152	"Yes," her father concurred, "so am I." **159**

First Timed Reading		Final Timed Reading	
Words Read in one minute	_____	Words Read in one minute	_____
Number of Errors	− _____	Number of Errors	− _____
Words Correct per Minute **Score**	_____	Words Correct per Minute **Score**	_____

Name _____ Date _____ Instructor _____

The Finish Line

	The man keeps running. His breath is coming with difficulty
10	now, and he can feel his heart beating rapidly. Just another
21	mile, he promises himself, that's all he has left to go. Behind
33	him, and on both sides, he can perceive other competitors
43	struggling, just as he is. Dozens of those other runners,
53	maybe even hundreds, are determined to beat him. Any one of
64	them might have the ability. So far, he has held his
75	insignificant edge, though.
78	He thinks of the years of training that have gone into making
90	him a champion athlete, the years of keeping his body in
101	exceptional condition. Every day of every one of those years is
112	focused into this race.
116	Now the man spots the finish line ahead. Out of the corner
128	of his right eye, he recognizes an opponent, coming fast. The
139	runner passes him with a final explosion of velocity. The man
150	summons up his last iota of strength, and regains
159	the lead. 161

First Timed Reading	**Final Timed Reading**
Words Read in one minute _____	Words Read in one minute _____
Number of Errors − _____	Number of Errors − _____
Words Correct per Minute **Score** _____	Words Correct per Minute **Score** _____

Name _____   Date _____   Instructor _____

Mae's Emergency

10	The jangling of the phone sounded urgent, but Jamie didn't realize that she was the only one in the house. After four
22	rings, the answering machine was activated, and Jamie
30	overheard her best friend's terrified voice speaking through
38	the contraption.
40	"Help, Jamie. Help me! If you're there, please pick up!"
50	Jamie galloped to the portable and scooped it up as swiftly as she
63	could, but, alas, it was already too late. There was silence on the
76	other end, nothing but an ominous dial tone. Without
85	hesitating for even a minute, she called her friend back.
95	"I'm here, Mae. What's going on?"
101	"Mom won't let me play soccer tomorrow unless I'm
110	completely done with my book report. But I haven't even
120	started reading that immense novel yet!"
126	"Yikes, is that all?" shrieked Jamie. "You got me petrified. I
137	thought it was some kind of horrendous emergency."
145	"This is an emergency!" cried Mae.
151	"Don't be so dramatic," bellowed Jamie. "You know perfectly
160	well that a homework assignment isn't an emergency!" 168

First Timed Reading	**Final Timed Reading**
Words Read in one minute _____	Words Read in one minute _____
Number of Errors − _____	Number of Errors − _____
Words Correct per Minute **Score** _____	Words Correct per Minute **Score** _____

Name _____   Date _____   Instructor _____

Pitcher Plants

11	We usually think of plants as being beautiful things that grow
	peacefully. Some plants, though, aren't so innocent. Pitcher
19	plants work very hard to trap and devour insects. There are
30	many different species of pitcher plants throughout the world,
39	and some of them even flourish right here in the United States.
51	All pitcher plants operate in a similar way.
59	The simplest pitcher plant resembles a long tube. At the top
70	of the tube is a leafy hood. When it rains, the tube fills partially
84	with water, and the plant gives off a scent that attracts
95	various bugs, like flies and mosquitoes.
101	The insects land on the hood and begin explorations. As
111	they move down the tube, they discover that its inside is
122	covered with slippery hairs that point downward. The insects can't
132	climb back up. They fall slowly until they land in the
143	water and drown. The pitcher plant leaves them there until they
154	start to decay into a soup. Eventually, that soup becomes
164	nourishment for the plant. **168**

First Timed Reading		**Final Timed Reading**	
Words Read in one minute	_____	Words Read in one minute	_____
Number of Errors	– _____	Number of Errors	– _____
Words Correct per Minute **Score**	_____	Words Correct per Minute **Score**	_____

Name _____ Date _____ Instructor _____

The Poetry Contest

	Jack had never particularly cared for poetry, and he was
10	certain that — ordinarily — he'd never be able to write a
20	poem that merited any exceptional praise. But a contest
29	was a contest!
32	"I'm going to enter that poetry competition at school," he
42	announced to his sister, Elaine.
47	"I was under the impression that you despised poems," she
57	said. Elaine was two years older than Jack, and always
67	enjoyed challenging whatever he said.
72	"I don't despise them," he corrected her. "I just don't like
83	those ridiculous ones that rhyme 'trees' and 'breeze', and 'moon'
93	and 'balloon.' I don't think the moon resembles a balloon,
103	and I can't imagine why anyone would go completely bananas
113	just because a breeze rustles through some trees."
121	"Then what will you write about, genius? Poems are usually
131	about those kinds of subjects."
136	"Not necessarily, though," said Jack. "I'm going to compose a
146	poem about our family. Mom and Dad will be in it, and you
159	will, too. So you'd better be nice to me, or else!" 170

First Timed Reading	**Final Timed Reading**
Words Read in one minute _____	Words Read in one minute _____
Number of Errors – _____	Number of Errors – _____
Words Correct per Minute **Score** _____	Words Correct per Minute **Score** _____

Name _____ Date _____ Instructor _____

Tojiro's River

9	A slight breeze rippled above, and wafted some cherry
19	blossoms off into the approaching night. The moon floated lazily
32	up out of the water, and began its slow ascent through the sky.
42	In the distance, a pair of red-crowned cranes fluttered gracefully,
	like shadows dancing in the last of the light.
51	Tojiro had come down to the river to think and to dream. It
64	was not unusual for the Japanese boy to come here at the end
77	of the day. The sound of the running water simultaneously
87	soothed his mind and stirred it. He felt that the river was a
100	wondrous place, created especially for him and his thoughts.
109	Tojiro stretched out on his back, and gazed at the stars. He
121	hearkened to the voice of the river, as it murmured slowly
132	along. Suddenly, he heard a rustle from behind, and turned to
143	see what it was. A girl was slogging clumsily toward the
154	bank of the river. Tojiro recognized her immediately. She was
164	Miyoshi, the entrancing daughter of the village carpenter. 172

First Timed Reading	**Final Timed Reading**
Words Read in one minute _____	Words Read in one minute _____
Number of Errors – _____	Number of Errors – _____
Words Correct per Minute **Score** _____	Words Correct per Minute **Score** _____

Name _____ Date _____ Instructor _____

Crunchy Doodle

10	"Now when the camera rolls," said the director to Sam, "take a spoonful of the cereal and give me a gigantic smile."
22	"I know what to do," said Sam, "because we've already
32	attempted taping this commercial twenty times. Why was
40	the last take unusable?"
44	The director was getting impatient. "Your smile just wasn't
53	gigantic enough for this delicious product," he complained.
61	"Remember, this isn't your typical cereal! It's extra
69	crunchable Crunchy Doodle!"
72	"I'm getting nauseous," said Sam. "I've already ingested six
81	bowls of this garbage."
85	"Now, Sam," coaxed the director in a soothing voice. "You
95	don't want to be unmanageable, do you? Just take one
105	more measly chomp."
108	The cameras rolled and Sam shoveled another mouthful
116	between his teeth. He couldn't summon up a smile, though.
126	"Cut!" hollered the director. Then he said to Sam, "You
136	didn't smile at all this time! What's going on?"
145	Sam indicated the cereal floating in the milk, and shook his
156	head. "That's supposed to be extra crunchable Crunchy Doodle,
165	correct?" he asked.
168	"Definitely," replied the director.
172	"Well," said Sam, "it got soggy." 178

First Timed Reading		Final Timed Reading	
Words Read in one minute	_____	Words Read in one minute	_____
Number of Errors	– _____	Number of Errors	– _____
Words Correct per Minute **Score**	_____	Words Correct per Minute **Score**	_____

Bibliography

TEACHING STUDENTS WITH SPECIAL NEEDS

Adams, Anne H. *The Reading Clinic*. London: The Macmillan Company, 1970.

Clark, Diana Brewster and Joanna Kellog Uhry. *Dyslexia: Theory and Practice of Remedial Instruction*. Baltimore: New York Press, 1995.

Cohen, Libby G., ed. *Children with Exceptional Needs in Regular Classrooms*. National Education Association, 1992.

Durkin, Delores. *Teaching Them to Read*. Massachusetts: Simon and Schuster, 1989

Alexander, J. Estill and Heathington, Betty S. *Assessing and Correcting Classroom Reading Problems.* Glenview, Illinois: Scott, Foresman and Company, 1988.

Fox, Christy. *Reading Comprehension*. 9/5/00. <http://acce.virginia.edu/go/cise/ose/information/ints/compre.html>.

Johnson, Dale D. and Pearson, P. David. *Teaching Reading Vocabulary*. New York: CBS College Publishing, 1984.

Olson, Judy L. and Platt, Jennifer M.. *Teaching Children and Adolescents with Special Needs*. New Jersey: Prentice Hall, Inc., 2000.

Roseberry-Mckibbin, Ph.D, Celeste. *Multicultural Students With Special Language Needs: Practical Strategies for Assessment and Intervention*. Fresno: California State University, 1995.

Simmons, Deborah C. and Kame'enui, Edward J.. *What Research Tells Us About Children With Special Needs: Bases and Basics*. New Jersey: Lawrence Erlbaum Associates, Publishers, 1998.

Renaissance Group. *Teaching Strategies.* 7/19/00. <http://www.uni.edu/coe/inclusion/strategies/inclusive_classroom.html>.

Wood, Karen D. and Bob Algozzine. *Teaching Reading to High Risk Learners*. Massachusetts: Allyn and Bacon, 1994.

PHONICS INSTRUCTION

Stahl, Steven. "The Utility of Phonic Generalizations in the Primary Grades." *The Reading Teacher*. Vol. 50, No. 3. November, 1996.

Vadasy, Patricia F., Jenkins, Joseph R. and Pool, Kathleen. "Effects of Tutoring in Phonological and Early Reading Skills on Students at Risk for Reading Disabilities." *Journal of Learning Disabilities*. Vol. 33, No.4. July/August, 2000.

TEACHING STUDENTS TO READ THROUGH TECHNOLOGY

Hammerberg, Dawnene D. "Reading and Writing Hypertextually: Children's Literature, Technology, and Early Writing Instruction." *Language Arts*. Vol. 78, No.3. January, 2001.

ASSESSMENT

Alexander, J. Estill and Heathington, Betty S. *Assessing and Correcting Classroom Reading Problems.* Glenview, Illinois: Scott, Foresman and Company, 1988.

Kopriva, Rebecca. *Ensuring Accuracy in Testing for English Language Learners*. Washington D.C.: Council of Chief State Officers, 2000.

Florida Department of Education. Feb. 1999. *Alternative Assessment*. (ESE 10211). Tallahassee, Florida.

Florida Department of Education. Feb. 1999. *Model Standards for Comparable Testing Procedures*.

Florida Department of Education. Aug. 1997. *Testing Modifications and Accomodations for Students with Disabilities.* (ESE 9603). Tallahassee, Florida.

STUDENT DISTRIBUTION

National Center for Education Statistics. *State Comparisons of Education Statistics: 1969-70 to 1996-97*. 8/30/00. <http://nces.ed.gov/pubs98/9801/#chap2a>.

The Condition of Education. *Racial and Ethnic Distribution of Elementary and Secondary Students.* 8/30/00. <http://nces.ed.gov/pubsearch>.

Leveled Books Story Questions Answer Key

Please Note: Question five asks the students to compare the Leveled Book with a selection in the textbook. If the students have not read the textbook selection, have them compare the Leveled Book with a selection or book they have recently read.

GRADE 5

Dan's Time

1. Dan is having his tenth birthday.
2. The watch belonged to Dan's great-great-grandfather. He got it in 1900 for his 40th birthday.
3. Answers will vary but may include: Grandfather gives Dan a watch that has been passed down through the family. Grandfather shares special moments with his grandson.
4. Time and traditions tie people and events together.
5. Answers will vary.

The Eye of the Hurricane

1. The walls of the storm were too high for them to fly over.
2. Small low-flying clouds called scud speed by overhead.
3. The movement of hurricanes is unpredictable. It changed course and the ship blundered into it.
4. Four friends on a dormitory ship, figure out a way to avoid the damage from a hurricane by remaining in the eye.

5. Answers will vary.

Franklin Delano Roosevelt

1. His parents doted on him, and he was born to wealth and privilege.
2. He mounted a vigorous and exhausting campaign to show that he had the strength for the job.
3. It gave him great determination, and even greater understanding of the suffering of others.
4. A disabled person can be a great leader.
5. Answers will vary.

Diego's Sea Adventure

1. The Armada is sailing to England to invade it.
2. The English used fireships. They had guns that could fire from a farther distance. The stormy weather wrecked many ships.
3. He experienced many dangers and watched how the captain and crew were able to handle them. Also, Rodrigo gave him some important advice,

which he can use in the future.
4. It is about the adventures of Diego, a Spanish boy, as he sails with the Armada in 1588.
5. Answers will vary.

From Dust to Hope

1. They destroyed the crops and left dust everywhere, including inside houses.
2. He could see their truck was from Oklahoma and he resented people from there.
3. She was trying to let Frances know that she should be proud of who she was and not be influenced by the names people might call her.
4. The difficulties of leaving the home you love and starting a new life elsewhere; dealing with people not liking you because of who you are and where you are from.
5. Answers will vary.

Through a Mountain...

1. Possible answers: dynamite, power tools such as jack hammers and power drills and giant

modern tunneling machines.
2. It connected England and France. It was the largest tunneling project in history.
3. Accept all reasonable answers.
4. It is about how tunnels are dug and built.
5. Answers will vary.

The Mills Green Team

1. She injured herself in a fall.
2. Their mother wanted them to.
3. She loved flowers and probably liked having them in the house, especially during the season when there weren't flowers blooming outdoors.
4. Two young children decide to help out a neighbor and, as a result of their kindness and work, many other people get involved in helping too.
5. Answers will vary.

Blue-faced Blues

1. He was an airline pilot and frequently out of the country.
2. It was not done in a realistic way.

3. It is a way of documenting his progress and giving the piece importance.

4. A young artist learns that not everyone will understand what he is doing, but after seeing other artists' unique styles, he realizes that he should stay true to himself and should continue his artistic pursuits.

5. Answers will vary.

Dancers in the Spotlight

1. All the "dolls" become alive and begin to dance.

2. With their body movements and facial expressions.

3. It is about young people. It also has many things they like in it, such as toys, and a holiday celebration.

4. Preparing for a ballet performance takes a lot of hard work.

5. Answers will vary.

Human Writes!

1. The Sumerians invented writing about 5,000 years ago.

2. A system using pictographs is the most difficult because of the number of symbols or characters needed.

3. Answers will vary,

but may include: to keep records, to share information, to preserve their culture and language.

4. The main idea of the book is how people developed writing from culture to culture through the ages.

5. Answers will vary.

Dear Diary

1. Answers will vary, but may include: women got the right to vote, talking movies replaced silent films, Charles Lindbergh made his historic nonstop flight across the Atlantic, the stock market crashed.

2. They were much lower. A movie ticket that costs $7.50 to $9.00 today cost 10 cents in the 1920s. Of course, wages were lower, too.

3. Some activities included attending movies, dancing the Charleston, listening to jazz, going to baseball games, doing crossword puzzles, and swimming at the beach.

4. It's about a young girl's way of life almost a century ago.

5. Answers will vary.

Maya's Mural

1. It showed Maya and her friends in the swimming pool.

2. Maya was rather lonely and unhappy at the beginning of the story. By the end, she was much happier and positive.

3. A lot of people will be able to see and enjoy these paintings; also working on a larger-than-life scale might give some artists a sense of freedom.

4. A girl, named Maya, crippled by polio, becomes well known in her community for painting murals.

5. Answers will vary.

Kelly in Charge

1. They had complained about having boring meats.

2. She knew that her parents were losing patience.

3. She probably learned that planning and cooking a meal is not as easy as she thought.

4. It is about a girl who has to prepare breakfast for her family. It is almost a disaster, but it turns out okay in the end.

5. Answers will vary.

On Track

1. He could sell stolen parts there.

2. If his bicycle was stolen and brought to the shed there would be only one set of his tire tracks.

3. He figured out how extra weight on a bicycle can affect the look of the tire treads.

4. Marshall and the other kids solved the thefts by observing drawings of the tire tracks and comparing them to those made by the thieves.

5. Answers will vary.

Tourist Trap Island

1. She loved all the natural things about the island: the animals, plants, and natural beauty.

2. He did not know if the island could raise the money necessary to put in the sewer system and did not want to get in trouble with the state.

3. Accept all reasonable responses.

4. It's about an island girl who helps her neighbors realize that their beautiful island is fine just the way it is.

5. Answers will vary.

Tornado!

1. From southwest to northeast.

2. Texas, Oklahoma, Kansas, and Nebraska. Some people consider the alley to extend all the way north to the

Dakotas.

3. Because so many trees and poles had been splintered open by the tornado.

4. It is about the 1998 tornado in Birmingham, Alabama, what destruction it caused, and how people kept themselves safe during the disaster.

5. Answers will vary.

The Riddle of the Sphinx

1. He was able to solve the riddle of the Sphinx.

2. He refused to believe Demos, that the Sphinx would turn him into stone, and he said he knew the answers to many riddles.

3. Answers will vary. One possibility is that very few people think of a cane being a third leg.

4. Oedipus solves the riddle of the Sphinx and saves Thebes from the monster.

5. Answers will vary.

On the Ball

1. Spheres, cones, cubes, cylinders, and pyramids.

2. The lead. It had more momentum and couldn't stop in time at the stop sign.

3. Answers will vary, but most likely students will say yes because the author ended the story on that note.

4. Bobby travels to the land of Orbis and learns about the shapes called spheres.

5. Answers will vary.

Teammates

1. He had had cancer and was recovering at home.

2. His team was doing poorly, and he missed the best player.

3. No, Robert did what he did out of compassion. We know because when he played with Ethan, he didn't shoot any better than the other team members.

4. It's mostly about how one boy displayed courage and compassion for a teammate with cancer.

5. Answers will vary.

Unusual Bridges

1. Ropes can be stretched across a gap and tied to each side. People can then climb across on the ropes.

2. A drawbridge might be built to prevent people from crossing a river or to allow boats to pass under or beside a bridge.

3. They are both record-breaking suspension bridges. The Royal Gorge Bridge is the highest bridge; the Akashi

Kaikyo Bridge is the longest.

4. It describes different types of unusual bridges throughout history and throughout the world.

5. Answers will vary.

Flight of the Trumpeters

1. Hunters killed for their feathers; some swans ate old lead pellets.

2. Because of a natural phenomenon called imprinting, the swans followed the first thing they saw after they hatched.

3. They do not want the birds to become extinct.

4. The author wants to inform readers about the trumpeters and what is being done to help them migrate so that year after year they will be able to return to their winter and summer homes.

5. Answers will vary.

A Matter of Time

1. She had been thinking about the future a few minutes earlier.

2. She volunteered to test the rocket, and she took a chance on using the "eject" button.

3. Answers will vary.

4. The past and the future may not always be what you expected.

5. Answers will vary.

Making Pipes is His Bag

1. It is made of wood-usually African blackwood-attached to a leather bag.

2. He loved the sound of the instrument and was fascinated by the machines used to make them.

3. Answers will vary, but may include; love of the instrument itself, sense of satisfaction from making something well.

4. The book is about a man who makes bagpipes, and the process of making pipes.

5. Answers will vary.

The Day My Grandpa Voted

1. It is told by Freddie, Amos's grandson.

2. He didn't go because he felt the white people in town would give him a very hard time when he tried to vote.

3. The authorities took it out of service so African-Americans couldn't cross the river to get to the polling place.

4. It is about one man's courage in standing up for his rights and the effect his actions had on his grandson.

5. Answers will vary.

GRADE 6

Knitting Circle

1. Because it's a popular club and her friends belong.
2. Possible answers: creative, willing to try things, has many interests.
3. She tells about her experience with the Knitting Circle and what she learned from it.
4. This story is mostly about a girl's refusal to be pressured by her peers into participating in an activity that she had no interest in.
5. Answers will vary.

Letters From Lila

1. London, Paris, Nice Florence, Rome, Venice, Athens, and Santorini
2. Food; language
3. Answers will vary.
4. A girl and her aunt traveling together and experiencing new cultures.
5. Answers will vary.

Crossings

1. He wanted to become a TV weather reporter.
2. They were each living in a place they didn't like and they were doing things that didn't fit into their plans for their futures.

3. Answers will vary. Their goals could be obtained if they each had the proper training.
4. Two families decide to trade places because each believes the other's place is where true happiness lies. The city family wants to live in the country, and the country family wants to live in the city.
5. Answers will vary.

Tornado Alley

1. The *Fujita-Pearson Scale*
2. At first he is excited about it, but then he becomes scared.
3. In case a tornado knocked out their electricity for a long time.
4. Mary and her family cope with a tornado that passes through their property.
5. Answers will vary.

A Summer Day

1. Learning can be fun.
2. How to clam and how to scuba dive. He'll also join the library's summer reading program.
3. Possible answers; because he is jealous; because he thinks they have nothing in common.
4. It is about a boy who learns that learning and growing are a fun

and important part of life.
5. Answers will vary.

Laurie in Charge

1. She checks him for blood and bruises.
2. To show that she is grown up and responsible.
3. She tells Mrs. Martin how responsible she is.
4. Laurie thinks she is responsible enough to baby-sit four-year-old twins. She finds out it is hard work but does a good job.
5. Laurie would do well. She has good problem-solving skills.

To the Rescue!

1. Fewer people died on the Andrea Doria because rescuers arrived on time, and the boat took longer to sink.
2. There is the danger that rescuers may break through the ice and become victims themselves; there is the danger of freezing to death in the water beneath the ice.
3. The rescuers must radio directions to the victims, who then must rescue themselves.
4. The main idea is that people and animals carry out rescues in dangerous situations.
5. Answers will vary.

The History of Karate

1. It is a form of self-defense intended to improve one's body, mind, and character.
2. He made karate a popular martial art. He taught thousands of people karate and even opened schools in America.
3. Possible answers: They were impressed to see that people could fight without weapons and win.
4. The main idea is that karate developed in China, Japan, Korea, and Okinawa.
5. Possible answer: She never used karate unless she was attacked first.

Ron's Story: Talking Baseball

1. He thought the exercises were immature and not very helpful.
2. Because they made him more nervous than other words. He was scared he wouldn't be able to say them without stuttering, so he stuttered.
3. Narrating a baseball game has a natural rhythm; he was therefore comfortable talking about it.
4. This story is mostly about a father who

tells his son how he overcame a stuttering problem.

5. Answers will vary.

George Balanchine...

1. A choreographer is someone who creates dances and trains dancers to perform.

2. A person needs to have a strong and flexible body, as well as discipline and the desire to work hard.

3. He fell in love with ballet while there and learned about all the training and practice a dancer and choreographer need to perform in ballets.

4. George Balanchine was a famous choreographer who worked hard to create dances that people would find beautiful and magical.

5. Possible answers: He would have wanted them to work hard; he would have had many interesting ideas for the play.

Meet the Band

1. Joe Moreno's instruments were lying around and they wanted a way to have fun.

2. They made decisions by having each band member contribute an idea and agree on the

one thing they liked best. Examples: choosing the band's name, which songs to record.

3. As a result of creating songs and music together, they made a recording and were introduced to the music world.

4. This story is mostly about the formation of a rock band and the recording of a CD.

5. Answers will vary.

Through Alexandra's Eye

1. Her three subjects are her cat, her dinner table and her grandmother in the snow.

2. They wanted her to join them. They also didn't understand her desire to paint.

3. Answers will vary. She would continue to paint but probably not start the business.

4. A little girl who loves to paint. She makes a friend, stays true to herself and starts a card business.

5. Answers will vary.

Nate, Steffi, and the Great Pyramid

1. He wanted to play baseball at home; he would miss his friends.

2. They have more advanced technology and equipment.

3. Answers will vary. Possible answers; Yes, he seemed to be getting more interested in the dig; No, he didn't think anything would ever be found.

4. It is mostly about a visit that two kids from Georgia made to the Great Pyramid.

5. Answers will vary.

Mining the Moon

1. She is connected to a school in Texas via satellite.

2. She finds it lonely and tiresome because there are no children her age living there.

3. Answers will vary.

4. Jillian's discovery of ice that enables the continued settlement of the moon. It is also about Jillian's own discovery that the moon adventure was and would be awesome.

5. Answers will vary.

Across the Country

1. They are going to meet their mother who is out West on business.

2. Because it is narrow, flat and black and seems to unroll before him.

3. Possible answers; scared, lonely, amazed.

4. A family trip shows a boy that, while things might not always be fun in the same old ways, there are new possibilities for enjoyment, as one grows older.

5. Answers will vary.

Sea of Treasures

1. The wind made the ocean currents too dangerous for swimming, so the two had to find something else to do.

2. Its beacon warns sailors away from the rocks, emergency equipment is kept there, and Jim is working on a special oceanography project there.

3. It is a sea capsule – a small, sealed vessel that moves along the ocean floor so that a person inside can study and photograph underwater debris and marine life.

4. One summer, a brother and sister visit a lighthouse and learn about the ocean from an oceanographer.

5. Answers will vary.

A Tune for Lucy

1. Sarah met Lucy when Lucy's cat Sebastian ran under Sarah's porch and she had to help Lucy get her cat back.

2. She brought the statue because she thought it might bring her good luck and help her make friends.
3. She was happy that she was able to teach kids again. Also, she was filled with joy that she was able to enjoy their company and listen to music, and that the girls wanted to spend time with her.
4. The story is mostly about an older woman who helps a child, and vice versa.
5. Answers will vary.

Hercules

1. He killed a lion that attacked the cattle he was guarding.
2. They would probably show his great strength and courage.
3. He means that because Atlas tried to trick him in the first place he tricked Atlas into taking back the weight of the sky.
4. It is mostly about how Hercules won his freedom by taking the golden apples from the garden.
5. Answers will vary.

John Glenn: Space Pioneer

1. Project Mercury's goal was to send Americans into space.

2. They did not want to alarm him; they hoped they could solve it themselves.
3. It provided data for research on aging; it showed that elderly people are capable of performing in zero G.
4. Answers will vary.
5. John Glenn is a hero whose space journeys sparked our imagination and provided us with useful information on space travel and aging.

Rosa Parks

1. Blacks had to attend segregated, inferior schools; they had to give up their bus seats to white people; they could not use the same restaurants, water fountains, elevators, and movie theaters as whites.
2. She saw an urgent need for black people to improve their lives, and she was tired of the gross injustices they faced. She felt she could help fellow blacks by sharing her skills with them.
3. She risked the danger of being beaten by the bus driver or the police; she risked being jailed and fined; she lost her job and received death threats, yet she never backed down from her protest.

4. Rosa Parks, an individual willing to stand up and challenge an unfair law, was able to help achieve justice for her people.
5. Answers will vary.

Last Summer at Camp Woodside

1. She was afraid of heights.
2. She arranged private lessons for Jenny.
3. Answers will vary. Possible answer: Diane knew that Jenny would truly be over her fear of heights if she competed in the final.
4. The story is mostly about how Jenny faces her fear of heights and goes on to win a wall-climbing contest.
5. Answers will vary.

Symphony Weekend

1. Monday
2. Answers will vary. Possible answer: Because it is an enjoyable, worthwhile experience.
3. Answers will vary. Possible answers: ticket sales, donations, fundraising events
4. The main idea is that all the musicians and staff of the Roanoke Symphony must work together to make a successful concert.

5. Answers will vary.

The Reluctant Princess

1. Ella was arrested for breaking Rule Number 1: Everyone must walk backward on Tuesdays.
2. Ella discovered that being a princess was a worthwhile job, because she had the ability to change the kingdom for the better.
3. Answers will vary.
4. The story is about a kingdom with silly rules and how Princess Ella gets the rules changed.
5. Answers will vary.

Lake Joy, at Last

1. The cold forced the kids to wear space suits that made them look like aliens.
2. He designs floats for the family.
3. They enjoy life and each other.
4. It's about a family that enjoys living in a variety of places.
5. Answers will vary.

Skills Intervention Scope and Sequence

COMPREHENSION

	Grade 1 Book A Pages	Grade 1 • Leveled Books	Grade 2 Book A Pages	Grade 2 • Leveled Books	Grade 3 Book B Pages	Grade 3 • Leveled Books	Grade 4 Book B Pages	Grade 4 • Leveled Books
Author's Purpose					102-105	Dragon Parade p. 254	104-107	Bookworm's Band p. 296
Cause and Effect	214-217	Spot's Trick p. 414 Fun Run p. 416	216-219	The Ghost on the Train p. 456	96-99	Simon Says "Go for It!" p. 236 Lost at Sea p. 240 Perry Mantis, Private Eye p. 242 How to Raise a Happy Tadpole p. 256	98-101	For Jamal p. 288 Doubles p. 316
Compare and Contrast	208-211	What's New at the Zoo p. 408 In the Lake p. 410	210-213	This Is Your Land p. 464	90-93	Winter in the Artic p. 238	92-95	The Zoom Lens Mystery p. 300 Saving the Black Rhino p. 322
Draw Conclusions	232-235	Pig's Play p. 426	234-237	John Muir p. 462 Africa: Animals at Night p. 466	72-75	Worlds Within Our World p. 270 The Missing Violin p. 274	74-77	Dolphins p. 304
Fact and Nonfact					114-117	Can Animals Talk? p. 262	116-119	Anansi and Turtle Share Dinner p. 302
Fact and Opinion							132-137	Ping's Pictures p. 294 Walking in Beauty p. 298
Form Generalizations	256-259		258-261	A Voice for Her People p. 478 Billy Fish p. 482	138-141	How the Narwhal Got Its Tusk p. 258	140-143	
Important and Unimportant Information					126-129		128-131	Helping Hands p. 310
Make Predictions	226-229	Gab and Sam p. 388 Cam and Luck p. 396	228-231	A House and a Garden p. 436 Hello, José p. 438	48-51	Riding Proud p. 284	50-53	The Ninth Inning p. 290 Nine Sense p. 312
Main Idea	202-205	Around Bug Town p. 402 Bat Helps Out p. 404	204-207	Everybody's Happy p. 480 Fall Is Fun! p. 418	66-69	The Night Jazz Came Alive! p. 244 Ben Franklin Alive! p. 264	69-71	Run Fast, Fly Far p. 282
Make Inferences	220-223	Fall Is Fun! p. 418	222-225	How Kids' Clubs Help People p. 448	84-87	An Ancient Art p. 248 The Secret Lives of Cats and Dogs p. 272	86-89	
Make Judgments and Decisions					120-123	Who's Afraid of the Wolf? p. 260	122-125	George Washington p. 292 Wolverine and White Elephant. 320
Problem and Solution	250-253		252-255	The More the Merrier p. 446 The Well Used Coat p. 450	60-63	The Family Game p. 230 Special Delivery p. 234	62-65	Postcards From Mari Vic p. 278 King for a Day! p. 318
Sequence of Events	190-193	Pig Digs! p. 392 Around Bug Town p. 402	192-195	Farmer Brown's Birthday Surprise p. 472	42-45	Robots on the Loose! p. 252	44-47	Jamie, the Junkyard Artist p. 286 Will Fox Ever Learn? p. 308
Steps in a Process					108-111	Journey Across the Desert p. 232	110-113	Comic Relief p. 306

COMPREHENSION (continued)

	Grade 1 Book A Pages	Grade 1 • Leveled Books	Grade 2 Book A Pages	Grade 2 • Leveled Books	Grade 3 Book B Pages	Grade 3 • Leveled Books	Grade 4 Book B Pages	Grade 4 • Leveled Books
Story Elements	196-199	Big? p. 398 The Box p. 400	198-201	The Wall p. 440 Janie in Old California p. 442	54-57	Journey to America p. 228 The Barn Raising p. 246	56-59	The Stony Creek Bandit p. 276 Sukey Johnson Builds a House p. 280
Summarize	244-247	Their Names Will Live On p. 434	246-249	Coyotes Rule! p. 470 I Live at the Museum p. 474	78-81	Stormy Weather p. 266 The All-American Girls p. 268	80-83	

VOCABULARY STRATEGIES

	Grade 1 Book A Pages	Grade 1 • Leveled Books	Grade 2 Book A Pages	Grade 2 • Leveled Books	Grade 3 Book B Pages	Grade 3 • Leveled Books	Grade 4 Book B Pages	Grade 4 • Leveled Books
Antonyms and Synonyms	324-327 330-333		326-329 332-335		158-161	Winter in the Artic p. 238 Perry Mantis, Private Eye p. 242 How the Narwhal Got Its Tusk p. 258	160-163	Postcards from Mari Vic p. 278 Sukey Johnson Builds a House p. 280 King for a Day! p. 318 Wolverine and White Elephant p. 320
Compound Words	318-321		320-323		152-155	Journey to America p. 228 Journey Across the Desert p. 232	154-157	Jamie, the Junkyard Artist p. 286 The Ninth Inning p. 290
Context Clues	276-279		278-281		146-149	Simon Says "Go for It!" p. 236 Lost at Sea p. 240 The Night Jazz Came Alive p. 244 The Barn Raising p. 246 An Ancient Art p. 248 Robots on the Loose! p. 252 Who's Afraid of the Wolf? p. 260 Can Animals Talk? p. 262 The Secret Lives of Cats and Dogs p. 272 The Missing Violin p. 274	148-151	Riding Proud p. 284 For Jamal p. 288 Bookworm's Band p. 296 Walking in Beauty p. 298 Will Fox Ever Learn? p. 308 Nine Sense p. 312 Doubles p. 316 Saving the Black Rhino p. 322
Contractions	288-291		290-293					
Figurative Language	348-351		350-353		188-191	Dragon Parade p. 254	190-193	Helping Hands p. 310
Inflectional Endings -ed	270-273		272-275					
Inflectional Endings -s	264-267		266-269					
Inflectional Endings -es	294-297		296-299					
Inflectional Endings -er, -est	300-303		302-305					
Inflectional Endings -ing	306-309		308-311					
Multiple-Meaning Words	342-345		344-347		176-179	Special Delivery p. 234 Little Fox and Big Coyote p. 250	178-181	The Stone Creek Bandit p. 276 Run Fast, Fly Far p. 282

VOCABULARY STRATEGIES (continued)

	Grade 1 Book A Pages	Grade 1 • Leveled Books	Grade 2 Book A Pages	Grade 2 • Leveled Books	Grade 3 Book B Pages	Grade 3 • Leveled Books	Grade 4 Book B Pages	Grade 4 • Leveled Books
Possessives	282-285		284-287					
Prefixes	318-321		320-323		170-173		172-175	The Zoom Lens Mystery p. 300 Comic Relief p. 306
Root Words					182-185	Ben Franklin p. 265 Worlds Within Our World p. 270	184-187	Anansi and Turtle p. 302 Dolphins p. 304
Suffixes	336-339		338-341		164-167	The Family Game p. 230 How to Raise a Happy Tadpole p. 256 Stormy Weather p.266 The All-American Girls p. 268	166-169	George Washington p. 292 Ping's Pictures p. 294 The First Emperor p. 314

STUDY SKILLS

	Grade 1 Book A Pages	Grade 1 • Leveled Books	Grade 2 Book A Pages	Grade 2 • Leveled Books	Grade 3 Book B Pages	Grade 3 • Leveled Books	Grade 4 Book B Pages	Grade 4 • Leveled Books
Parts of a Book	356-261		156-161		196-201		196-201	
Graphic Aids	362-367		362-267		208-213		208-213	
Various Texts	368-373		368-373		214-219		214-219	
Reference Sources	374-379		374-379		202-207		202-207	
Library/Media Center	380-385		380-385		220-225		220-225	